THE CAPITAL EXPENDITURE DECISION

THE IRWIN SERIES IN FINANCE

EDITORS

Myron J. Gordon
University of Rochester

Robert W. Johnson
Purdue University

The Capital Expenditure Decision

by

G. DAVID QUIRIN
Associate Professor
University of Toronto

1967
RICHARD D. IRWIN, INC.
Homewood, Illinois

First Printing, January, 1967
Second Printing, September, 1967
Third Printing, May, 1968
Fourth Printing, January, 1969
Fifth Printing, July, 1969
Sixth Printing, April, 1970
Seventh Printing, June, 1971

Library of Congress Catalog Card. No. 66-27456

Printed in the United States of America

For Jean

Preface

This volume is intended to provide a systematic and thorough treatment of the theory of capital expenditure management for students and for managers faced with problems in this area. Treatment of the topic in the standard textbooks on business finance is necessarily brief. The journal and monographic literature is extensive but scattered and is inaccessible to many would-be users, particularly to those in industry. Examination of this literature also reveals a number of gaps and unresolved conflicts. I have sought to fill the former and to suggest tentative solutions for the latter.

Preliminary drafts of this material have been used as a text for advanced undergraduate and graduate courses in financial management at the University of British Columbia; it will also be useful for those parts of courses in business finance and public finance which deal with capital expenditure decisions. Most of the material can be handled without any special prerequisites, although a course in intermediate price theory would be useful. Portions of chapter 9 require an acquaintance with linear programming, while chapters 10 and 11 require some knowledge of statistics and probability.

My indebtedness to other workers in the field will be obvious to the reader. Many people have helped more directly in a number of ways. In particular, I should like to thank my students for forcing me to clarify my own thinking. Valuable criticisms on various parts of the text were contributed by the editors, Professors Myron Gordon and Robert Johnson, and by a number of present and former colleagues including Professors Harvey Babiak, David Blazouske, James Bray, William Hughes, Peter Lusztig, and Ronald Ma. I have perpetrated the remaining errors in spite of their wise counsel. Other friends and colleagues, particularly Professor Leslie Wong, Chairman of the Division of Finance at the University of British Columbia were generous with their advice and encouragement. Computations for the linear programming examples in chapter 9 were performed at the Computing Centre, University of Chicago, while the author was attending the Ford Foundation Faculty Research Workshop in Finance in the summer of 1965. Special thanks are also due to Miss Elizabeth Werts, who typed most of the manuscript several times.

TORONTO, ONTARIO   G. DAVID QUIRIN
December, 1966

Table of Contents

CHAPTER 1

An Introduction to
Capital Expenditure Management

1.1 What Are Capital Expenditure Decisions?

An automobile manufacturer is contemplating building a new assembly plant. The corner service station is thinking about buying a new cash register which will greatly simplify its bookkeeping procedures. Construction of a tunnel under the English Channel to link the Continent to Great Britain has been considered on several occasions by the British government. John and Ethel Smith are wondering whether they should buy a home and move out of the apartment which they now rent. All of these decision-making units face problems which are of the same type, in that they must decide whether or not to undertake capital investment projects.

A capital investment project may be defined as any project which involves the outlay of cash in return for an anticipated flow of future benefits. The latter may be monetary, as they are in the first two examples given above, or they may be nonmonetary, or only partly monetary, as they are in the case of the tunnel or the new home. It is the exchange of a present expenditure for future benefits which is the distinctive feature of the capital expenditure situation. The accounting treatment of the expenditure, i.e., whether it is charged to an asset account or directly to expense is really irrelevant, except as it affects the tax status of the expenditure. For example, advertising and research expenditures are made with a view to benefiting a firm with an increase in future sales. They can and should be analyzed as capital expenditures, although accounting custom has decreed that such expenditures are to be written off as they are incurred. From the manager's point of view capital expenditures are made primarily to acquire a stream of future benefits, and only secondarily to acquire the tangible or intangible assets which yield the benefits.

1

As the examples cited at the beginning of this section indicate, capital expenditures are made by business firms, by governments, and by individuals or households. The basic problem which must be resolved in deciding which expenditures to make out of the infinity of available alternatives is very similar in all cases, irrespective of the sector of the economy in which the decision maker is located. In the chapters which follow, the basic similarity of capital expenditure decision problems will be examined in more detail, although the complicating features affecting different types of decisions made by different types of decision-making units will also be examined.

Our analysis will be restricted to investment in assets which produce continuing benefits. Investment in assets which turn over rapidly, such as inventories, accounts receivable, and other working capital items will not be considered explicitly. While parts of the analytical apparatus to be developed here, particularly the treatment of costs of capital in Chapters 5 and 6 are of importance in considering such investments, a complete analytical framework for them is beyond the scope of this book.

1.2 Why Are Capital Expenditure Decisions So Important?

At this point, the reader may well ask why capital expenditures deserve to be treated in a different manner than consumption expenditures or routine purchases of any kind. Surely all expenditures, at least those of equal amounts, are of equal importance, and are deserving of equal consideration. While this is a tempting observation, there are several practical reasons for placing greater emphasis on capital expenditure decisions.

First of all, the consequences of capital expenditures extend into the future, and will have to be endured for a longer period than the consequences of current operating expenditures. John and Ethel Smith's decision about their house will determine the kind of housing they will have for some time to come. Government capital expenditure decisions determine where roads and railways will be built, what water supplies will be available in what localities, and in some countries what types of public utility services will be provided, and where. Such decisions go a long way toward determining where business firms will locate and where population will grow and decline, and they may have a profound effect on the nature of society within the country.

In the case of the manufacturing firm, capital expenditure decisions are going to determine what plants will be built, where they will be built, and how they will be equipped. These factors in turn largely determine what can be made in the plants. Such decisions shape the basic character of the firm, or its "image", and as such may be very important.

Capital expenditure decisions are quite often irreversible, because there is little or no secondhand market for many types of capital goods. (Some intangible capital assets, such as an individual's professional education, may be inherently nontransferable.) The only alternative to continuing to use the asset is to scrap it, recognize the loss, and start anew. Because of these two features, capital expenditures effectively commit the firm to a given technology, and significantly determine the future pattern of operating expenditures, so the dollar-and-cents importance of the commitment goes far beyond the initial outlay.

In his classic study of economic development, Schumpeter focused attention on the importance of innovation and the role of entrepreneurship in the process of economic growth. To Schumpeter, innovation is the introduction of new production functions into the general equilibrium framework of the economy.[1] In this process, the ideas of entrepreneurs are translated into reality through the medium of capital expenditures. The growth process is essentially generated and given direction by capital expenditures, and the efficiency of the capital allocation process is one of the key factors in economic growth.

A final reason for focusing so much attention on capital expenditure decisions is that there are conceptual problems involved which necessarily make the decision process more complex. While this makes things more difficult for the decision maker, it also makes the problem more challenging.

1.3 Why Do Capital Expenditure Decisions Pose A Problem?

There are three basic reasons why capital expenditure decisions pose difficulties for the decision maker. In the first place, the hoped-for benefits will be derived in the future. The future, in the real world, is never known with certainty, though it may be convenient for the economic theorist to assume for some purposes that it is.

Secondly, even if the benefits were certain, some might be exceedingly difficult to measure in quantitative terms. This is a problem of

---

[1]J. A. Schumpeter, *The Theory of Economic Development*, trans. R. Opie (From the German ed. of 1911) (New York: Oxford, 1961), pp. 74-94.

particular importance in the case of decisions made by many government agencies and by households, but it is not entirely absent in decisions made by business firms. It is obviously desirable to measure benefits and costs in terms of Marshall's "measuring rod of money," but though we may expect a new mural in the employees' lunchroom to improve morale and productivity, it would indeed be a brave man, and perhaps an exceedingly foolish one as well, who attempted to derive a dollar-and-cents estimate of the benefits to be expected from such an investment.

Finally, even if we were able to miraculously solve the two preceding problems and measure all costs and benefits in dollar-and-cents terms (and it will be argued below that this can be done with a sufficient degree of accuracy in an important class of cases), we would still not be out of the woods. Benefits received, and costs incurred, at different points in time are not, strictly speaking, comparable. A dollar received now is not the same as a dollar to be received next month or next year, and cannot be directly compared with it.

Economic theorists and practical administrators have grappled with these three problems for years, in an attempt to formulate rational decision rules for capital expenditures. While none of the three can be regarded as completely solved, except perhaps in the simplest cases, relatively more success has been attained in resolving the third problem, at least in theory. The practical usefulness of the solutions derived unfortunately depends on the extent to which the estimates of benefits and costs used satisfactorily pass the first two hurdles. This is rather a tall order, but it must be recognized that the imprecision of such estimates is a matter of degree. While many estimates are sufficiently accurate to warrant examination within a fairly rigorous analytical framework, others are not.

The usefulness to the administrator of the analytical techniques to be described here does not, fortunately, depend on their ability to produce perfectly optimal solutions. It will be sufficient that they produce an adequate level of improvement over other techniques available. Here we stand on firmer ground. While their adoption by many business firms and government departments may have some of the earmarks of a fad, the consensus seems to be that the results justify the effort.

1.4　Interest and the Problem of Intertemporal Comparisons

Economic theory has made much progress in resolving the problem of comparing sums received at different points in time. True, it has done so in the most part by ignoring, or assuming away (which to the practical man may seem like the same thing) the problems posed by risk and uncertainty and the difficulties of measuring benefits, but let us not belittle the extent of the accomplishment. The intellectual problems posed managed to baffle most of the world's greatest minds for centuries, as a casual examination of the rather depressing literature on usury from Aristotle to some of the later scholastic philosophers indicates only too well.

The reason why a dollar today is worth a different amount than a dollar to be received next year lies in the existence of interest. If I have a dollar today, I can lend it and get more than a dollar back next year. Interest is the price at which claims to money now exchange for claims to money in the future. Just as the price of apples and oranges may be used to measure both apples and oranges by a common yardstick, to derive the value of a basket of fruit, the interest rate enables us to measure receipts at different dates and find the value of a series of payments. We need not be concerned here with the question of why interest exists, as we are interested only in behaving rationally in a world in which it does exist.

1.5 The Concept of Present Value

Just what is the relationship between the value of payments received at different dates? This relationship will be of fundamental importance to us in later chapters. An approach to its understanding can be gained by asking ourselves just what sum, to be received a year from now, we would regard as equivalent to a dollar in our pocket today. Suppose that if we have a dollar today, we can lend it and be sure of being repaid a year hence with interest at 6 percent. If we lent it on this basis we would get $1.06 a year from now. With this opportunity available, it is clear that $1.00 today can be exchanged for $1.06 a year from now, and is its equivalent in value. It is conventional to speak of $1.06 as the *amount of $1.00* invested *for one year* at simple interest of 6 percent, or as the *future worth* of $1.00 for one year at 6 percent.

In the general case, with an interest rate r per period, expressed as a fraction of the initial sum S, the future worth W_1 of S dollars after one year is given by:

$$W_1 = (1+r)S \qquad\qquad (1)$$

Where we look at periods longer than one year, we will recognize that the amount $S(1+r)$ received after one year can be reinvested for another year at the same interest rate, so that after two years we have:

$$W_2 = S(1+r)(1+r)$$

$$= S(1+r)^2 \tag{2}$$

and for longer periods:

$$W_n = S(1+r)^n \tag{3}$$

In many instances we already know the amount we are going to receive at some future date and are interested in knowing the present sum to which it is equivalent. It is intuitively obvious that if $1.00 is going to be worth $(1+r)$ dollars after a year, we need only $1/1+r$ dollars today to have a dollar a year from now. This amount is called the *present value of a dollar due in a year at r percent*.

In general, where Q_t is a sum to be received in t periods, and the interest rate is r, its present value V is given by

$$V_0 = \frac{Q_t}{(1+r)^t} \tag{4}$$

The process of finding present values is sometimes referred to as *discounting*, and the interest rate r used for the purpose as the *discount rate*.

Using Formula (4) we can find the present value of a sum due at some time in the future. To find the present value of a series of payments which differ from one another, it is necessary to find the present value of each payment and add, in accordance with

$$V_0 = \frac{Q_1}{1+r} + \frac{Q_2}{(1+r)^2} + \frac{Q_3}{(1+r)^3} + \cdots + \frac{Q_n}{(1+r)^n} = \sum_{t=1}^{n} \frac{Q_t}{(1+r)^t} \tag{5}$$

A special case where this is not necessary is the case of an *annuity* where the annual payments are equal. The present value of an annuity of $Q per year for n years can be found by solving:

$$V_a = Q \frac{1 - \dfrac{1}{(1+r)^t}}{r} \tag{6}$$

or by consulting tables such as those found in Appendices A and B.

A more specialized case is the perpetuity, which is simply a perpetual annuity. The present value of a perpetuity is given by:

$$V_p = \frac{Q}{r} \tag{7}$$

While truly perpetual income streams are uncommon, the formula is a useful approximation where the length of the stream is indefinitely long.[2]

The theoretical models built by many economists speak of "the" interest rate as if it were unique. The more careful ones admit that they are able to pull this rabbit out of the hat because they put it there in the first place, by assuming the existence of only one type of credit instrument or claim with a single maturity and a specified degree of risk (frequently zero). In fact, as nearly all point out, there are a number of interest rates for different types of claims of varying degrees of risk and various maturities, so that there is a structure of interest rates rather than a unique rate.[3] Economists often use the term "interest" indiscriminately to refer to the yield on capital investment represented by all types of claims, equity as well as debt. This is somewhat confusing to the layman and at variance with the definition of the term used by accountants and lawyers, all of whom tend to understand interest as a payment made for the use of borrowed money. In the following chapters, we shall be concerned at some length with the relationships between debt and equity financing, and in order to avoid the confusion caused by the indiscriminate use of the terms "interest" and "interest rate," the terms "discount," "yield," "cost of funds," and "discount rate" will be used as appropriate when the form of financing is immaterial. The former terms will be reserved for the debt case.

_____

[2]These formulas assume annual compounding. For the complications arising from other assumptions regarding compounding, the reader is referred to any of the standard texts on the mathematics of finance.

[3]Regarding the term structure of interest rates, see F. A. Lutz, "The Structure of Interest Rates," *Quarterly Journal of Economics*, Vol. LV (1940-41), pp. 36-63, reprinted in W. Fellner and B. F. Haley (eds.), *Readings in the Theory of Income Distribution* (Philadelphia: Blakiston, 1946), pp. 499-529, or see B. G. Malkiel, "Expectations, Bond Prices, and the Term Structure of Interest Rates," *Quarterly Journal of Economics*, Vol. LXXXVI (May, 1962), pp. 197-218. For the risk structure of rates on corporate debt, see L. Fisher, "The Determinants of Risk Premiums on Corporate Bonds," *Journal of Political Economy*, Vol. 67 (June, 1959), pp. 217-37, reprinted in H. K. Wu and A. J. Zakon (eds.), *Elements of Investments* (New York: Holt, Rinehart and Winston, 1965), pp. 268-96.

1.6   The Meaning of Rationality in Capital Expenditure Decisions

Economics is concerned with the allocation of scarce resources which have alternative uses to meet desired ends. Capital is a scarce resource, and the uses to which it may be devoted as well as the ends it may serve are many, so its allocation is an economic problem. We shall say that a decision maker is rational in his behavior if he allocates the capital available to him *efficiently*, i.e., so as to reach a preferred position in terms of his set of goals, which will be defined for the present as an ordering of the available ends in terms of their desirability to him (or to those whom he represents). We will leave the goal set itself completely undefined for the moment. Obviously, it will be substantially different for a spendthrift and a miser.

Rationality is merely the allocation of resources in a manner consistent with the wishes of decision makers. Given the goal set, and given transitivity in the ordering,[4] it is feasible to establish decision rules which will enable its attainment.

Ordinarily, however, it will pay to place certain constraints on the goal set. Certain types of goals are sufficiently common to warrant detailed study and the specification of decision rules for their attainment. Much of the book will be concerned with this problem. In the case of the firm, the specification of benefits and costs is relatively simple, and it will suffice for most purposes to regard the cash receipts and expenditures of the firm as synonymous with benefits and costs. We shall argue below that the maximization of the market value of the firm is a particularly suitable goal for a large class of business firms.

1.7   Rationality in Public Expenditures

It is somewhat more difficult to specify suitable goals for governments. Many of the traditional criteria of popular demagoguery can be shown to be either meaningless or self-contradictory. For example, Bentham's slogan "The greatest good for the greatest number" is of little use in choosing between two projects, one of which will yield benefits worth $1,000 to each of 1,000 citizens, and the other of which will yield benefits of $100 each to 9,000 citizens. There have been many more subtle and sophisticated attempts to resolve this problem, but these have run into a few snags as well.[5]

---

[4]An ordering is said to be transitive if it is consistent and does not contain the following sort of statements: A is preferred to B, B is preferred to C, and C is preferred to A.

[5]A. Burk (Bergson) "A Reformulation of Certain Aspects of Welfare Economics,"

There are several difficult problems, partly interrelated, which must be resolved in some fashion if public expenditure decisions are to be made on rational grounds. Some of the problems are theoretical, with profound and ill-understood philosophical implications. The others are merely practical, but no more tractable on that account.

The most fundamental difficulty is the problem of defining a "social welfare function"; it is on this bed of thorns that most of the recent discussion by economic theorists, cited above, has been impaled. The problem is simple. A fully satisfactory solution, if possible, is difficult. The problem arises because, in the strictest sense of the word, it is impossible to speak of social benefits and social costs. Benefits are enjoyed by individuals, and costs must, in the end, also be borne by individuals. The net social gain (loss) resulting from any project which creates benefits and costs within the social group is simply the sum of individuals' satisfactions created and destroyed by the project. Unfortunately, satisfactions are personal and psychological and can neither be compared nor added in any meaningful sense, unless it is possible to define a social welfare function telling us how individuals' satisfactions are to be measured, weighted, and added up.

The economists' perplexity over the problem of making interpersonal comparisons of utility must seem amusing to the practical politician, who has been making them for years. He knows, in his reflective moments, that he has made a few mistakes, but his success in politics has rested on his ability to make such comparisons and make use of them in a manner satisfactory to his constituents. He knows for example that it usually improves social welfare to take fifty cents apiece from a couple of city dwellers and give a dollar to a farmer, for the farmer's vote is apt to be worth twice as much as the city dweller's and is more likely to be bought for a dollar than are both the city dwellers' to be lost for fifty cents apiece. In fact, one can only gaze with wonder and admiration at the intricacy of some of the interpersonal comparisons regularly made by political leaders.[6]

Since this book is aimed at the practical administrator it is pro-

---

Quarterly Journal of Economics, Vol. LII (February, 1938), pp. 310-34; K. J. Arrow, *Social Choice and Individual Values* (New York: Wiley, 1951); W. J. Baumol, *Welfare Economics and the Theory of the State*, (Cambridge: Harvard, 1952); I. M. D. Little, *A Critique of Welfare Economics* (2nd ed.; London: Oxford, 1957); J. Rothenberg, *The Measurement of Social Welfare*, (Englewood Cliffs, N.J.: Prentice-Hall, 1961).

[6]Impending reapportionment in most states will change the relative weighting of votes and will provide an interesting test of the flexibility of the politicians' evaluation procedures.

posed to skirt this particular problem rather than try to solve it. The problem is important, and while the future of democracy may depend on its solution, its present problems unfortunately cannot wait for such utopian solution but must be solved with the materials at hand. It will accordingly be assumed that the administrator has some sort of a social welfare function and knows, for example, that benefits received by farmers are to be given a weight of two, costs borne by them a weight of three, that city folks count for one each, and perhaps that utility corporations count for five (or minus five, depending on the location) before elections and nothing after.

The incomparability problem aside, some formidable difficulties remain in the public expenditure field. Assuming we know how to add up the benefits and costs imposed on different individuals we are still faced with the problem of measuring them and determining their incidence. How much is the nuclear deterrent worth to a city dweller in New York? To a farmer in North Dakota? Less extreme examples abound. This problem is bad enough in the business firm, but is magnified in the political context because the benefits and costs are frequently intangible and because market prices may be an inappropriate guide even for the tangible ones in certain cases where external economies or diseconomies are involved or when unemployed resources are being used for the project. This problem exists purely at the practical level but is a serious one. It is complicated by the natural propensity of those proposing a project which will benefit them (and these are often the only ones who give it detailed scrutiny) for magnifying real benefits and creating imaginary ones to the limits of decency, and sometimes beyond, while sweeping as many of the costs as possible under the carpet.[7]

The public decision problem is, like the corporate one, twofold. The spending authority is (or should be) concerned first of all with allocating its budget efficiently, in such a manner as to maximize the excess of public benefits over public costs, as defined by the social welfare function, regardless of the size of the budget. The second half of the problem is knowing where to stop, i.e., determining what the size of the budget ought to be. This problem is not too serious for the corporate decision maker, for market forces operate in such a way as to keep him in line, but there is no such constraint on the public decision

---

[7]See, for example, the examples cited by J. Hirshleifer, J. C. DeHaven and J. W. Milliman, *Water Supply, Economics, Technology and Policy* (Chicago: University of Chicago Press, 1961).

maker who can call upon the taxing powers of the state or the money-printing powers of the central bank.

This question is really crucial, for the answer given determines the size of the public sector in the economy, and conflicting answers to it have been the source of much of the political controversy of our time. An easy answer, and a wrong one, is that if public benefits exceed public costs, a project is worthwhile and should be undertaken. It is wrong because it ignores the fact that capital expenditures in the private sector create social benefits as well, and if resources are diverted from the private sector to the public sector and used there to produce smaller benefits (as measured by the social welfare function) than they would have in the private sector, then society is worse off as a result. These problems will be examined in more detail in Chapters 4 and 7.

1.8 Needed: A Systematic Approach to Capital Expenditure Management

While our primary focus is on the decision problems involved in the administration of capital spending, there is more to administration than just decision making. Successful use of capital, whether by a business firm, a household, or a government requires the generation and analysis of proposed projects, deciding which projects to carry out, and the execution of the project selected. In the going concern, it also requires the exercise of continuing control over the entire process.

The importance of generating proposals ought to be self-evident. Even if a perfect solution to the decision-making problem existed, which is not the case at the present time, its application to an ill-assorted lot of generally deficient proposals will not lead to the efficient utilization of capital resources. While many possible uses for funds just appear (particularly in governments) there is little doubt that the relative lack of success of many firms is due to a failure to generate enough profitable outlets for funds. The current fad for institutionalized research and development activity is the result of efforts to systematize the generation of investment opportunities rather than waiting for them to happen along. There is an economic limit to this process, brought about by the fact that it costs money to generate projects and to consider them. Our understanding of the process of innovation is highly imperfect, and there is little doubt that there is much room for improvement in this area.

It has been argued that, because of this, the emphasis on evaluation and decision-making procedures in the literature on capital expenditure management has been misplaced, and that most of it should be scrapped, or at least that economists should stop pestering businessmen and politicians to improve their decision-making procedures.[8] The germ of truth contained in this position should not be permitted, however, to become an excuse for sloppy or inappropriate evaluation procedures. The generation of a large volume of investment proposals means, inevitably, the generation of a lot of paperwork for their evaluation. Evaluation procedures can be made relatively routine, and it is not demonstrably more expensive to evaluate projects correctly than to evaluate them incorrectly. The only cost is the added cost (if any) of getting the evaluation system right in the first place or of changing a bad system for a good one. For a firm adding to its assets by as little as $50,000 per year, an improvement of 2 percent in the average return on investment after taxes could justify an expenditure of over $90,000 on overhauling the firm's capital budgeting system if the firm's cost of capital were 12 percent. For a firm spending $1 million yearly, the corresponding amount is $1.8 million. This book is clearly a great bargain and should be on the desk of everyone in your firm.

The best of projects, carefully chosen, are no guarantee of success. Execution is not always just a matter of giving the appropriate orders. However, this is not a treatise on administration, and we will assume here that the administrator either knows how to get things done or can find out somewhere else.

PROBLEMS

1. Considering your education as an investment project, can you identify *(a)* the benefits, *(b)* the costs, which you would use in an analysis to determine its economic desirability? Which of these can be measured in monetary terms? What difficulties arise in attempting to measure them?

2. What is the present value of the following future payments, assuming annual compounding?

Amount due	Due in	Interest rate
100	1 year	6%
350	3	4
200	2	5
600	4	8
1,000	50	20
1,000	100	3

[8]W. W. Haynes and M. B. Solomon, Jr., "A Misplaced Emphasis in Capital Budgeting," *Quarterly Review of Economics and Business* (February, 1962), pp. 39-46.

3. Show that

$$V = \sum_t \frac{Q_t}{(1+r)^t}$$

reduces to

$$V = Q_t \frac{1 - \dfrac{1}{(1+r)^t}}{r}$$

where Q_t is a constant.

4. Show that

$$V = Q \frac{1 - \dfrac{1}{(1+r)^t}}{r}$$

approaches

$$\frac{Q}{r}$$

as t increases.

5. Examine a recent legislative enactment (national or local) involving the raising of funds by a specific tax and their expenditure. Can you identify the implicit weights used by the legislature in evaluating the contributions to and from the particular groups affected? Are these weights consistent with other enactments of the same legislature?

CHAPTER 2

The Capital Expenditure
Decision Process

2.1 Introduction

The capital expenditure process in any economic unit involves several distinct steps. Proposals to spend money must be generated, alternatives must be weighed against one another, decisions must be made to carry out specific projects, and action must be taken on these decisions. These steps, which we will refer to as project generation, project evaluation, project selection, and project execution are necessary in any organization which makes capital expenditures. Executive action which is directed at control of the capital expenditure process must concern itself with each of these steps and will usually find it necessary to add additional steps to keep the process under control. Thus it may impose budgetary controls on the execution of projects to see that authorized expenditure limits are not exceeded without review. Where appropriate, it may establish a system of "postaudit," i.e. following up the results of completed projects, either within the organization's regular cost accounting system or in addition to it, to provide a continuing check on the effectiveness of the decision-making process.

The extent to which the process needs to be formalized and systematic procedures established depends on the size of the organization, on the number of projects which must be considered, and on their complexity and diversity. What's good for General Motors may not be good for the corner store. While even the latter may face occasional decisions calling for careful evaluation along the lines to be discussed here, it must be remembered that increasing sophistication costs money and that the cost of the decision-making process should not be increased beyond the savings likely to result from the superior decision.[1]

[1]W. J. Baumol and R. E. Quandt, "Rules of Thumb and Optimally Imperfect Decisions," *American Economic Review*, Vol. LIV (March, 1964), pp. 23-46.

In most organizations, ultimate control over capital expenditures is reserved to the highest levels of management. Such expenditures affect the long-term spending patterns of the organization, and their effects may not be as easily reversed as decisions over the allocation of current operating expenditures. One does not buy a furnace without committing himself to a succession of fuel bills, the size of which may very well depend on the kind of furnace chosen. Because of this characteristic, capital expenditure decisions are among the class of decisions which are best reserved for consideration by the highest levels of management.[2] This does not mean that the entire process has to be confined to the top levels, but it does mean that, where parts of it are to be decentralized, care must be taken to establish policies and procedures which retain effective control of the entire process in the hands of the group ultimately responsible for its results, even though some authority may be delegated.

2.2 Project Generation

It is normally not too difficult to obtain a set of proposals for spending money. The trick, however, is to obtain the *right* set of proposals.

The decision to establish a firm, is, in nearly all cases, a decision to undertake certain capital expenditures. Based on their studies of the market for the proposed product, the promoters will examine alternative plans for meeting the demand and will select, using capital budgeting criteria, the alternative which appears to be the most economic. Here the investment proposal originates within the entrepreneurial group, though they may call on technical specialists for advice.

Once the firm has been established as a going concern, investment proposals may be generated at several levels within it. These will normally fall into one of the following classifications:

1. *(a)* Proposals to add new products to the product line. *(b)* Proposals to expand capacity in existing product lines.
2. Proposals designed to reduce costs in the output of existing products without altering the scale of operations.

In the literature on capital theory, decisions of type 1 involve the choice of "scale" and lead to so-called "capital widening," while decisions of type 2 involve the choice of "technique" and lead to "capital deepening." The distinction is for the most part of theoretical rather than

---

[2]W. H. Newman, "Basic Objectives which Shape the Character of a Company," *Journal of Business*, Vol. 26 (October, 1953), pp. 211-33.

practical importance,[3] and in practice many proposals include elements of both. Either type of proposal may originate at any level within the firm, from the board of directors down to the production line worker, and it is probable that a large proportion of proposals originate in a rather haphazard fashion. New products are suggested by the sales force or by plant foremen who see a way of utilizing idle capacity, while improvements in technique may result from suggestions coming from the factory floor. Few managements seek to discourage new ideas, and the ubiquitous "suggestion box" may sometimes yield something more valuable than discarded gum wrappers.

However, because of the eventual obsolescence of most products and the desire of management for sustained growth in the firm, many firms have found that it pays to be more systematic in the search for new investment opportunities. A firm which does not generate enough investment proposals to keep its funds fully employed is not going to grow but is going to decline and vanish sooner or later. A firm which merely generates this volume is unlikely to do much better. The healthy firm is one in which there is a continual flow of profitable investment proposals, and one in which the problem of choice between proposals is serious.

The search for opportunities of type 2 is most frequently systematized by continuous review of production operations, either as part of the responsibility of line managers or by separate work study or industrial engineering groups in staff positions, or both. These same sources are likely to be involved, along with marketing management, in proposals to increase the scale of operations.

In the early Industrial Revolution, and well into the 20th century, ideas for new products tended most frequently to originate with inventors, who either started new enterprises with the aid of promoters or took their ideas to existing firms.[4] One of the outstanding features of the continual evolution of capitalism has been the assimilation of the process of invention into the firm itself and its subsequent systematization. This has led to a continuous search for new and better products to supplement or supplant those currently produced. One of the results which is a favorite target of social critics has been the phenomenon of "planned obsolescence." While there may be aspects

---

[3]See, e.g., F. A. Hayek, *Prices and Production* (2d ed.; London: Routledge, 1935) for an analysis of possible relationships between capital deepening and the business cycle.

[4]J. Jewkes, D. Sawers, and R. Stillerman, *The Sources of Invention* (London: Macmillan, 1958).

of this which deserve criticism, it should be remembered that if the firm itself didn't plan to make its own products obsolescent, its competitors would, so that we would probably get to the same place but more slowly, with more turnover in the business population, dislocation in the labor force, losses to investors and disruption of communities. The wastes resulting from planned obsolescence within the firm are easily seen and noted, while the wastes that would have resulted from its alternatives didn't occur, are less obvious, and are easily ignored. The other alternative is to forbid change entirely, which is not a possible alternative in a free society.

This institutionalization of the inventive process has come about through the growth in science and technology as formal academic disciplines and the establishment of engineering departments and research departments in business firms. The firm which wants to stay healthy must organize itself in this fashion if it is to continue to innovate and grow.

In government, there is perhaps less danger of a shortage of proposals for spending money. In North America, traditional political beliefs concerning the role of government in the economy tend to inhibit its activity as an innovator. In spite of this, its scope has been continuously growing. Within the boundaries it has set for itself, however, there are two possible approaches to the allocation of funds. Roads can be built where the political pressures are too great to resist, or they can be built as part of a coherently planned highway system. While there have been undoubted improvements in the way governments approach problems of this type, there is still a great deal of room for improvement. The growth of government activity has occurred without any systematic search for investment opportunities, with few standards for evaluation, and without the discipline of the market place. As a result, large sums have been invested in the pet projects of pressure groups, the rates of return on which, by any rational system of evaluation, are exceedingly low, if not negative. Other projects, also within the political responsibility of government but which could yield very high social rates of return, have been neglected. While lack of standards for evaluation must bear part of the blame, a large part must be attributed to the passive, haphazard nature of the government's search for investment opportunities.

There is a need, in government, to adopt and adapt the practices of industry in this regard. This must embrace the search for all types of socially profitable investments, whether of the cost-reducing, scale-increasing, or "new product" variety, within its defined sphere of activity. The systematic search for cost-reducing projects has been a routine practice in industry for well over half a century. The reports of the Hoover Commission in the United States and the Glassco Commission in Canada indicate the extent of the lag. While steps are being taken to systematize generation of cost reduction projects, public funds will continue to be frittered away until the entire process is rationalized to a greater extent than it is at present.

This requirement is even more pressing for the developing countries. Many of these envisage a greater role for government in the economy, which, whatever its possible philosophical merits, offers greater opportunities for waste if the whole expenditure process is not brought under control. While waste may be tolerated in more affluent societies, it may spell the difference between success and failure in reaching self-sustained growth in countries where capital for both the private and public sector is scarce and the margin between success and failure is paper-thin.

2.3 Project Evaluation

The basic steps in project evaluation are the estimation of benefits and costs and the conversion of such estimates into measures of desirability.

The basic difference between the evaluation process within the firm and within government is in the estimation of benefits and costs; the measures of desirability are formally identical. The firm need only concern itself with the private benefits and costs accruing to the firm, which are usually expressed in the values of the market place. Governments, on the other hand must identify and measure social benefits and costs which are frequently not measurable from market data and must further identify the incidence of such benefits and costs on particular groups in society, then apply appropriate weights to the different interests involved before the estimates can be converted into measures of desirability.

It has sometimes been argued that it is a fundamental social responsibility of business firms to take account of social benefits and social costs in their operations. While the firm is certainly at liberty to do so if it wishes, its suitability, as an institution, for this social role is questionable. This is particularly true in those cases where there are large discrepancies between private and social costs on the one hand, and benefits, on the other. In the first place, if the firm is operating in a highly competitive industry and competitive factor markets, the attempt to provide for social costs (e.g., smoke, industrial diseases) is a royal road to competitive ruin, unless competitors do likewise. Ignoring them may be the key to success. It is essential for the state to intervene in such instances to make private costs equal to social costs for all firms if the socially irresponsible are not to drive the socially responsible out of the industry. This principle has been recognized, at least in part, since the first Factory Acts in England in the early 19th century.

Even if the firm has sufficient market power to assess the full social cost of its operations against the consumers of its product, the desirability of its doing so is open to question. Such a decision involves a value judgment to the effect that compensation should be paid, and another to the effect that customers should be assessed to pay for it. Such a decision is clearly political in nature, and corporate managements do not have any express mandate from the electorate to make them. To the extent that the state does not intervene in the exercise of such judgments, there is an implicit delegation of authority, but this is hardly enough. Such responsibility is unsought, and its exercise calls for judgments of a type qualitatively different from normal managerial decisions. If society wishes to equalize social and private costs and to redistribute real income, then it should do so systematically, through political processes, rather than expect corporate management to fill the power vacuum.

As a concrete example, consider the following case. Company A has substantial control over the price of its product, through the possession of market power and is faced with a strong union under a closed shop agreement. The product is of minor importance in the economy. The rest of the economy, and the labor market, is perfectly competitive or nearly so.

Suppose further that pension costs may fairly be considered as part of the long run social cost of labor. In the competitive sector of the economy, labor sells for a price dominated by short run conditions, i.e., containing no element of pension. Nor can employers in the competitive sector offer pensions unilaterally because their competitors will not. If A grants its unionized employees a pension, its management is behaving in a "socially responsible" manner. To the extent that the pension costs are met through higher prices, it is transferring real income to its employees from its customers, most of whom do not have pensions. To the extent that pension costs are met out of profits, it is transferring real income away from its shareholders, who may not have pensions either. The equity of such an arrangement is at least open to question, though we shall not pursue the matter further here.

There are few cases in which benefits and costs are known precisely beforehand, so their estimation inevitably involves forecasting. Because the future is uncertain, such estimates may differ widely from the ultimate results. This has at least two implications for evaluation.

Outcomes are, a priori, random variables. Single-value estimates may represent the expected value of the probability distribution of outcomes, or may be systematically biassed. In either case the relative dispersion of outcomes and the consequent risks associated with different projects usually differ, and this should be taken into account in the decision process. We will examine various ways of doing this later. The important point to be noted here is that some analysis of possible alternative outcomes must be an integral part of the evaluation process.

The other implication is that evaluation ought to be done by an impartial group which has no axe to grind. Operating departments are prone to want the latest in equipment for reasons having little to do with productivity, and this may consciously or unconsciously affect their estimates of the potential benefits to be derived from it. Good salesmen are by nature or by training optimistic and may not be the best source of estimates of the marketability of a new product. All projects ought to be scrutinized carefully by a staff group which has no vested interest in their adoption, and evaluation should be subject to review to insure that objectivity remains their basic concern and isn't replaced with mere conservatism.

As mentioned above, evaluation also involves converting measures of benefits and costs into measures of desirability. Once desirability measures are established, such conversion is a routine clerical operation or can be easily programmed on a computer. Care should be taken, however, that the desirability measures chosen do not unconsciously discriminate in favor of certain types of projects rather than others which may be more productive but unusual in some respect. While many of the criteria proposed may give similar results on most of the types of projects examined by the company, they may seriously misrank the unusual project. Criteria chosen should be as general in application as possible.

2.4 Project Selection

As indicated, responsibility for the results of capital expenditures rests on top management. Top management may delegate authority to approve certain types of capital expenditures, while limiting the amount, controlling the criteria used in selection, and holding the lower levels accountable for the results.

In a healthy organization, actual selection among projects which have been proposed must be done by the responsible line executives. Much of the evaluation of projects will ordinarily be done by staff specialists, and the calculation of measures of desirability is essentially clerical in nature. While a great deal of screening must be done at the evaluation stage, care should be taken to insure that the function of line management is not reduced to one of rubber-stamping capital budgets prepared in all their essentials by the staff group. A sufficiently large number of proposals should survive the evaluation process to insure that the real decisions are being made at the appropriate level in the organization and to insure that no unusual but worthwhile proposals are eliminated. Judgment must be exercised ultimately by those responsible and will remain, inevitably, as a factor modifying the specialists' evaluation. Proposals passed to management for ultimate selection should be presented with sufficient detail and supporting data to enable the estimates of the evaluation group to be checked and modified where necessary.

When the final selection has been made, funds are appropriated and the budget system takes over.

2.5 The Budgetary System

The funds appropriated for capital expenditures make up the capital budget, which is administered by the accounting department of the organization. While appropriation of funds normally constitutes approval in principle for the expenditures, control must be exercised to ensure that funds are spent as intended. Before signing contracts, those responsible for the execution of projects will apply through the controller for formal authority to spend the funds. After comparing the proposed expenditures with the budget, the controller will authorize the expenditures. Then, as invoices appear, they will be charged against the budget. Monthly budget reports will indicate the status of all projects, i.e., total appropriated, outstanding authorizations, and actual expenditures made. Most systems will permit individual appropriations to be exceeded by some small margin to allow for errors in estimating, the balance to be transferred from other projects. Major overruns will ordinarily require supplementary appropriations from the approving authority, while minor ones will usually require explanation. There are, of course endless variations of the above basic system in actual use. There is no point in pursuing the accounting technicalities here.

Besides the control of expenditures, the accounting department will be responsible for preparing the data for budget reviews, separating the costs and revenues associated with particular projects for several years after their completion in order to provide a check on the operation of the evaluation and selection process. Without this feedback relationship, estimates can diverge further and further from reality without anyone being the wiser.

The budgetary process in most government bodies is deficient in several respects. There is control over expenditures but seldom any followup. Costs are frequently recorded in ways which make followup impossible. The budgets themselves are deficient in that all expenditures, capital and operating, are scrambled up in a single bulky document with little explanation and no supporting data. Most operating expenditures are virtually nondiscretionary and result from programs started in prior years. A great deal of legislative time is spent plowing through such estimates which might better be concentrated on the capital expenditures which effectively commit the government to future operating expenditures. In addition, the practice of annual appropriations may mean that parts of a project appear in several successive annual budgets, while the project as a whole is never examined in all its ramifications. Budgetary practices have been the subject of unfavorable comment in reports by commissions on government organization. The adoption of their proposals is an urgently needed reform, even if it means altering some of the cherished traditions of parliamentary procedure.

2.6 Capital Budgeting Criteria and Project Design

It is of course important that all levels of management understand the budgeting system and the criteria by which proposals are selected. Communication should embrace not only the criteria but the approximate standards required for acceptable projects. Nowhere is this more important than in the engineering design of new projects. Good engineering practice seeks optimal *economic* solutions for technical problems and considers economic data in addition to technical data. Design personnel require an understanding of the standards used for selection if they are to do their job effectively. In particular, when a cost-of-capital criterion is used for deciding between alternative projects on the basis of their prospective rates of return, or when a cutoff rate is used, it is essential that the discount rate assumed for design purposes *be* the cost-of-capital rate or the cutoff rate if design engineers are not to be working at cross-purposes with the rest of the organization. The most economical plant, designed on the assumption that the cost of capital is 6 percent, will not be the most economical plant for a firm whose cost of capital is 15 percent. The techniques selected will be too capital-intensive, and the scale too large. This failure of communication, if carried far enough, can lead to the design of projects which are never acceptable. Alternative designs based on varying assumptions about the cost of capital could be prepared but the designing of plants is expensive.

The need to know the appropriate cost of capital for design purposes well in advance of the actual proposal of projects is one of the basic reasons for using estimated cost of capital or some other criterion known in advance, rather than a rule which determines the effective cutoff rate by considering the availability of funds on some arbitrary basis. It is also a practical objection to the suggestion of Gordon that estimation of the cost of capital is not necessary since both the cost of capital and the optimum budget may simultaneously be determined using an investment decision model.[5] While the theoretical case for the Gordon position is excellent, it cannot be applied in practice unless the model can be broadened to incorporate project design as well.

2.7   Budget Review and Followup Calculations

The information feedback provided by a review of the results of projects carried out has been mentioned as a necessary part of the structure of controls. Obtaining the necessary information may require some modification of existing information systems in the business firm and may require more elaborate gathering of statistics in a government body.

In the business firm, the only change normally necessary will be to keep direct cost and sales records on a sufficiently detailed basis to enable the identification of those revenues or costs associated with a particular project. It will ordinarily suffice to compare actual cash outlays and expenditures with those forecast; there is no need to get unduly elaborate. Additional coding on data inputs will normally be

---

[5]M. J. Gordon, *The Investment, Financing, and Valuation of the Corporation* (Homewood, Ill.: Irwin, 1962), p. 219.

required along with some additional reports. What should normally be avoided is an attempt to integrate data for this purpose into an all-purpose cost accounting system. Fully distributed costs may be useful for many purposes, but the essence of project evaluation is the consideration of what are essentially direct and marginal costs, on a cash basis rather than an accrual basis, so that fully distributed costs are of little use in checking evaluation estimates. It should be noted that the eventual outcome of a project will be only one of the possible outcomes that was considered in the initial evaluation. Even if a probability distribution of outcomes was explicitly considered, only one can emerge. There are serious difficulties in attempting to evaluate the performance of the valuation group, insofar as its estimates of probabilities are concerned, on the basis of accounting data. This problem has yet to be resolved.

There will always be some subjective elements in the review. Insofar as the selection of a project means the rejection of alternatives, there will not be any "actual" figures for the alternatives. It will ordinarily suffice if the projected cash flows of the adopted alternative turn out to have been reasonably consistent with the results.

In government bodies, benefit-cost studies on completed projects are fraught with many difficulties similar to those involved in preparing the initial projections. Many of the benefits and costs will be external, not appearing in the government's accounts, and others will be non-monetary in nature and difficult to measure in monetary terms. Still other benefits and costs may have been overlooked. While we must, because of the nature of the data and the projects, be willing to make allowances for uncertainty, there is no excuse for failure to attempt an objective appraisal of results, even (or especially?) if the project was undertaken by the opposing party.

PROBLEMS

1. Which of the following groups do you think would be the most suitable to assume responsibility for evaluating proposed capital expenditures in a medium-sized firm? Why?

   (a) The accounting department,
   (b) The engineering department,
   (c) A special group reporting to the sales manager,
   (d) The purchasing department,
   (e) Someone else.

2. *(a)* Distinguish between the following projects as (i) capital widening, (ii) capital deepening.

   (1) Construction of a new restaurant by a chain,

   (2) Installation of automatic dishwashers in one of its restaurants,

   (3) Construction of a parking garage adjacent to one of its restaurants,

   (4) Acquisition of a frozen-foods processor by the restaurant chain.

   (b) Should this classification make any difference in the selection process? Why?

3. Construct flow charts showing the steps in the capital expenditure process in (a) the federal government, (b) a system you would regard as ideal. Ignore the actual evaluation procedure and decision criteria, but focus your attention on identifying the location of responsibility for various steps in the overall process, the structure of controls, and the information feedbacks in the system. Compare the two.

CHAPTER 3

The Evaluation Process:
Criteria for Measuring Desirability

3.1 Basic Requirements

A systematic review of the literature on investment decisions will reveal a bewildering variety of suggested criteria on which to base them. Terborgh, in a review of the literature down to 1948, found several dozen proposed rules for equipment replacement decisions alone, most of which as he stated "are theoretical orphans," and many of which "border on superstition."[1] If the whole literature on investment decisions, including that dealing with government decisions, is included, many more could be added to the list, though it is questionable whether more light would be shed on the problem in the process.

Our discussion will be confined to the most widely accepted criteria and will attempt to produce some order out of the chaos.

Part of the conflict between different criteria arises out of the possible multiplicity of goals which it is sought to serve. In most of this chapter, it will be assumed that the goal sought is either maximum profit, in the case of the firm, or maximum efficiency in the use of capital, in the case of society as a whole, subject to a constraint on risk.

In considering capital expenditure decisions, in which time must enter as an explicit feature of the calculation, maximization of profits will be taken to mean maximization of the *present value* of profits. Present value is used to provide a common yardstick, enabling us to resolve conflicts between present and future profits. Later on we shall consider some special criteria that can be applied when other goals are sought. We shall assume throughout that benefits and costs are suitably measured, postponing the discussion of what constitutes suitable measurement until later chapters.

---

[1]G. Terborgh, *Dynamic Equipment Policy* (New York: McGraw-Hill, 1949), p. 271.

Any criterion must provide, at least, a means of distinguishing between acceptable and unacceptable projects. It must also solve the problem of choosing techniques; if there are two acceptable ways of doing something, it must choose between them. For a number of reasons we would also like it to provide us with a ranking of projects in order of their desirability. In some respects, it may seem simpler to provide a ranking than a clear-cut "yes" or "no." This is because of the uncertainties surrounding the cost-of-capital question, to which Chapters 5 to 7 are devoted. On the other hand, alternative criteria which produce identical accept-reject decisions may not produce identical rankings, so we must tread warily and understand the reasons for this inconsistency if we are to use the appropriate criterion in the appropriate circumstances.

In reaching decisions, any suitable criterion must respect the following two fundamental principles:

(a) The "Bigger the Better" Principle.
     Other things being equal, bigger benefits are preferable to smaller ones.
(b) The "Bird in the Hand" Principle.
     Other things being equal, early benefits are preferable to later benefits.

As the "other things" which must be held equal for each of these includes the variable on which the other depends, and as other things are seldom equal in any event, these principles themselves can hardly be used as criteria, and some means must be found of taking account of both in a single yardstick.

Finally, it must be a criterion which is applicable to any conceivable investment project. As long as the investments being considered are fairly similar in term of size, life, and the time-shape of the earnings streams, many of the proposed criteria will do a tolerable ranking job. When something of a different nature comes along they may fail signally to give it an appropriate ranking among the conventional alternatives.

3.2 Urgency

The use of "urgency" as the stated criterion for the selection of investment projects is often little more than a semantic cover for the lack of any criterion at all. Yet many firms and governments continue to use it as a criterion, or at least claim that it is the criterion they use.

The only objection to urgency is that unless it is defined in a certain way it is totally lacking in objectivity and is not quantifiable. Its use means the acceptance of projects on the basis of nothing more substantial than the persuasiveness of their proponents. The only valid measure of urgency in a firm which seeks to maximize profits is the contribution of the project to that goal. If a project does not contribute to the attainment of the goals of the organization, then it is a figment of the imagination to describe it as urgent.

Merely to insist that urgency is a derivative characteristic, not an intrinsic one, is not to deny the existence of urgency, properly understood, or its importance. "Urgency" may in certain circumstances of genuine emergency be a suitable and sufficient justification for undertaking a project. For example, if a minor machine breaks down, causing a complete stoppage of production, the cash flow resulting from its replacement is the entire cash flow of the operation, so the return on the investment will, in fact, be astronomical. In such circumstances insisting on calculations of rates of return, and so on, prior to replacement would be somewhat irrelevant and possibly even harmful if the result is to delay the resumption of production.

The basic problem, of course, is in deciding when real urgency exists. If appropriate controls are not enforced, there will be a tendency on the part of some operating managers to undertake pet projects, not otherwise acceptable, on grounds of supposed urgency. The problem should be kept within manageable proportions by giving operating managers authority to make emergency appropriations up to a suitable limit on their own authority, but with subsequent review elsewhere in the organization to see that they conform to acceptable criteria.

3.3 Payback

Pride of place in any discussion of investment criteria should be assigned to payback, not because of its merits but because of its wide usage. It is popular not only with North American business executives, but under the name "recoupment period" with Soviet planners as well.[2] The former apparently avoid more complicated computations involving present value calculations because they don't understand them, or fear their superiors won't, the latter because the concepts of interest and profit are anathematized in Marxist dogma.

---

[2]This is provided as an additional argument for junior managers seeking to get rid of obsolete systems relying on payback.

Payback is simply a measure of the time required for the cash income from a project to return the initial investment to the firm's treasury.[3]

The basic ranking depends on the length of the payback period, projects having quicker paybacks being preferred. The method can be extended to the analysis of the problem of choosing between more and less capital intensive techniques by calculating the payback (out of the difference in cash flow between the two projects) on the additional investment required for the more expensive of two conflicting and mutually exclusive projects, as shown in Table 3-1. If the payback period on the incremental investment for the more expensive project exceeds the minimum standard required, then the more expensive alternative should be adopted. In the example shown in Table 3-1, if the required payback standard is three years or less, project *A* should be adopted rather than project *B*, for although project *B* meets the standard, the part of it representing the increase in investment over *A* does not.

TABLE 3-1
APPLICATION OF PAYBACK ANALYSIS TO
TECHNIQUE PROBLEM

	Project A	Project B	Incremental
Initial Cost	$5,000	$7,000	2,000
Cash flow year:			
1	2,000	2,500	500
2	2,000	2,500	500
3	2,000	2,500	500
4	2,000	2,500	500
Payback	2.5 years	2.8 years	4.0 years

Is payback a suitable criterion for evaluating projects? It is difficult to give an unequivocal answer, for it does have certain advantages. In the first place, it is easy to calculate. All that is needed are estimates of the cash flows for the first few years, and the ability to subtract these successively from the initial investment and to calculate the fractional remainder. Its apparent simplicity also accounts for its widespread popularity.

On deeper examination, however, its understandability is a little more questionable. Is what it measures a reliable index of profitability?

---

[3]In its simplest and most logical form. Other versions use book profits, after deducting depreciation, and may make some provision for interest.

The answer unfortunately must be, in general, no. It ignores the "bigger the better" principle completely, in that it does not take any account of cash flows after the investment has been recovered. It gives some attention to timing, but doesn't adequately satisfy the "bird in the hand" principle either because it gives all receipts prior to recovery a weight of one and all subsequent receipts a weight of zero. The pairs of projects shown in Table 3-2 *(AB, XY)* would be ranked equally by the payback criterion. Are they really equally desirable?

TABLE 3–2
AMBIGUITY OF THE PAYBACK CRITERION

	A	B	X	Y
Initial cost	$5,000	$5,000	$6,000	$6,000
Cash flow year:				
1	2,500	2,500	3,000	1,000
2	2,600	2,600	2,000	2,000
3	0	2,800	1,000	3,000
4	0	3,000	500	500
5	0	3,200	0	0

There are cases where all projects have long lives, substantially in excess of the payback period, and where income streams are equal from year to year. In such cases, the payback criterion is a good approximation to the reciprocal of the internal rate of return criterion discussed below. However, we seek a criterion usable with any conceivable project type, for short lived projects as well as long, for highly irregular cash flows as well as regular ones, and if such projects may have to be considered, payback is not an adequate criterion.

Some administrative difficulty arises because of the need to determine a cutoff point. This is not too serious a problem, however, as most sources of long term funds have the characteristics noted above, so that the reciprocal of the cost of capital rate (see Chapters 5-7) may be used as a maximum acceptable payout period, e.g., if the cost of capital is 25 percent, paybacks must be less than four years.

All is not black and white, however. While recognizing the desirability of using lifetime earnings estimates, and giving due weight to each year, many investments are made where the income from the investment is highly uncertain and its life expectancy more so. (Can you make a 10-year cash flow forecast for a hula-hoop bender?) Under such circumstances, payback may become important, not so much as a measure of profitability but as a means of establishing an upper bound on the acceptable degree of risk. Where one can appraise the near future with some confidence, but is completely in the dark about longer term prospects, a short payout period may be an adequate guarantee against loss, investment being undertaken as a sporting proposition in the hope that some of the projects will last long enough to make the whole operation profitable. In such circumstances any attempt to maximize profits is really a shot in the dark.

3.4 Accounting Rates of Return

This general heading is used to describe a number of similar approaches which use accounting records or proforma statements to measure profitability as an annual percentage of the capital employed.[4] Much smoke, and little light, has been generated by a discussion of whether these are "true" rates of return.[5] The answer in brief, is that they are, if that is how you want to define the "true" rate of return, but whether the results are useful as an investment criterion is another story.

The most elaborate version, and the most thoroughly consistent one, takes average income, as measured by a series of proforma income statements, as a percentage of average investment; i.e., average book value after deducting depreciation.

Table 3–3 indicates the calculations for a project costing $5,000 with scrap value of $1,000 and annual incomes as shown.

TABLE 3–3
ACCOUNTING RATE OF RETURN: VERSION I

	Year 1	Year 2	Year 3	Year 4	Average
Cash income	1,500	2,000	2,500	3,000	2,250
Depreciation	1,000	1,000	1,000	1,000	1,000
Net income	500	1,000	1,500	2,000	1,250
Book value:					
Jan. 1	5,000	4,000	3,000	2,000	
Dec. 31	4,000	3,000	2,000	1,000	
Average	4,500	3,500	2,500	1,500	3,000

$$\text{Rate of Return } \frac{1250}{3000} \times 100 = 41.7\%$$

[4] It is not intended to imply that they are used solely by accountants or that they have the endorsement of the accounting profession in general or of any responsible group of accountants.

[5] See the similarly depressing discussions in Congress and the Canadian Parliament of bills requiring disclosure of the "true" rate of interest in installment contracts.

A second version uses original cost rather than average book value as the denominator, i.e., $1250/5000 \times 100 = 25$ percent. This is a little less consistent, in that income is averaged but investment is not, but if someone wishes to do it this way, we have no particular reason to stop him. As an approximation to the internal rate of return (Sec. 3.8), this usually gives better results than using average investment.

How about these as criteria? The calculations are not more difficult than those for payback, except that they must be extended to cover the project's entire life. The notion of a rate of return is easy to grasp for all but the most obtuse managers. If one has difficulty in explaining it, one can always ask the individual whether he'd rather put his money in a bank that paid 4½ percent or one that paid 4 percent. (It isn't wise to make the spread any wider, because of the danger of introducing extraneous considerations having to do with the solvency of the banks).

These criteria can be extended to the analysis of the technique problem by an approach similar to that used in Table 3-4. There is little difficulty in relating them to measures of the cost of capital for purposes of determining a cutoff point, for they are both expressed as a percentage. (This does not necessarily imply that the percentages are comparable, however.) Version I is probably more consistent with conventional methods of measuring cost, at least of debt capital.

As far as our two basic principles are concerned, they are compatible with the "bigger the better" principle but not with the "bird in the hand" principle, for equal weight is given to profits earned in the first and last year. Related to this problem is the fact that the calculated year-by-year rates of return vary from year to year in Version I, even if income is perfectly stable, which is annoying to some and disconcerting to many. As a result, they resolve the choice between A and B in Table 3-2 but not that between X and Y.

A second type of accounting measure is the "single year" rate of return. This, as the name implies, is a measure of profit in a single year, which may be the first year, the "first full year" or some other equally elusive standard. It may be applied either against average investment over the life of the project, against average investment in the year selected for study, or simply against initial cost. Table 3-4 shows the calculations for these six variants, for the project analyzed in Table 3-3, assuming year one is the first year and year two the "first full year."

The widely varying results point to the desirability of ensuring uniformity of practice if an accounting measure is to be employed. These versions ignore all years other than the one studied, so contravene both our basic principles. Their dangers when applied to projects having anything except a stable income are too obvious to require elaboration. Needless to say, they resolve the ambiguities of Table 3-2 but not necessarily in a desirable fashion.

TABLE 3-4
ACCOUNTING RATE OF RETURN: VERSION III, IV

	Version III (first year)	Version IV (first full year)
Cash income	1,500	2,000
Depreciation	1,000	1,000
Net income	500	1,000
Book value:		
Jan. 31	5,000	4,000
Dec. 31	4,000	3,000
Average	4,500	3,500
Rate of return:		
(a) On lifetime average investment	$\frac{500}{3,000} \times 100 = 16.7\%$	$\frac{1,000}{3,000} \times 100 = 33.3\%$
(b) On average investment in year studied	$\frac{500}{4,500} \times 100 = 11.1\%$	$\frac{1,000}{3,500} \times 100 = 28.5\%$
(c) On initial cost	$\frac{500}{5,000} \times 100 = 10.0\%$	$\frac{1,000}{5,000} \times 100 = 20\%$

A final measure similar to the accounting rates of return is the payback reciprocal. If payback is 4 years, the payback reciprocal is 25 percent, if 3 years 33⅓ percent and so on. Needless to say, this criterion doesn't acquire any magical virtues by being stood on its head. If income is fairly stable, and the life of the project long, it may give a reasonable approximation to the internal rate of return discussed in Sec. 3.8.[6]

3.5 Benefit-Cost Ratios: Undiscounted

A benefit-cost ratio is, as the name implies, simply a ratio between the sum of the benefits, measured in some manner, and the costs of the project. In the undiscounted version, the benefits are taken at face value, while in the discounted versions, to be discussed in the next section, calculations are complicated by a discount factor.

There are two versions of the undiscounted benefit-cost ratio, which

[6]M. J. Gordon, "The Payoff Period and the Rate of Profit," *Journal of Business* (October, 1955) reprinted in E. Solomon (ed.), *The Management of Corporate Capital* (Glencoe: The Free Press, 1959), pp. 48-57.

we may label "gross" and "net" respectively. In the former, benefits are calculated without deducting depreciation, then added and the sum divided by the investment cost. In the net version, depreciation is deducted in computing the benefits.

In symbols, if Q_t is the cash flow in period t, D_t the depreciation charge in period t, and C the cost of the asset, the following formulas may be used to calculate benefit-cost ratios:

$$\text{B.C.R. (undiscounted, gross)} = \frac{\sum_t Q_t}{C} \tag{1}$$

$$\text{B.C.R. (undiscounted, net)} = \frac{\sum_t (Q_t - D)_t}{C} \tag{2}$$

The equation used is a matter of indifference, since both give identical rankings. In fact, the net ratio equals the gross ratio minus 1.0. As the gross ratio is slightly easier to calculate, this relationship makes it simpler to arrive at the net ratio.[7]

These are easy to calculate, and it is easy to understand what they purport to measure. They are compatible with the "bigger the better" principle, since all income is taken into account, but not with the "bird in the hand" principle, since early receipts are given identical weights to those late in the project's life.

3.6 Benefit-Cost Ratios: Discounted

A discounted benefit-cost ratio is a somewhat more sophisticated tool. It is the ratio of the present value of the future benefits, at a specified rate of discount, to the present value of the present and future investment outlays and other costs, at the same rate.

It may be gross or net, net being simply gross minus one.

Algebraically, the gross discounted benefit-cost ratio is

$$\frac{\sum_t Q_t (1+k)^{-t}}{\sum_t C_t (1+k)^{-t}}$$

where Q_t represents the net cash inflow during a period t when the

---

[7]Which follows from the relationship $C = \sum_t D_t$.

net flow is positive, C_t represents the net cash outflow during a period t when the net flow is negative,[8] and k is the required yield per period expressed as a fraction.

The discounted benefit-cost ratio takes account of all income, whenever received, and to this extent complies with the "bigger the better" principle. The introduction of compound interest into the calculation effectively gives more weight to early receipts than to late ones, so that this is the first criterion we have examined which gives effect to both principles.

Administratively, it requires more computation than some of its less sophisticated brethren, but less than some of its competitors. It is not as easy to understand, at least for those people who flee in horror at any calculations involving compound interest.

It can be used to solve problems of choosing techniques by calculating the incremental benefit-cost ratio on the incremental investment required for the more expensive project.

There are, of course, as many ratios as there are possible values of k, so the analyst is faced with the problem of picking k. This is not as simple as it sounds and is of crucial importance, since rankings will not be independent of the value of k chosen. Consider the following two projects:

A costs $100.00 and returns $106.00 in a year.

B costs $100.00 and returns $112.36 in two years time.

Table 3-5 shows the results of calculating discounted benefit-cost ratios at 5 percent, 6 percent and 7 percent respectively. If the discount rate is 5 percent, project B is better, while if it is 7 percent project A is better. The fact that we're indifferent between them at a rate of 6 percent is not calculated to increase our confidence in the approach at this point. This is, however, no barrier to its use in giving accept-reject decisions. In fact, if k is the company's cost of capital, a ratio of 1.0 or better indicates that the project will at least cover its cost. In the example given above, the yield is exactly 6 percent. If the required rate of return is 6 percent, we can be indifferent whether we accept either or both. If it is 5 percent, both are profitable, while if it is 7 percent neither is.

---

[8]This is the customary definition, in which if $C_t > 0$, $Q_t = 0$ and vice versa. There are some merits, which we will examine in Chapter 5, in using an alternative definition which does *not* net out the annual cash flows but simply gives a ratio between total expected inflows and total expected outflows.

TABLE 3–5

EFFECT OF CHANGING DISCOUNT RATES ON PROJECT
RANKING BY BENEFIT COST RATIO

	Gross Benefit Cost Ratio at:		
	5%	*6%*	*7%*
Project *A*	1.01	1.00	0.99
Project *B*	1.02	1.00	0.98

Calculations are relatively simple as the following examples show:

Example 1

Required:

To calculate the benefit-cost ratio, at a discount rate of 10 percent, of a project costing $10,000 and yielding annual returns of $4,000, $5,000, and $6,000 in the three years of its useful life.

Calculations:

Year	Annual Benefits		Discount factor (appendix A)		Present value
1	4,000	×	0.909	=	3,636
2	5,000	×	0.826	=	4,130
3	6,000	×	0.751	=	4,506
Sums	15,000				12,272

Benefit-cost ratio (gross) = $\dfrac{12,272}{10,000}$ = 1.23

(net) = 0.23

Example 2

Required:

To calculate the benefit-cost ratio at 10 percent for a project costing $10,000 and yielding annual returns of $1,000 per year for 20 years.

Calculations:

Because the annual payments are uniform it is possible to use the formula for the present value of an annuity. From Appendix B, the present value of an annuity of $1.00 per year for 20 years at 10 percent is $8.514. The present value of the benefits in this case is simply $1,000×8.514 or $8,514 and the gross benefit-cost ratio 0.85.

Example 3

Required:

To calculate the benefit-cost ratio for a project costing $10,000 and yielding annual benefits of $2,500, $2,000, and $1,500 for the first three years of its life and of $1,000 for the next seven.

Calculations:

This is a hybrid case consisting of three unequal payments followed by an annuity lasting for seven years. While it is possible to use the technique indicated in Example 1 for the entire problem, the calculations can be simplified by treating the first three years in this manner, the last seven as a deferred annuity. The present value of an annuity of $1.00 for 10 years at 10 percent is, from Appendix B, $6.145 while the present value of a three year annuity is $2.487. The value of a seven year annuity beginning in the fourth year is simply the difference or $3.658. The complete calculations follow:

Year	Annual Benefits		Discount Factor		Present Value
1	2,500	×	0.909	=	2,273
2	2,000	×	0.826	=	1,652
3	1,500	×	0.751	=	1,127
4-10	1,000	×	3.658	=	3,658
Sums	13,000				8,710

Benefit-cost ratio (gross) = 0.87
(net)   = (negative)

3.7 Annual Costs and Benefits

A formula quite widely used in engineering studies converts capital costs, including an interest component, into an equivalent annual payment, which is then compared with average annual savings or profits to evaluate the desirability of alternative projects. This is a variant of the benefit-cost ratio approach as the following discussion will indicate.

Finding the equivalent annual payment is simply equivalent to finding the size of the annual annuity which has a present value equal to the cost of the asset. (This ignores salvage value.)

Example

Required:

Find the annual cost and benefits at a 10 percent discount rate of a project costing $10,000 and yielding $1,000 per year over a 20 year period.

Calculations:

Since the flow of benefits is uniform, the annual benefit is simply $1,000. To find the annual costs, we must find the size of an annuity which has a present value of $10,000. The 20 year annuity factor, from Appendix B is 8.514, and the annual cost is found by solving the following expression for x

$$10,000 = 8.514x$$

The resulting annual cost is $1,175.

If the annual benefits are divided by the annual costs, the resulting benefit-cost ratio is

$$\frac{1,000}{1,175} = 0.85$$

Referring back to Example 2 in Sec. 3.6, we note that this problem is identical with the one discussed there, and that the result is identical.

Where annual benefits are equal, it is a matter of indifference whether the annual benefits-annual cost approach or the conventional discounted benefit-cost ratio is used. Where annual payments are irregular (as they would be even in this case if there were any scrap value) the use of the annual benefits-annual costs approach requires that benefits be converted into an equivalent annual stream. To do this requires first of all that the irregular benefits be discounted to find their present value, and, as a second step, that an equivalent annual income be calculated in the same manner used to calculate equivalent annual cost. This is computationally more cumbersome than calculating the discounted benefit cost ratio, which merely requires finding the present value of receipts, avoiding the calculation of equivalent annual values, and leads to identical results. The additional computation is thus pointless, not to mention confusing to those who are not intoxicated by compound interest calculations, and had best be avoided.

3.8 Net Present Value

The "net present value" method is an alternative which is closely related to the benefit-cost ratio. Net present value is simply the difference between the present value of benefits and the present value of costs, or

$$\text{N.P.V.} = \sum_t Q_t (1+k)^{-t} - \sum_t C_t (1+k)^{-t}$$

Like the benefit-cost ratio, it takes account of all income and its timing with appropriate weights. Calculations are similar, except that instead of taking the ratio of the sums of benefits and costs, we take the difference. Thus for Example 1 in Sec. 3.6, net present value is simply $12,272 − $10,000 = $2,272; for example 2 it is $8,514 − $10,000 = − $1,486.

The profit-maximizing rule, using the net present value criterion, is to accept all projects having a positive net present value at the company's cost of capital rate. It can be used to solve problems of choosing between mutually exclusive projects by considering whether the incremental investment yields a positive net present value. When used in this fashion, net present value yields decisions which are identical to those reached using benefit-cost ratios. The choice of which to use is a matter for personal preference. We prefer the benefit-cost ratio for many purposes, but where the analysis is fitted into a more elaborate model, as in Chapters 9 to 11, net present value may be more convenient.

Ranking projects in order of net present values will, in general, give a different ranking than that resulting from ranking by benefit-cost ratios. Only the latter, however, reflects the *relative* profitability of various projects. Since it is relative profitability that is of interest in the capital-rationing situations for which a ranking is required, benefit-cost ratios are more appropriate in most applications.

One of the advantages claimed for net present value is that the ranking of projects is independent of the discount rate chosen for the analysis.[9] This is simply not so. Consider two projects, each costing $50.00, but returning

(a) $106 after one year
(b) $112.36 after two years.

At 5 percent, project (a) has a net present value of $50.95, project (b) a net present value of $51.91. At 7 percent, project (a) has a net present value of $49.07, project (b) a net present value of $48.14. The ranking is reversed by the change in discount rates.

3.9   The Internal Rate of Return

The internal rate of return is another widely used measure of investment worth that takes the interest factor into account. It is also

---

[9]H. Bierman, Jr. and S. Smidt, *The Capital Budgeting Decision* (New York: Macmillan, 1960), p. 30.

known as the "marginal efficiency of capital,"[10] or the "rate of return over cost,"[11] and by a number of other names.

By definition, the rate of return is the rate of discount which will equate the present value of the net benefits with the cost of the project. It can be found by solving the following equation for r

$$\sum_t Q_t(1+r)^{-t} = \sum_t C_t(1+r)^{-t}$$

where r is the rate of return and the other symbols have the meanings previously assigned. In the following discussion, we shall denote the present value of benefits as V

$$V = \sum_t Q_t(1+r)^{-t}$$

and that of costs as C

$$C = \sum_t C_t(1+r)^{-t}$$

The calculations required to find r are somewhat more complex than those we have encountered to date. We are required in effect to solve a polynomial in r, and in most instances one of high degree which can only be solved by trial and error. The approach is to pick an estimated rate (the payback reciprocal, while limited in value as an investment criterion, may be helpful in picking a starting point). The present values are then calculated and summed to find $V - C$. If $V - C$ is positive, a higher rate must be tried, if it is negative, a lower rate. If $V - C = 0$ the initial guess was indeed fortunate and the rate has been found. Otherwise, this procedure continues until a rate is found for which $V - C = 0$ or, in practice since not all values for r are tabulated, two rates are found for which, respectively, $V - C$ is

---

[10]J. M. Keynes, *The General Theory of Employment, Interest and Money* (London: Macmillan, 1936), pp. 135-36.

[11]Irving Fisher, *The Theory of Interest* (New York: Macmillan, 1930), p. 168. Professor Alchian disputes this identification claiming that Fisher, elsewhere, uses the concept to measure return on an opportunity cost basis, starting with the cheapest project and expanding its size only if the incremental returns on the additional investment meet the usual tests. It should be noted that the alternative to the cheapest investment is not investing at all, and the procedure outlined here appears to be consistent with Fisher in all respects. See A. A. Alchian, "The Rate of Interest, Fisher's Rate of Return over Costs (Sic) and Keynes' Internal Rate of Return," *American Economic Review*, Vol. XLV (December, 1955), p. 938.

positive but small and $V-C$ is negative but small. The correct value is then found by interpolation. The necessary calculations can, of course, be easily and efficiently performed on a computer.

Example

A project costs $10,000 and promises cash flows of $5,000, $4,000, $3,000 and $2,000 over a four year life.

Required:

Find the rate of return.

Calculations:

Using the payback reciprocal $1/2.3 = 0.40$ approximately, select a rate of 40 percent for the initial trial.[12] Calculate the present value of the income stream.

Year	Cash flow		Discount factor 40%		Present value
1	5,000	×	0.714	=	3,570
2	4,000	×	0.510	=	2,040
3	3,000	×	0.364	=	1,092
4	2,000	×	0.260	=	520
Sums	14,000				7,222
	$V-C = 7,222 - 10,000 = -2,778$				

The $V-C$ calculation indicates that this rate is far too high. Try 20 percent, then 18 percent, and 16 percent, with the following results:

Year	Q_t	20%		18%		16%	
1	5,000	0.833	4,165	0.847	4,235	0.862	4,310
2	4,000	0.694	2,776	0.718	2,872	0.743	2,972
3	3,000	0.579	1,737	0.609	1,827	0.641	1,923
4	2,000	0.482	964	0.516	1,032	0.552	1,104
			9,642		9,966		10,309
$V-C$			-358		-34		309

The rate which makes $V-C=0$ lies somewhere between 16 percent and 18 percent. By interpolation, it is

$$16 + \left(\frac{309}{343} \times 2\right) = 17.8 \text{ percent approximately.}$$

---

[12]This is a bad selection for this particular example. The payback works best for long-lived projects having relatively stable cash flows.

That this is the rate of return on the outstanding balance can be shown by deducting this return from the cash flows in each year, using the balance of the cash flow to reduce the amount outstanding each year:

Year	Cash in	17.8% Return on balance	Reduce investment	Balance at year end
0	0	0		10,000.00
1	5,000	1,780.00	3,220.00	6,780.00
2	4,000	1,206.84	2,793.16	3,986.84
3	3,000	709.66	2,290.34	1,696.50
4	2,000	301.97	1,698.03	(1.53)

The $1.53 overrecovery results from the rounding of the initial return estimate and/or the use of straight line interpolation.

The internal rate of return satisfies both our fundamental requirements. It can solve technique problems, by giving us the rate of return on the incremental investment required for the more expensive or capital intensive technique.

Example

Project A costs $1,000 and produces receipts of $500 per year for three years. Project B costs $1,200 and produces receipts of $600 per year for three years.

Required:

What is the incremental return on the extra investment in B?

Calculations:

Adopting B can really be regarded as equivalent to adopting two projects, A^1 identical to the actual project A, and $B - A^1$, the income stream for which is the difference between B's and A's.

Year	B	A^1	$B - A^1$
0	(1,200)	(1,000)	(200)
1	600	500	100
2	600	500	100
3	600	500	100

Rate of Return on $B - A^1 = 23.7$ percent.

Computationally, finding a rate of return is more difficult than using any other criterion we have discussed. However, it is not *that* difficult and computer programs can be written which will find a rate of return in seconds. This is a lot of artillery which may not be necessary, or readily available, however,

Conceptually, the notion ought to be simple enough, for it is identical to that of the yield on a bond or a savings bank deposit, but it may prove frightening to some because it involves compound interest.

An added advantage often cited is that it provides a ranking which is independent of any assumptions about the cost of capital. This is only apparently true, however.

One point against it is that it may not give a unique answer for all proposals. While all can be forced into the mold one way or another, its Procrustean properties force us into a fairly complicated examination of some hidden assumptions to be discussed below. It should be noted at this point that this criterion and the discounted benefit-cost ratio are the only ones which satisfy our basic requirements, so that our choice of an evaluation criterion must involve one or the other (or perhaps both).

3.10 Selection Rules Which Maximize Net Benefits

If we measure the cost of a project (the present value of costs) along the x-axis and the benefit cost ratio along the y-axis we can construct a rectangle, the area of which corresponds to the present value of gross benefits to be derived from a project (*OABC* in Fig. 3-1). The present value of costs can be represented by a rectangle having the same length along the x-axis and a height of 1.0 (*OAED* in Fig. 3-1).

FIGURE 3-1

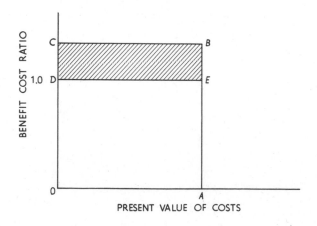

The net addition of the project to the present value of the firm, or net benefit created by it, is simply the difference between the two rectangles, or the cross hatched rectangle *BCDE* in Fig. 3-1.

If we rank all projects in order of descending benefit-cost ratios, construct rectangles of this type for them, place them side by side, and smooth out the rough edges, we obtain Fig. 3-2.

FIGURE 3-2

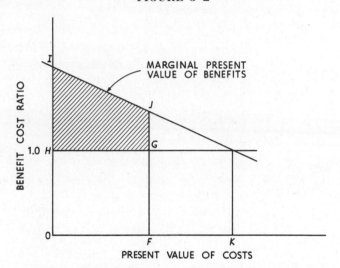

The net addition to the present value of the firm which results from the adoption of a budget committing the firm to additional costs having a present value *OF* is simply the area *GHIJ*. It is clear that we can increase this net addition by extending our commitment as far as *OK*, but not beyond. In other words, the net addition to long run profits is maximized when we accept all projects having a benefit cost ratio of 1.0 or greater.

For well-behaved projects having a single internal rate of return, the condition that benefit-cost ratio equal 1.0 is equivalent to the condition that the internal rate of return equal the cost of capital. If we use the internal rate criterion, the profit maximizing rule is to accept all projects having positive present values at the cost of capital rate, for which the internal rate of return is greater than or equal to the cost of capital.

In the absence of risk, or where the risk of individual projects is unlikely to make any substantial difference in the riskiness of the firm, the optimum capital budget for the firm is the one which conforms to the rule stated above. Many companies do not, in practice, carry investment to this margin, for a variety of reasons. Before succumbing to any of the reasons for such failures to maximize net worth, management should recognize the extent of the profits being foregone by adhering to alternative policies.

The most frequent departure from the maximization policy is one which sets a maximum limit on the budget, because of some real or imaginary limit on the funds available, or because limited managerial skills and shortages of personnel limit the capacity of the firm to digest growth. While the operative restrictions are different, both situations have in common a more or less arbitrary upper limit on capital expenditures, with which management must do the best they can, and are generally referred to as "capital-rationing" situations. These will be examined in Chapter 9.

3.11   The Formal Relationship between the Benefit-Cost Ratio and the Internal Rate of Return

The fact that both these criteria satisfy our "bigger the better" and "bird in the hand" conditions suggests that the two concepts are, if not mathematical twins, at least cousins. And so they are. Bringing the cost of capital into the picture for a moment, the profit maximizing rule, using the benefit-cost ratio criterion, can be stated as follows:

Accept all projects for which the gross benefit-cost ratio V/C is greater than 1.0, using the cost of capital as the discount rate.

The equivalent rule for the internal rate of return criterion is:

Accept all projects for which the rate of discount making $V = C$ (or $V/C = 1.0$) is greater than the cost of capital.

The marginal investment to which we are indifferent will, in either case, be that for which the rate of return equals the cost of capital and the benefit-cost ratio equals 1.0.

Mathematically, if

$$V = \sum_t Q_t(1+r)^{-t}$$

and $$C = \sum_t C_t(1+r)^{-t}$$

we have the benefit-cost ratio defined as

$$\frac{V}{C} = \frac{\sum_t Q_t(1+k)^{-t}}{\sum_t C_t(1+k)^{-t}}$$

where k is given and V/C is to be found.

For the internal rate of return we have

$$\frac{\sum_t Q_t(1+r)^{-t}}{\sum_t C_t(1+r)^{-t}} = 1.0$$

where V/C is given and r is to be found. Note that $V/C=1.0$ implies that $r=k$, and conversely.

Despite the formal near-identity of these expressions, there are differences, which may result in their giving conflicting rankings. This should be no surprise, since the rankings given by benefit-cost ratios using different discount rates may themselves conflict.

The relationship may be examined in more detail by considering the graph of $V-C$ as a function of r. Present values of benefits are calculated at a number of different discount rates, costs (or present values of deferred costs, if a net outflow occurs) are deducted and the resulting values are plotted on a graph measuring $V-C$ along the y-axis and r along the x-axis. We will refer to the resulting graph as a "present value profile."

Example

Required:

Construct a present value profile for the example given in 3.8 above.

Calculations:

We have present values for four discount rates in the calculations for the example. For a zero discount rate, $V-C$ is simply the sum of expected receipts minus the cost of the asset. Adding a couple of intermediate values, we have the following, which are plotted in Fig. 3-3.

r	$V-C$
0	4,000
0.05	2,626
0.10	1,468
0.16	309
0.18	−34
0.20	−358
0.40	−2,778

FIGURE 3-3
PRESENT VALUE PROFILE-EXAMPLE

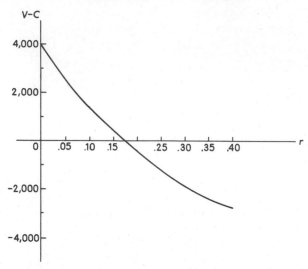

The typical profitable investment, that is, one which involves an initial outflow of funds followed by inflows which more than repay the initial investment, has a present value profile that looks something like that shown in Fig. 3-3, in that it has a positive y-intercept and slopes downward monotonically to the right (we are not concerned with the portion to the left of the y-axis).

However, this shape is all that different projects have in common, and it is quite possible to have situations such as that depicted in

FIGURE 3-4
SOURCES OF CONTRADICTION IN PRESENT VALUE RANKINGS

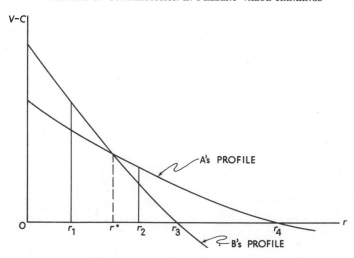

Fig. 3-4 where the present value profiles of two proposals cross. This is how contradictory rankings arise. If A and B both cost the same amount, and benefit cost ratios are calculated at a discount rate r_1, B will be ranked ahead of A. At a rate of r_2, or at any rate in excess of r^*, A will be ranked ahead of B, as it will by the internal rate of return criterion since its internal rate, r_4, is higher than B's internal rate, r_3. This contradiction may arise whenever there is a difference in the time shapes of the benefit streams.

If we are interested only in accept or reject decisions, the contradiction is unimportant. Our profit maximization rule says, using the benefit-cost criterion, to accept all projects for which the benefit cost ratio exceeds 1.0 (or equivalently, for which $V - C > 0$) when discounted at the company's cost of capital, while the rate of return rule says to accept all projects for which the rate of return exceeds the cost of capital.[13] If the cost of capital is below r_3, both projects will be accepted regardless of what criterion is used, if it is between r_3 and r_4, only A will be accepted, and if it is above r_4, neither will be accepted. So, the choice of criteria need not affect accept-reject decisions since either leads to the same results.

Yet the world is not always so simple. We might be forced to omit or postpone some of the projects which we would like to include under the profit maximization rule stated, and the choice of which ones to reject requires a ranking. If our starting capital cost is r_1, we might decide to drop A, with its lower benefit cost ratio. Yet this "capital rationing" procedure implies an opportunity cost for funds substantially in excess of r_1, and if this opportunity cost is in fact above r^*, A might be the better choice. Capital rationing will be examined in more detail in Chapter 9.

3.12 The Multiple Rate of Return Problem

Occasionally, if present value calculations are made at a number of discount rates, present value of benefits will be found to equal costs at more than one discount rate. In other words, the project has more than one rate of return. As it is quite easy for the analyst to quit after he has found one rate, there is a possibility, indeed a strong likelihood that in many projects for which this is true, it is overlooked. It is for this reason that we have advocated the sketching of present value profiles in all cases. A number of suggestions for the interpre-

---

[13]Making the appropriate selection in each case from among sets of mutually exclusive alternatives.

tation of multiple rate cases have been made in the literature. Before examining these, however, it is necessary to have an understanding of the reasons for their existence.

Fig. 3-5 shows sketches of present value profiles for a number of cases in which multiple rates can be found. Type *(b)* is probably the most common.

FIGURE 3–5
MULTIPLE RATES OF RETURN

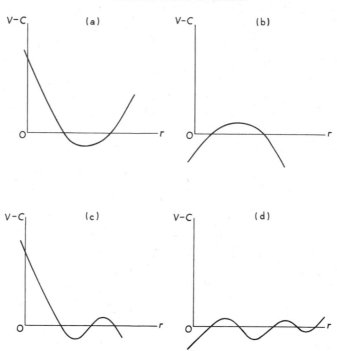

What have these cases in common? This is not too clear at first glance. Types *(a)* and *(c)* have positive intercepts on the *y*-axis, indicating that *undiscounted* benefits exceed costs, but *(b)* and *(d)* do not. Adding a requirement that undiscounted benefits must exceed costs for a project even to be considered is a device that will eliminate some multiple rate cases, including the most common, but it will not eliminate the others, and is wrong anyway. A well-behaved type of "project" (in that it has only one "rate of return") is a normal loan contract. Since the amount of money eventually to be repaid to the lender exceeds the amount borrowed, benefits of the loan are exceeded by the undiscounted costs and the present value profile looks like Fig. 3-6. The "rate of return" in the normal loan case is more familiar as the

FIGURE 3–6
PRESENT VALUE PROFILE: NORMAL LOAN

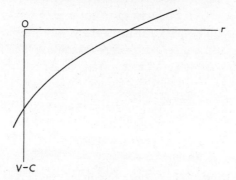

interest cost of borrowing. It makes no more sense to exclude multiple rate projects having negative $V-C$ from consideration than it does to exclude the possibility of borrowing. They are, in fact, an equivalent to, or more accurately, a substitute for borrowing, as we shall see presently.

If we consider cash outflows as having negative signs, cash inflows as positive, the typical single rate investment has a cash outflow succeeded by a succession of inflows, an income stream of the type sketched in Fig. 3-7. $V-C$ is really the *sum* of the discounted values of the stream (after we adopt the sign convention just suggested).

FIGURE 3-7
INCOME STREAM: TYPICAL INVESTMENT

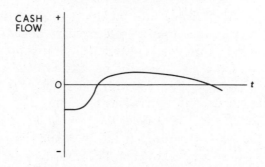

In the normal case, we can find a positive rate of return if undiscounted benefits exceed costs because, as r is increased, benefits lying further in the future than costs are reduced by a proportionately greater amount than costs, so that, for some finite value of r, they are reduced to equality. This is the process used in finding a rate of return, and it depends for its success on the alteration in sign between the initial outflows and the succeeding inflows. If there were no alteration in sign, we could never reduce the present value of the income-outlay stream to zero. An alteration in sign is, mathematically, a necessary condition for the existence of a finite rate of return.

Similarly, the existence of *two* reversals in sign is a necessary condition for the existence of two rates, three for three rates and so on. These conditions are not sufficient, however. The mathematical conditions for the existence of multiple roots are discussed in some detail in the appendix to this chapter.

FIGURE 3-8
INCOME STREAM: DUAL RATE CASE

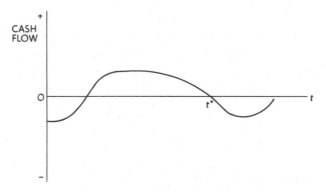

Are multiple rates really a problem? Since they require an income stream such as that shown in Fig. 3-8, wouldn't it be simpler to discontinue the operation at time t^*, thus avoiding the subsequent losses and, incidentally, the multiple rate problem?[14] Unfortunately, things aren't so simple. Many projects involve positive abandonment costs. Old buildings must be torn down, abandoned oil wells plugged, and so on. Failure to do so is apt to incur the penalties of the law and result in an even larger terminal cost. The firm is committed to the abandonment cost at the moment it undertakes the project.

Even if it weren't, our resolution of the techniques problem involves calculation of the rate of return on the incremental investment involved in more expensive techniques. The cash flow in such cases is found by subtracting that of the cheaper project, year by year, from that of the more expensive. Such a process can easily lead to a multiplicity of sign reversals, as shown in the following:

---

[14]C. S. Soper, "The Marginal Efficiency of Capital, A Further Note," *Economic Journal*, March, 1959, p. 175.

Year	Cash flows Project A	Cash flows Project B	Incremental Cash flow $(B-A)$
0	(10,000)	(15,000)	(5,000)
1	6,000	4,000	(2,000)
2	5,000	5,000	0
3	4,000	6,000	2,000
4	3,000	7,000	4,000
5	3,000	8,000	5,000
6	3,000	8,000	5,000
7	3,000	2,500	(500)
8	3,000	0	(3,000)
9	3,000	0	(3,000)
10	3,000	0	(3,000)

The existence of multiple rates raises a problem concerning their interpretation. Are all equally valid, or are some more valid than others?

There are two basic possible interpretations. One attempts to distinguish between "genuine" and "spurious" rates. The other treats all rates as equally valid but recognizes that the internal rate criterion must be supplemented in cases where multiple rates exist.

A number of authors have chosen to define as genuine those rates at which the value of $V-C$ is falling as r increases.[15] A convention has also been offered for deciding which of the "genuine" rates is to be regarded as "the" rate.[16] The reason for regarding these rates as genuine is "because for higher rates of interest ... the project is unprofitable. That is, it is the highest rate of interest it would be worthwhile to pay on borrowed money.[17]"

Making a distinction on this basis would require that only rate r_3 in Fig. 3-9 be accepted as genuine, for this is the only rate which is "genuine" in accordance with the verbal basis for distinguishing between rates. Yet this is not the procedure followed by Wright, who identified r_3 and r_1 as genuine, and r_2 as spurious.[18] McLean offers no reason for his requirement, while Massé offers a convention which requires consideration of the value of $V-C$ at the company's cost of capital rate. While his procedure will generally lead to correct results,

---

[15]J. G. McLean, "How to Evaluate New Capital Investment," *Harvard Business Review*, Vol. XXXVI (November-December, 1958), p. 59; J. F. Wright, "Notes on the Marginal Efficiency of Capital," *Oxford Economic Papers* (N.S. Vol. 15) July, 1963, p. 125.

[16]P. Massé, *Optimal Investment Decisions* (Englewood Cliffs, N. J.; Prentice-Hall, 1962), pp. 21-23.

[17]J. F. Wright, *loc. cit.*

[18]J. F. Wright, *op. cit.*, p. 128.

FIGURE 3–9
THREE RATE CASE

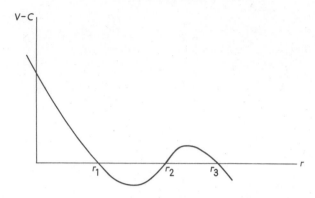

it is really tantamount to making a decision using the benefit-cost ratio criterion and subsequently picking a rate of return which justifies it.

An alternative solution which has been proposed in the literature uses the cost of capital to discount negative portions of the income stream to a point where they can be deducted from positive flows and succeeds in producing a single rate.[19] The rate so produced, however, is not the equivalent of the rate found by the regular discounting process for normal single-rate projects, mathematically or otherwise, thus cannot be used to rank multiple-rate projects in with the others. It is thus useless except for accept-reject decisions, for which it is unnecessary, as will be seen below.

Mathematically, there are no grounds for distinguishing one rate from another, as all are roots of a single polynomial equation.[20] The verbal distinction offered by Wright is inconsistent with his practice, and would, if applied, frequently lead to inappropriate decisions. What we are interested in is reaching correct decisions, and the quest for a "genuine," or "correct," or "true," internal rate of return is irrelevant unless it leads to making better decisions. As it contributes nothing to our understanding which improves our ability to make decisions, the concept had better be dropped. The appropriate question to be

------

[19]E. Solomon, *The Theory of Financial Management* (New York: Columbia, 1963), pp. 130-31; A. S. Merrett and Allen Sykes, *The Finance and Analysis of Capital Projects* (New York: Wiley, 1963), pp. 162-65.

[20]The only roots capable of interpretation as rates of return are, of course, those which are real numbers, and negative rates are of little economic interest.

asked is not "what is the correct rate of return?" but "under what circumstances does it pay to invest in a project exhibiting multiple rates of return?"

The answer to this is clear from an examination of the present value profiles. If $V-C$ is positive at the company's cost of capital, the project adds to the present value of the company and should be undertaken. If it does not, it should be rejected. This principle holds irrespective of the number of rates of return there are, and irrespective of whether the undiscounted benefit-cost ratio is above or below 1.0.

To see why this is so, examine the case of an investment which costs $6.00, returns $100 after one year and involves a terminal outlay of $100 at the end of the second year. This project has an undiscounted $V-C$ of *minus* $6.00 and two rates of return, 6.8 percent and 1443.0 percent. Its present value profile is sketched in Fig. 3-10. If the cost of capital is 10 percent, the value of $V-C$ is $2.26, and the project is profitable. This project is not dissimilar to borrowing $100 for a year, but paying $6.00 interest a year in advance of receiving the loan. It pays, if the cost of capital is 6.8 percent or greater, because it can be viewed as an alternative temporary source of funds

FIGURE 3-10
DUAL RATE CASE
$(-6, 100, -100)$

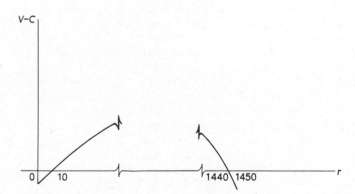

during the period for which cumulative inflows exceed cumulative outflows.

For accept-reject decisions, if any multiple rate cases are present, the internal rate criterion used alone cannot give an unequivocal answer, but the benefit-cost criterion is quite satisfactory.

APPENDIX TO CHAPTER 3

Conditions for Multiple Rates of Return

The simplest case in which multiple rates can exist is one in which the investment produces income in the two succeeding periods. In this case, finding the internal rate of return involves solving the following expression for r:

$$\frac{Q_1}{1+r} + \frac{Q_2}{(1+r)^2} - C = 0 \tag{1}$$

where C is the cost and Q_1, Q_2 the respective receipts.

This is a quadratic equation in r, which may be rewritten in more familiar form:

$$-Cr^2 + (Q_1 - 2C)r + (Q_1 + Q_2 - C) = 0 \tag{2}$$

Like any other quadratic, this has two roots which can be found from

$$\frac{-(Q_1 - 2c) \pm \sqrt{(Q_1 - 2C)^2 + 4C(Q_1 + Q_2 - C)}}{-2C} \tag{3}$$

Roots may be real or complex and may be positive or negative. The only roots which admit of an economically meaningful interpretation as internal rates of return are positive real roots. By Descarte's Law of Signs, the number of positive real roots is given by the number of changes in sign between the successive coefficients of r in (2). For the normal investment project, in which C is positive, the sign of the first coefficient is negative. The sign of the second is uncertain and dependent on the numerical values in the given case, as is the sign of the third. Where the undiscounted benefits exceed the costs, however, the third coefficient is positive, which means that the sequence of signs must be either $- - +$ or $- + +$. As both of these contain only one reversal, there is only one real, positive root. In the two period case with positive C, an excess of undiscounted benefits over costs is a necessary and sufficient condition for the existence of a single internal rate of return.

For a dual rate to exist in this two-period case, it is necessary that undiscounted benefits be less than costs, i.e., that the constant term in (2) be negative. As this could imply either $- - -$ or $- + -$, it is not a sufficient condition for dual rates. Unless $Q_1 > 2C$, there will be no roots at all. Where $Q_1 > 2C$, there will be an outlay, a substantial inflow of funds, and subsequent outlay, but the availability of funds from period 1 to period 2 may make the whole venture profitable at certain rates of discount. The present value profile of this case is sketched in Fig. 3-5b.

In the loan case, the conditions are reversed, and the present value profile is sketched in Fig. 3-5a.

In the general case, we have

$$\frac{Q_1}{1+r} + \frac{Q_2}{(1+r)^2} + \cdots + \frac{Q_n}{(1+r)^n} - C = 0 \tag{4}$$

which reduces to

$$- Cr^n + \cdots + \left(\sum_{t=1}^{n} Q_t - C \right) = 0 \tag{5}$$

Here there can be as many as n roots. For there to be at least one positive real root, i.e., one internal rate of return, it is sufficient that the undiscounted benefit-cost ratio be greater than 1.0.

PROBLEMS

1. Calculate internal rates of return for the following projects:

	A	B	C	D	E
Initial Cost	10,000	12,000	15,000	11,000	20,000
Benefits:					
Year 1	6,000	3,000	6,000	2,000	5,000
Year 2	4,000	4,000	8,000	4,000	5,000
Year 3	3,000	5,000	9,000	6,000	5,000
Year 4	2,000	6,000	9,000	8,000	5,000
Year 5	1,000	7,000	9,000	10,000	5,000

2. Assuming the cost of capital to be 12 percent, calculate benefit-cost ratios for the projects listed in Problem 1.

3. Calculate annual benefits and costs for the projects listed in Problem 1, using an assumed cost of capital of 12 percent.

4. *(a)* Sketch present value profiles for the following projects:

	A	B
Initial Cost	10,000	10,000
Benefits:		
Year 1	2,000	7,000
Year 2	4,000	5,000
Year 3	6,000	4,000
Year 4	8,000	2,000

(b) What is the internal rate of return for each project?

(c) For what range of capital costs is project A preferable to project B? Why?

5. Projects C and D are mutually exclusive. If a firm's cost of capital is 15 percent, which should it choose?

	C	D
Initial Cost	20,000	30,000
Benefits:		
Year 1	8,000	8,000
Year 2	9,000	9,000
Year 3	10,000	11,000
Year 4	10,000	13,000
Year 5	10,000	17,000

6. A mining company calculates that by continuing operations at the present rate, ore reserves will be exhausted in 10 years, with an annual net cash flow, after taxes, of $10,000 during this period. By introducing a mechanized digger, it can double output and raise the annual net cash flow to $20,000 after taxes. The digger costs $30,000. (Assume for this problem that any tax credits for depreciation are taken into account in reckoning the net cash flow). It estimates its cost of capital at 8 percent.

    (a) Calculate the cash flow stream resulting from installing the digger.

    (b) Should the company install the digger?

    (c) What is peculiar about this project?

7. "A firm which maximizes the rate of return on its assets does not thereby maximize its profits." Is this proposition correct? Explain.

8. "A firm which seeks to maximize its long run profits should seek to maximize the ratio of its receipts stream, suitably discounted, to its discounted stream of expenditures." Is this proposition correct? Explain.

CHAPTER 4

Measuring and Evaluating Benefits and Costs

4.1 Some Basic Rules

The evaluation of projects involves calculating the benefits and costs which will result from the construction of projects and the use of these estimates to evaluate the desirability of the projects. Alternative measures of desirability have already been discussed; in this chapter we will examine their application to the data of specific cases. We will not be concerned here with the mechanics of estimation, which is a problem requiring the special skills of engineers, market researchers, and other specialists, but with the conceptual problems involved in deciding which costs and benefits are to be considered in the analysis. There are a number of possible concepts of costs and benefits, but many of these are inappropriate for decision making purposes. Decisions as to what should be included are difficult enough in the context of the firm; in the public sector they are still more complex. It is here that the judgment of the analyst is critical, for once estimates are prepared, application of the decision criterion is almost routine.

The basic principles to be applied in the analysis are relatively simple. They may be summarized as follows:

1. The analysis should embrace all costs and benefits resulting from the adoption of the proposed project, from the standpoint of the optimizing unit, i.e., the firm in the case of private sector decisions and society or the economy as a whole in public sector decisions.
2. It should be on an incremental basis, taking the difference between the resulting streams of costs and benefits with and without the project respectively.
3. External effects, i.e., indirect benefits or costs, should be taken into account to the extent appropriate to the decision-making unit.

59

4. Care should be taken to compare total benefits with total costs. The practice of offsetting certain benefits against certain costs or vice versa can in many cases lead to misranking of projects.
5. Double counting should be avoided.
6. Opportunity costs are the relevant standard.
7. An appropriate period should be considered. Application of these principles is best illustrated by the examination of certain rules. In the following discussion we will assume that the decision criterion is the discounted benefit-cost ratio, either on a project lifetime or annual basis, or the internal rate of return. Other criteria are decidedly inferior and should not be used as the basic measurement of desirability.

4.2   Be Careful of Depreciation and Similar Charges

The appropriate cost of an asset to be charged against operations during any given period is the opportunity cost of using it during that period, or, technically, its user cost for that period.[1] Obviously, when we are considering a new capital expenditure, the relevant cost to be considered is the entire capital cost, to be regarded as an outlay in the period the asset is acquired, minus its residual value on disposition, to be regarded as a cash receipt at the time it is disposed of. Depreciation or depletion should not be charged against the income produced, since provision for this is implicit in the procedure of comparing or equating the discounted benefit and cost streams. To deduct it again would involve us in counting the same cost twice.

In the case where assets are already owned and their continued use is involved in the decision, the appropriate cost is user cost, i.e., the reduction in disposal value resulting from the continued use of the asset for the period in question. This is particularly relevant in the replacement problem, which involves other complications and will be discussed below in Sec. 4.10. It also enters other decisions such as the following:

Example 1

A firm has a plant which was used for the manufacture of a discontinued line. The equipment in the plant has been disposed of, and it is currently vacant. The plant is fully written off on the firm's books, while the land is carried on the books at is original cost of $10,000,

---

[1]This concept is developed by J. M. Keynes in his *General Theory of Employment, Interest and Money* (London: Macmillan, 1936), pp. 66-73, to which the reader is referred for more detail.

incurred 40 years ago. The property could be sold for $150,000 today net, after taxes. It is estimated that the remaining life of the building is 10 years, after which it will be a candidate for demolition. Because of this, and because of its location in a declining neighborhood, its estimated (aftertax) value 10 years from now is only $70,000. The firm is considering using this property to house a new manufacturing operation, equipment for which costs $70,000 and which is expected to produce income having a *present value* of $140,000 after taxes. The cheapest alternative location would cost $100,000. Should the process be housed in the old plant or should it be undertaken at all?

If one adheres to accounting conventions, the project is highly desirable. On a conventional accounting basis, it will show a profit, since no charge will be made for the fully depreciated plant nor for the land which is, of course, not depreciable. It is clear, however, that a decision to undertake the process in this location involves a rejection of the $150,000 which could currently be realized on the sale of the property, so that an opportunity cost is incurred. Besides this, there is an outlay of $70,000 for the equipment bringing the opportunity cost of the venture to $220,000, against which we have the present value of income of $140,000 and the future value of the property, $70,000, which must be further reduced to a present value basis. On this basis, it is clear that the project as a whole is unprofitable, when the alternative of selling the property is taken into account. If the benefit-cost analysis is to lead to the appropriate decision, these costs must be taken into account in the evaluation process, though they are not out-of-pocket costs nor costs which will appear on the books.[2]

Example 2

In other circumstances depreciation may appear on the books but should be ignored. A mining company has a mill which costs $2,000,000 and was installed three years ago on a concession in a remote corner of South America where the ore body unexpectedly petered out. Its estimated life was 20 years and it has been depreciated on a straight line basis, so that its book value is $1,700,000. The company's new geologists have found another ore body which would, if developed at

---

[2] A thorough accounting analysis will reveal that nonrecurring profit, on the sale of the asset, will be reduced by holding it. Unless present values are taken into account, however, it may still show the project to be profitable, e.g., if the undiscounted operating profits total in excess of $150,000.

a cost of $500,000 after allowing for tax credits, produce concentrates having a present value of $1,400,000, after taxes. The scrap value of the mill in its present location is nil.

Should the company proceed to develop the new ore body? Some of the company's management thought not, arguing that it was silly to throw $500,000 in good money after $1,700,000 bad, in order to recover ore with a net present value of $1,400,000. After this group had convinced the board of directors not to proceed with development of the mine, the accountant quit and incorporated a company of his own. Several months later he was able to convince the management to sell him the concession, complete with mill, for $50,000. After all, they had analyzed it and concluded it was worthless. Having obtained title to the property, our intrepid hero approached a member of the board and offered to sell the concession back to the company for $500,000. He was able to convince the board that the purchase would be extremely profitable, since although they would pay $500,000 for the property, and another $500,000 to develop the mine, the present value of the ore was $1,400,000, offering a benefit-cost ratio of 1.4.

After due consideration, the board decided to buy the concession from him, and offered him a job as president of their company, the former incumbent having been taken suddenly ill.

In this case, the company's initial decision was wrong. Because the mill had no value in any alternative use, no opportunity cost was involved in utilizing it to develop the new ore body. No provision should have been made for depreciation in the benefit-cost analysis because no outlay was involved, and no opportunity sacrificed. This is, of course, an instance where the classic adage "sunk costs don't matter" applies. The loss has already been incurred by building the mill. While it wouldn't pay to build the mill to develop the new ore body, it does pay to use it if it is already there and can't be used for anything else or disposed of. The fact that the loss will appear as annual losses in future income statements is merely one of the vagaries of the accounting process. They will, however, be less than if the ore body had not been developed. If desired they could be avoided by writing down the book value of the mill immediately, this is probably preferable but may not be desired for tax reasons.

4.3 Compare Total Benefits with Total Costs

This rule is one which is frequently ignored in practice. In theory, ignoring it is unlikely to lead to incorrect decisions, if all projects having benefit-cost ratios in excess of 1.0 or offering prospective rates of return in excess of the cost of capital are adopted. With few exceptions, the practice of deducting future costs from future benefits and comparing the net benefits with the initial capital outlay is not going to make a desirable project appear unprofitable, or vice versa.

In a risk-free world, the practice is often perfectly permissible. Where risk is present, however, it can make projects or combinations of projects which are, in fact, highly risky, appear as desirable as less risky projects. It is, of course, preferable to have an evaluation system which makes explicit allowance for riskiness, as outlined in Chapters 10 and 11. Many, if not most, existing budgeting systems do not make explicit provision for risk, and in such systems care should be taken to avoid netting, which leads to errors of the type illustrated below.

Example 1—Narrow vs. Wide Margins

Project A has an initial cost of $250,000. It produces revenues of $55,000 annually for ten years, from which annual operating costs of $5,000 may be deducted, giving net benefits of $50,000 per year. Project B also costs $250,000, but produces annual benefits of $200,000 for ten years. Operating costs are $150,000 per year, so net benefits are once again $50,000 per year.

If future costs are deducted from future benefits, and net benefits are used in the evaluations, the two projects appear equally desirable. At a cost of capital of 10 percent, the benefit-cost ratio is 1.23, the internal rate of return is 15 percent. But are they equally desirable?

There are some reasons for preferring project A. Its adoption implies the commitment of resources having a present value of $280,723 (initial cost plus present value of operating expenses) to the production of output having a present value of $337,953. The benefit-cost ratio on this gross basis is 1.20. Adoption of project B, on the other hand, implies the commitment of resources having a present value of $1,171,690 to produce output worth $1,228,920. Its benefit-cost ratio on a gross basis is only 1.05. The relative gain from the resources committed to A is greater than from those committed to B. Using net benefits overstates the true benefit-cost ratio in both cases, but the overstatement is greater in the case of the marginal project. The whole *rationale* of the internal rate of return calculation is based on netting benefits against costs and finding the rate of discount which equalizes them. On this basis, both projects appear equal. This is a clear case of a situation where its power to discriminate is inferior to that of the benefit-cost ratio.

If the firm is operating on a profit-maximizing basis, it should accept both projects. If there is a capital rationing problem, however, and the firm is ranking projects on the basis of benefit-cost ratios it may prefer to adopt project A, because of the lower implicit commitment to future expenditures. Strictly speaking, however, both projects make the same addition to the firm's present value and are equally desirable uses of this year's budget.

At a more practical level, consider the effects of risk, with which we will be dealing more systematically in Chapters 10 and 11. Here, if risk is present, we are presumably using expected values of benefits and costs. Benefits and costs are estimated separately and may fluctuate to some extent independently of one another (though there may be some correlation between the two). If the variability of benefits and costs is proportionate to their size, then B is a much more risky venture than A. Suppose revenues have been overestimated by 10 percent, as the result of unforeseen competition. Then A's gross benefits drop to $50,000 per year, but the project remains profitable. If B's annual revenues were cut to $181,819, the present value of benefits would be only $1,117,205, and it would be clearly unprofitable.

For an impartial ranking, it is necessary to estimate benefits and costs as two separate streams and compare their present values.

Example 2—Deduction of Borrowing Costs and Benefits

A second case in which the netting process can lead to inappropriate results is the situation where the effects of borrowing (real or notional[3]) are netted against the results of the investment itself.

Consider two machines, both costing $37,900, producing cost savings of $10,000 per year for five years. Project A, however, can be financed in part with a $30,000 loan at 8 percent repayable in 5 annual installments of $7,513. Project B can be financed with a $20,000 loan at 6 percent repayable in 5 annual installments of $4,748. If the sum borrowed is deducted from the cost of the machine, and the repayments from the cost savings, the cash flows appear as follows:

---

[3]As in the approach suggested by E. Solomon, "Measuring a Company's Cost of Capital," *Journal of Business*, October, 1955, reprinted in E. Solomon (ed.), *The Management of Corporate Capital* (Glencoe: The Free Press, 1959), p. 140, where borrowing power contributed by a project is deducted from its cost and amortization of the "loan" is deducted from the benefits.

Year	Project A	Project B
Initial . . . .(7,900)		(17,900)
1 2,487		5,252
2 2,487		5,252
3 2,487		5,252
4 2,487		5,252
5 2,487		5,252

Internal rates of return calculated on these cash flows are approximately 17 percent and 14 percent respectively. Benefit-cost ratios, at a 10 percent assumed cost of capital, are 1.19 and 1.11. Yet the machines themselves produce identical outputs. On a gross basis, the rate of return is 10 percent and the benefit-cost ratio 1.0. In this case netting has distorted both the rate of return and the benefit-cost ratio.

The decision to acquire the asset should be distinct from the decision to finance and made separately. In this case as we shall see, if the marginal cost of capital is 10 percent, this cannot be evaded by borrowing at a lower rate, for adjustments in the cost of equity will offset part or all of the apparent saving from using debt. In this case the projects are identical, and a choice might eventually be made on the basis of the financing. But usually there will be a difference between projects which can only be obscured by lumping consideration of the projects and their financing into the same calculation. However, if the marginal cost of capital is 10 percent, both of these projects are on the margin of indifference and might just as well not be adopted at all, a fact which is obscured by the inappropriately calculated rates of return and benefit-cost ratios.

Example 3—Treatment of Associated Costs

In many public expenditure decisions, there are not only costs incurred by the public treasury but other costs incurred by individuals or firms in the private sector in utilizing the facilities made available through the public investment. For example, where public investment is made to develop an irrigation scheme, farmers must also make substantial investments to shift to more capital-intensive agriculture. Occasionally, financing for the project itself comes from several levels of government. Our criterion would require that all costs, public and private, go into the denominator, and all benefits into the numerator of the benefit-cost ratio.

Different practices in this regard are followed by different agencies of the government. In the United States, for example, the rule stated above is followed by the Department of Agriculture, but other agencies follow different rules. The Bureau of Reclamation deducts associated costs (in the private sector) from the benefits, as does the Corps of Engineers, although the latter includes contributions to project cost from local sources on the cost side.[4] The differences in results may lead to serious incomparabilities in the comparison of projects undertaken by different agencies, and, worse, may lead to inconsistent selection of priorities among projects having a different mix of federal and state costs. Differences in evaluation resulting from the different approaches are illustrated by the following example:

	Present Worth
Direct federal cost	$10 million
Direct state and local cost	2 million
Associated private cost	3 million
Benefits	20 million

Benefit-cost ratios:

(a) Recommended basis (Dept. of Agriculture) $\dfrac{20}{10+2+3} = 1.33$

(b) Corps of Engineers basis $\dfrac{20-3}{10+2} = 1.41$

(c) Bureau of Reclamation basis $\dfrac{20-5}{10} = 1.50$

Both *(b)* and *(c)* overstate the correct benefit-cost ratio, tending to make the projects more attractive than they really are.

Professor Eckstein has recommended that the relevant denominator be the costs incurred by the agency making the appraisal and that all other costs be considered as deductions from benefits.[5] This rule is derived by considering the size of the budget as fixed and attempting to maximize benefits subject to a fixed budget constraint.[6] In our view this is incorrect.

First of all, one cannot take the budget as fixed and independent of the available projects. The evaluation process can go a long way toward determining the size of the budget itself, as we shall see in Chapter 7. All projects with a benefit-cost ratio in excess of 1.0, when an appropriate cost of capital is used, should be adopted. To do less leads to resource misallocation. A similar approach, deducting subsidies from cost, may be justified in the private sector, where selfish con-

---

[4] O. Eckstein, *Water Resource Development: The Economics of Project Evaluation* (Cambridge: Harvard, 1961), p. 65.

[5] *Ibid.*, Ch. 3.

[6] *Ibid.*, p. 75 *et. seq.*

siderations are valid. It is not acceptable in government where the criterion is supposedly the general welfare.

The use of this approach is allegedly justified by the fact that it leads to the maximum benefit for a given level of (in the examples used) federal government expenditures. This ignores, and treats as virtually irrelevant, costs borne by the private sector and other levels of government. Even if capital rationing is necessary, it is unacceptable because it will lead to the acceptance of inferior projects simply because a larger portion of their costs will be borne by other agencies. Consider the following projects (all benefits and costs are stated on a present value basis):

	A	B
Federal cost	5 million	10 million
Private cost	5 million	
Benefits	14 million	15 million
Benefit-cost ratios:		
Eckstein basis	$\frac{14-5}{5}=1.8$	$\frac{15}{10}=1.5$
Recommended basis	$\frac{14}{10}=1.4$	$\frac{15}{10}=1.5$

While use of the Eckstein criterion may not lead to serious misallocation of funds by the federal government (though one may be forgiven for skepticism) it can lead to particularly bad decisions at lower levels of government, where the inferior project may be eligible for federal grants of 90 percent. Compare the following:

	A	B
Local costs	1 million	10 million
Federal costs	9 million	
Benefits	11 million	15 million
Local benefit-cost ratio:		
Eckstein criterion	$\frac{11-9}{1}=2.0$	$\frac{15}{10}=1.5$
Recommended criterion	$\frac{11}{10}=1.1$	$\frac{15}{10}=1.5$

Application of the Eckstein criterion under capital rationing conditions will generally lead to the acceptance of projects part of whose cost is borne elsewhere in lieu of equal or better projects whose cost is borne wholly by the government in question. It is equivalent to attempting to evade the budget constraint by inducing other people to spend their money to supplement it, giving the spending authority control, albeit indirect, over more funds than have been appropriated to it. Not only does it lead to a misallocation of resources on an economy-wide basis, but it tends also to destroy the fundamental control of the legislature over the purse strings which is a basic necessity in a democratic society.

4.4 Make Comparisons on an Incremental Basis

While it is important to include all benefits and costs resulting from the project in the analysis, as the above examples show, care must be taken that the benefits and costs included are on an incremental basis and actually result from the project. Thus, care should be taken to avoid the use of "fully distributed" costs which may overstate the true costs.

Consider the case of a company considering a small expansion in plant capacity to produce subassemblies which were formerly purchased. On a discounted basis, the following present values are relevant to the decision:

Saving on subassemblies formerly purchased $1,500,000
Direct operating cost of producing subassemblies   1,000,000
Cost of plant expansion   200,000

The comptroller derived a benefit-cost ratio of 1.13, after allowing for income taxes estimated at $150,000 on a present value basis. The plant manager, who may have had enough headaches already, claimed that the expansion would be unprofitable, as it had not been allocated its fair share of overhead, which the comptroller was in the habit of passing on to operating departments at 32 percent of their direct costs. His calculations showed:

Saving on purchases $1,500,000
Direct operating costs 1,000,000
Overhead   320,000
                                           180,000
Plant cost   200,000
Benefit-cost ratio 0.9

He made no allowance for taxes since, on a distributed cost basis, the project was unprofitable.

In a case such as this, it is unlikely that overhead will be increased at all. Thus, it should not be taken into account in the decision. If the plant manager is paid on the basis of results, and if he is to be held accountable for the overhead allotted to his department, his position is understandable. Of course, he would not be in this position under a rational system of allocating responsibility.

There may be other instances when overhead will be increased. For example, when a new branch plant is established which will require additional traveling and other communication costs for senior executives who must oversee it, a charge for overhead is quite appropriate. If such a charge is to be made, it must be the best available estimate of the actual additional costs likely to be incurred and not some rule-of-thumb allocation. Generally, projects of the cost-reducing or replacement variety will not involve additional overheads, but major expansions of capacity will.

Another frequently included and often arbitrary provision is an allowance for working capital. Here again the use of a company-wide average, based on sales or expenses cannot be justified. Any such allowance must be based on a careful analysis of the effects of the project on required cash balances, inventory, and receivables, and take into account the funds provided by expense accruals. Since some projects may have the effect of reducing working capital requirements (e.g., by reducing required inventories) it is impossible to establish any rule. Where the projects are small, and the amount involved insignificant, working capital may as well be ignored. In other cases (e.g., major capacity expansions) the effect on working capital will be considerable, and must be taken into account. Still other projects, e.g., a warehouse network or materials-handling systems, may be justified primarily on the basis of their effect on working capital.

4.5 Treatment of Taxes

It goes without saying that any appropriate measure of benefits and costs in the private sector must take account of the effects of taxes on property and incomes. In theory, this can be done equally well by considering either benefits and costs on a before-tax basis, using a cost of capital suitably adjusted on a similar basis to complete the evaluation, or by making all calculations on an aftertax basis. In practice, however, because of accelerated depreciation and other factors, the appropriate adjustment to the cost of capital for various projects may be difficult to understand, so that it is much simpler to make all evaluations on an aftertax basis.

The incremental effect on the tax bill resulting from proposed projects should be carefully calculated at the company's marginal tax rate and included in the cash flows. While depreciation must not be directly included in the cash flows, it affects tax liability and must be considered in the tax calculation. For this purpose, the basis of the depreciation charge should be that actually used for tax purposes, not that used for financial reporting purposes. Where accelerated depreciation is available for one project but not another, this should be recognized in the evaluation, both from the point of view of shareholders, legitimately interested in maximizing aftertax profits, and from that of society, which presumably established the accelerated rates to provide an incentive which can only be effective if calculations are made on this basis. Tax liability should thus be stated on the basis of the tax actually payable as a result of the project. The method of reporting is of no consequence. Where accelerated allowances are available in early years, the tax liability in later years is increased, relative to that which would be incurred in later years under normal depreciation practices. The net result is to increase the discounted benefit-cost ratio or the internal rate of return by shifting benefits to the earlier years which are most heavily weighted under these criteria. It is in their ability to deal with subtleties of this kind effectively that these criteria derive their principal advantage over the older, simpler methods of evaluation.

Where there are external effects within the firm (i.e., in other divisions, Sec. 4.6) the tax implications of such external effects must, of course, be taken into account.

The treatment of taxes in public expenditure decisions is an area fraught with controversy and uncertainty. Government operations as such are usually tax exempt, so there is no tax liability to be considered in a formal sense. There may be taxes on the other side, i.e., in the form of user charges, but these are seldom an appropriate measure of benefits and are best ignored. (The only exceptions are projects designed to improve the tax-collecting machinery. Here, additional collections may be a measure of benefits.)

However, implicit taxes cannot simply be ignored in government expenditure decisions. One of the things we hope to get from our evaluation of public expenditure projects is some indication of the optimum size of government budgets, or the extent to which resources should be devoted to the different activities for which government is responsible, and we cannot do this unless we can make evaluations on a basis comparable with that used in the private sector.

It is theoretically quite feasible to make allowance for implicit tax payments out of the benefits estimated for public sector expenditures. This may be the appropriate policy for commercial and quasi-commercial government enterprises (e.g., the post office and publicly owned power plants) and a number of Canadian federal government enterprises go through the ritual of making notional book entries for an implicit tax on income, allegedly to ensure that they compete with private enterprises on a "fair" basis.

For most government operations, where the benefits are not marketed, any attempt to reduce benefits by some notional tax allowance is likely to be an exercise in futile make-believe. Just as it is most natural to consider benefits in the private sector net of tax and to use an aftertax cost of capital in their evaluation, it is most natural to consider benefits in the public sector on a nontaxed basis, using a before-tax cost of capital for evaluation purposes. The problem of selecting an appropriate cost of capital which will place public projects on a basis comparable with those in the private sector will be discussed in Chapter 7.

4.6 Treatment of External Effects

The external effects of a project are those benefits and costs which do not accrue to the decision-making unit. While they occur both within the private sector and the public, their relative importance is usually greater in the public sector; indeed the importance of external effects is one of the major reasons for the incorporation of certain activities, for example, the provision of police and fire protection, within the public sector. Where they occur within the private sector, they may lead, in the absence of government intervention, to troublesome discrepancies between private and social costs which prevent the attainment of an efficient allocation of resources through the functioning of the market mechanism.[7]

Ideally, from the point of view of welfare economics, all decision-making units should take account of the external consequences of their acts and behave accordingly, for it is only in such conditions that an ideal allocation of resources will be attained. As a practical matter, however, there are important differences between the ability of firms or individuals and that of the government to take account of external factors, and in the extent to which they should. External effects of a firm's projects are those which affect other firms, or other members of the community. Where a firm is decentralized, and decisions are made at the divisional level, there may be external effects on other divisions of the firm. Where this type of external effect is involved, optimum behavior at the level of the firm will only result if they are included in the decision-maker's calculations, just as opti-

---

[7] For the classical treatment of these problems, see A. C. Pigou, *The Economics of Welfare* (4th ed.; London: Macmillan, 1932).

mum performance at the economy-wide level requires consideration of external effects by all firms. Such external effects at the divisional level, however, affect the firm's profits and losses so are not external from the point of view of the firm itself but have direct financial consequences and should normally be taken into account.

It is not always so with true external effects—those which are felt outside the firm. These are of many possible types. Classic examples are those involving pollution. Pollution usually imposes costs on the rest of the community far beyond those it imposes on the polluter. For the firm to prevent pollution would require costly additional equipment or a change in location. Pollution is usually regarded as antisocial behavior, and roundly, perhaps justifiably, condemned. Where the industry is purely competitive, so that profit margins are merely normal, the financial ability of its members to provide protection against pollution is determined by the most antisocial firm. If the latter is able to avoid the costs of preventing pollution and is otherwise efficient, the ruling price for the product will be one which does not cover the social costs of producing it, if we included pollution among the latter. If other firms are to prevent pollution, they can do so only at the expense of their shareholders and to the detriment of their abiltiy to raise additional capital. If there are extra social costs involved in producing a product, they should, at least at first glance, be borne by those who benefit by consuming the product. The only way out of such an impasse is for the state to intervene and require all firms to prevent pollution. (A private cartel might accomplish the same objective but might be tempted to pursue less altruistic goals as well and is not ordinarily regarded as an acceptable type of regulation in North America.)

It is, of course, possible for a firm having a sufficient degree of monopoly power to take account of such external effects. However, to the extent that the exercise of such power leads to a reduction in output and an increase in price from the competitive level, consumers are presumably paying for pollution prevention already, though they may not be getting it. To the extent that costs are taken into account, prices raised, and output reduced further, "socially responsible" behavior of this type is no clear guarantee of ideal output. If, however, the firm is following a price-output policy consistent with that of a competitive industry,[8] such costs should be taken into account. It is,

---

[8] W. J. Baumol, *Business Behavior, Value and Growth* (New York: Macmillan, 1959), Chaps. 6-8.

perhaps, not possible to do more here than suggest that firms having substantial market power should behave in a socially responsible fashion on both counts.

Appropriate behavior in the public sector can be more easily defined. The government, as custodian of the general welfare, should take account of all external effects, except possibly those costs borne by foreigners, such as downstream pollution of international rivers. (Presumably these can be the subject of international negotiations; to abstain from the threat of harming your neighbor while he is in a position to harm you may be virtuous, but passes up a good opportunity to protect yourself against his future misdeeds.)

The problem, however, becomes more complex when several levels of government with differing jurisdictions are involved. That it is serious is shown by the extent to which municipal sewage disposal plants are involved in the water pollution problem. Most regional and local governments are under no constitutional obligation to consider benefits and costs external to their jurisdiction, nor do they in practice. Again it is easy to suggest that they should consider such effects, but in practice here, as in the private sector, the lowest common denominator may set the standard. A city which installs expensive sewage treatment facilities may be handicapped in its ability to attract population or industry compared with a suburb which is a flagrant polluter, whether such treatment is financed by user charges or out of the general tax revenues.

Where there is widespread disregard of external effects, and the offenders are local governments having powers granted by charter from a senior government, a tolerable solution can often be obtained by negotiation and agreement between individual government units. Where it cannot, it can be imposed by the senior government either by the imposition of charter provisions enforcing conditions on behavior, or by the establishment of specialized authorities having geographical jurisdiction coterminous with the extent of the external economies or diseconomies.

Where the offending governments have sovereignty with a federal system, as have the state governments or the provincial governments in Canada, difficulties are compounded. Some solutions may be attainable by interstate compact, but the small number of such agreements is indicative of the difficulty of reaching them. Since the activity is within the jurisdiction of the regional government, constitutional difficulties usually prevent the federal government from applying an imposed solution, though it may take the lead in attempting to bring the states together and may be able to use its financial strength and the promise of funds, virtually its only weapon in such a case, to encourage resolution of the problem. T.V.A. is perhaps the outstanding example of this approach.

Constitutional amendment, to place the activity within the sphere of the federal power, is of course another alternative, but it is a cumbersome device. However, there is always the heartening experience of Prohibition to look back on as a reminder of its possibility.

Since most public sector decisions will involve external benefits and costs, we will not look at special examples here. We will examine, however, "external" effects within the firm.

Example 1—Economies External to the Division

The pipeline subsidiary of a major oil company is considering the extension of its line to a new field and the construction of a gathering system within the field. The field produces 2,000 barrels per day, of which 1,000 are produced by the parent company, the balance by competitors. Crude from the field is currently carried by a nonaffiliated trucking company to the existing pipeline terminus at a cost of $0.30 per barrel.

The line is under I.C.C. regulation which limits its return to 7½ percent on a depreciated rate base. Anticipated cost of the line is $200,000, salvage value nil. Output is prorated, and is expected to remain at 2000 b/d for 10 years, at the end of which time the field will be depleted. Operating expenses are estimated at $40,000 per year.

Estimated tariff to be charged users is a flat rate of $0.103 per barrel, calculated to produce an accounting rate of return of 7½ percent after taxes, over the life of the line, calculated as follows:

	Cost per year
Operating expenses	$40,000
Depreciation	20,000
Return (7½% of average investment)	7,500
Income taxes (50%)	7,500
Total required	$75,000 = 0.103 per barrel

From the pipeline's point of view, the investment will produce a cash flow of $27,500 per year for 10 years on an investment of $200,000, giving an internal rate of return of 6.3 percent. This rate of return is respectable enough, for a pipeline investment, but is below the parent company's cost of capital of 13 percent. If this were all that was considered, there is a good chance the proposal would be rejected.

But the line also affects the earnings of the parent company, saving it 19.7¢ per barrel in transportation charges, increasing wellhead prices by an equivalent amount. This is a gross flow of $72,000 per year, reduced by income tax calculated as follows:

```
Gross earnings from price increase . . . . 72,000
Less depletion allowance 27½% . . . . . . 19,800
Taxable earnings . . . . . . . . . . . . . . . 52,200
Tax (50%) . . . . . . . . . . . . . . . . . . 26,100
```

Total annual cash receipts to the firm as a whole are as follows:

	Pipeline subsidiary	Producing department	Consolidated
Receipts:			
Trucking charge saved	–	$109,500	$109,500
Pipeline charge	75,000	(37,500)	37,500
Total receipts	75,000	72,000	147,000
Outlays:			
Pipeline operating	40,000	–	40,000
Income tax.	7,500	26,100	33,600
Total outlays	47,500	26,100	73,600
Net receipts	27,500	45,900	73,400
(after tax)			

which provides a handsome rate of return of 35 percent on the pipeline investment of $200,000. In this case the "external" savings form the major portion of the benefit. This is one of the factors which have led oil companies to extend pipeline systems aggressively rather than wait for other investors to do so.[9] Prospective returns to them are much greater than they are to outside investors. As a consequence, nearly all crude oil pipeline systems are owned by oil company subsidiaries.

By providing this line however, an equal external benefit is provided for other operators in the field. If these can be induced to share its cost 50:50 by setting it up as a joint venture, the company can reduce its investment to $100,000 while its annual receipts fall only to $59,650, boosting its internal rate of return on the venture to about 60 percent.[10] Since its incremental rate of return on the $100,000

---

[9]For other factors see L. Cookenboo, Jr., *Crude Oil Pipelines and Competition in the Oil Industry* (Cambridge: Harvard, 1955).

[10]Pipeline receipts fall by 50 percent to $13,750, producing department receipts are unchanged.

extra investment required for full ownership is only 6½ percent, it will prefer, if possible, to negotiate such a deal. Such a deal would have the incidental advantage of eliminating the likelihood of squabbles from nonintegrated producers over alleged tariff discrimination, "secret rebates," and so on. For both parties, it offers the additional attraction of being able to cut the tariff below the I.C.C. level, so that no return is earned on the pipeline, where it is taxable at the full rate, thus augmenting the price by an equivalent amount, of which only 72.5 percent is taxable, thanks to the depletion allowance.

Example 2—"External Diseconomies" within the Firm

The Feline Division of the Universal Motor Car Company is considering the introduction of a sports model, tentatively named the Cheetah. Market surveys indicate sales, at a manufacturers' net price of $2,000, growing as follows:

First year	15,000
Second year	25,000
Third year	35,000
Fourth year	40,000
Fifth year	45,000
Thereafter	50,000

Labor and materials cost is estimated at $1,000 per unit. Some assemblies can be produced in the division's existing plants, but new plant space costing $20 million will be required. This can be written off for tax purposes at a straight line rate of 5 percent. Initial tooling cost is estimated at $20 million of which $8 million can be written off at once, as it relates to the current year's model, the balance over a ten year period. Costs of annual model changes are estimated at $3 million for the second year, $5 million in the third, and $10 million in the fourth year, a pattern which is expected to repeat itself indefinitely. An advertising campaign costing $20 million will be required to establish the new line, while $10 million annually is expected to be sufficient to maintain its market position at the projected level of sales. The company is subject to a 50 percent marginal tax rate. Its cost of capital is 12 percent after taxes. For investment decision purposes, it does not carry analyses beyond the tenth year, as an arbitrary protection against risk.

Table 4-1 shows the estimates of cash flows derived by the division from the above data. It appears reasonably profitable on the above basis, with an internal rate of return of 31 percent and a discounted benefit-cost ratio of 1.08.

TABLE 4–1
CASH FLOWS FROM NEW MODEL, FELINE DIVISION
($000)

Year	Revenue	Labor & materials	Plant & tooling	Advertising	Tax outlays	Net cash flow
1	30,000	15,000	40,000	20,000	(7,600)	(37,400)
2	50,000	25,000	3,000	10,000	4,900	7,100
3	70,000	35,000	5,000	10,000	8,900	11,100
4	80,000	40,000	10,000	10,000	8,900	11,100
5	90,000	45,000	3,000	10,000	14,900	17,100
6	100,000	50,000	5,000	10,000	16,400	18,600
7	100,000	50,000	10,000	10,000	13,900	16,100
8	100,000	50,000	3,000	10,000	17,400	19,600
9	100,000	50,000	5,000	10,000	16,400	18,600
10	100,000	50,000	10,000	10,000	13,900	16,100

Internal rate of return $= 31\%$
Benefit-cost ratio $(k = 0.12) = 1.08$

What the analysis carried out by the division ignores, however, is that the Canine Division of the same company produces another sports model, the Mongrel, which currently has 40 percent of the market for this type of car. Of the sales achieved by the Cheetah, at least one-third will be achieved at the expense of the Mongrel. This will lead to a reduction in sales of the other division, to a reduction in their expenses for materials and labor, and to a reduction in taxes, as shown in Table 4-2.

TABLE 4–2
ANALYSIS OF NEW MODEL, AT CORPORATE LEVEL,
INCORPORATING EXTERNAL EFFECTS ON DIVISION
($000)

Year	Canine Division					Feline Division net cash flow	Total corporate net cash flow
	Lost sales	Lost revenue	Reduced expenses	Reduced taxes	Net cash flow		
1	5,000	10,000	5,000	2,500	(2,500)	(37,400)	(39,900)
2	8,333	16,667	8,333	4,167	(4,166)	7,100	2,934
3	11,667	23,333	11,667	5,834	(5,833)	11,100	5,267
4	13,333	26,667	13,333	6,167	(6,166)	11,100	4,934
5	15,000	30,000	15,000	7,500	(7,500)	17,100	9,600
6	16,667	33,333	16,667	8,334	(8,333)	18,600	10,267
7	16,667	33,333	16,667	8,334	(8,333)	16,100	7,767
8	16,667	33,333	16,667	8,334	(8,333)	19,600	11,267
9	16,667	33,333	16,667	8,334	(8,333)	18,600	10,267
10	16,667	33,333	16,667	8,334	(8,333)	16,100	7,267

Internal rate of return $=$ just below 12%
Benefit-cost ratio $(k = 0.12) = 0.99$

The full analysis indicates that the proposed addition to the Feline Division's product line is unprofitable for the corporation as a whole, if its cost of capital is 12 percent. The profit-maximizing solution for the company as a whole requires that such effects, external to the division, but internal from the point of view of the firm, be taken into account. Ensuring that they are so taken into account is a major problem in the design of a decentralized capital budgeting system where capital expenditure decisions are delegated to the divisions. This can be accomplished either by subjecting divisional budgets to a central review or by limiting the delegation to types of projects not likely to have "external" effects. Specifying these a priori may be somewhat difficult, as even cost-reducing projects may have external effects.[11]

Since many firms have decentralized decision-making systems which do not take full account of such external effects, some comment on the results of such failure should be added at this point. Such "external" effects on the revenue side only exist where the firm is sufficiently large for the sales of one division to have some impact on the other divisions, so they may be presumed to be limited to firms having some degree of monopoly power. In such a firm, failure to consider such effects will lead to an expansion of output beyond the profit-maximizing output in the conventional price-theory-textbook, analysis of monopolistic competition. In the language of the latter, discounted benefits are (long-run) marginal revenues, discounted costs are (long-run) marginal costs. Failure to take full account of external effects will lead to incorrect estimates of both. While there is no general way of predicting the outcome, an examination of the most likely types of error leads to the surmise that, in the limiting case, the competitive output and price will be attained. The examination of market concentration at the corporate level is likely to give an overestimate of the extent of monopolistic influences in the market to the extent that such practices persist. Insofar as continuation of the practice is likely to lead to price-output results more nearly approximating the competitive ideal, it is socially desirable that it be continued. We are concerned here, however, with laying down the conditions under which the firm, whether possessed of monopoly

---

[11]See J. Hirshleifer, "On the Economics of Transfer Pricing," *Journal of Business*, Vol. XXIX (January, 1956), pp. 172-84; "Economics of the Divisionalized Firm," *Journal of Business*, Vol. XXX (April, 1957), pp. 96-108.

power or not, can maximize its profits, not with whether it should, and need not pursue the matter further.

"External" effects can, of course, also exist on the cost side. Here their existence is independent of market structure. Such effects arise when the realization of economies of scale by one division is affected by the output decisions of another.

4.7 Mutually Exclusive Projects: The Choice of Techniques

Whenever there are two or more ways of achieving some objective, the decision maker is faced with the problem of choosing between alternative techniques. In practice, such decisions often incorporate problems of choice of scale, as for example, the choice between dams of different size with different generating capacity on the same site; however, this added complication does not seriously affect the decision process.

In the pure technique case, benefits are identical. The decision problem resolves itself into one of picking the alternative for which gross discounted costs are the lowest, or for which the rate of return is the highest.

In cases where problems of both scale and technique are involved, the decision requires consideration of a series of fictitious projects constructed in the following manner. Suppose we have three alternative projects, A, B, and C, listed in order of increasing cost. Substitute for the latter two the fictitious projects B' and C'. The cost of B' in each time period is the excess of its cost over the cost of A; the cost of C' is the excess of its cost over B''s. Benefits may be similarly defined, in the mixed case, though these will be identical in the pure "choice of technique" situation. Project A and the fictitious projects B' and C' are included in the list of budget proposals and the latter processed in the normal manner. If the accepted budget includes both A and B' and not C', then project B should be constructed. If, it includes all three, proceed instead with C. If only A is included, this is the appropriate choice. For other problems involving mutually exclusive projects, see Sec. 4.8 which follows.

Example 1—Mutually Exclusive Projects: The Pure Technique Case

A company intends to manufacture a minor part which it now purchases from an outside supplier at a cost of $20,000 per year. There are three processes it may adopt, having the following characteristics:

	Initial cost	Annual operating expenses (including taxes)
A	8,000	15,000
B	12,000	14,000
C.	20,000	12,000

At the company's cost of capital of 12 percent, the present value of benefits over 10 years is $130,000 in all three cases. The present value of costs for the three projects is:

A	$92,750
B	91,100
C	87,800

Project C should be adopted. Internal rates of return for the three projects are 62 percent, 49 percent, and 38 percent respectively.

Example 2—Mutually Exclusive Projects: Mixed Scale and Technique Case

A government agency is considering two proposals for the development of a dam for irrigation purposes. Project A will cost $1,000,000 initially, $50,000 per year to operate, will irrigate 5,000 acres, and will produce annual benefits of $200,000 for 50 years. Project B will cost $1,500,000 initially, $150,000 per year to operate, and will irrigate 10,000 acres including some which are not cultivable for other reasons, and will produce annual benefits of $320,000 for 50 years. The agency's cost of capital is 10 percent. Which alternative should be chosen?

Project A has a benefit-cost ratio of 1.48, project B a ratio of 1.12. Both are acceptable, but only one site is available, so the question is how intensively it should be developed. The following estimates can be derived for the fictitious project B'.

	Project B	Project A	Project B' (B − A)
Initial cost	$1,500,000	$1,000,000	$500,000
Annual operating	150,000	50,000	100,000
Annual benefits	320,000	200,000	120,000

B' has a benefit-cost ratio of only 0.39, hence would not be built if it were a separate, individual project. Project A should be chosen.

4.8   The Problem of Horizons

The choice of a horizon refers merely to the selection of the time period which the decision maker will consider in evaluating benefits and costs.

Some projects have a well defined life, dependent on physical or legal circumstances, e.g., the construction of a service station on a leased site. Others have indefinitely long lives, and may still be yielding benefits 300 years from now.

Is there any rule for establishing a horizon? In general, we must answer no, whether we are considering the private sector or the public sector. There is no reason for attaching any higher or lower weight to future benefits, other than that implicit in the discounting process. Even if the owners of a firm plan to retire in five years, maximizing the market value of their holding at that time probably requires that it be sold on a going-concern basis, and its sale price will be dependent on capitalized earnings past that point. However, as a practical matter, at the rates of discount which cost of capital considerations require us to use, benefits and costs don't count for much if they occur very far in the future. At 8 percent a dollar to be received 25 years from now is worth only $0.15 today, one due in 50 years only $0.02. The most practical way of resolving the horizon problem is to let the discount rate take care of it.

In practice, many firms impose a shorter limit on benefits and costs to be considered for many types of projects. The argument for the practice is that the future is uncertain, that forecasts beyond a certain length are unreliable, so that benefits beyond a certain point are largely conjectural. The short horizon is imposed as a crude limit on risk.

Most analyses prepared by federal agencies in the United States use a 50-year horizon though 100 years is used in some cases.[12] The former limit has been criticized as favoring present generations to the exclusion of future. However, the importance of the difficulty is also related to the choice of a discount rate. If public sector discount rates are those suggested in Chapter 7, the difference between a 50-year and 100-year limit is negligible.

The analysis of projects with lives considerably shorter than the effective planning horizon contains a built-in horizon which may hamper the application of particular criteria to arrive at appropriate decisions. Which is better, to invest $10,000 in a project lasting 5 years and promising an internal rate of return of 17 percent or to invest

---

[12]O. Eckstein, *op. cit.*, pp. 83 *et. seq.*

it in a project lasting 10 years and promising an internal rate of return of 15 percent? The two projects have built-in horizons, of 5 and 10 years respectively, and cannot be directly compared. To see why, it is necessary to review the sense in which the internal rate of return is a rate of return on the sum invested.

Consider project A which costs $10,000, and returns, net of taxes, the following amounts at the end of the years listed.

First	2,700
Second	3,530
Third	4,190
Fourth	2,680
Fifth	2,340

This project has an internal rate of return of 17 percent as verified by the following (cf. Sec. 3.8):

TABLE 4–3
INTERNAL RATE OF RETURN: PROJECT A (5 years, $R = 17\%$)

Year	Unamortized balance of investment Jan. 1	Cash flow Dec. 31	Of which: Return 17%	Of which: Recovery of capital
1	10,000	2,700	1,700	1,000
2	9,000	3,530	1,530	2,000
3	7,000	4,190	1,190	3,000
4	4,000	2,680	680	2,000
5	2,000	2,340	340	2,000
6	0			

The internal rate of return is the return earned *on that portion of the investment which has not yet been recovered.* It is the true rate of return on the unrecovered investment in that it is the largest amount which can be withdrawn each year and allow recovery of the initial investment by the expiry of the project. As a measure of profitability, it is merely an index of the profitability of the remaining investment in the project and not of the contribution of the project as a whole to the profitability of the firm.

Depending on the available opportunities for investing the funds set free, such a project may contribute less to the firm's ultimate profitability than another which offers a lower rate of return but ties up funds for a longer period.[13]

---

[13]E. Solomon, "The Arithmetic of Capital Budgeting Decisions," *Journal of Business* (April, 1956), reprinted in Solomon (1959), *op. cit.*, pp. 74-79.

To see how this may happen, consider project B, which offers a 15 percent internal rate on a $10,000 investment having the cash flow indicated below:

TABLE 4-4
INTERNAL RATE OF RETURN: PROJECT B (10 years, $R = 15\%$)

Year	Unamortized balance of investment, Jan. 1	Cash flow, Dec. 31	Return 15%	Of which: Recovery of capital
1	10,000	2,500	1,500	1,000
2	9,000	2,350	1,350	1,000
3	8,000	2,200	1,200	1,000
4	7,000	2,050	1,050	1,000
5	6,000	1,900	900	1,000
6	5,000	1,750	750	1,000
7	4,000	1,600	600	1,000
8	3,000	1,450	450	1,000
9	2,000	1,300	300	1,000
10	1,000	1,150	150	1,000

From the second year on, there is more still "invested" in project B than in project A, and it is producing a rate of return of 15 percent on this amount, whereas A is producing 17 percent on a smaller amount.

Because of the rapidly shrinking amount still "invested" in Project A, the portion of cash receipts from Project B which can be regarded as return on the remaining investment is larger than the portion of A's cash flow which can be so regarded, from the third year onward. If the opportunities for profitable reinvestment of the funds which are recovered from the two projects are limited, it may well be that B is to be preferred to A. To make a direct comparison of their effects on the profitability of the firm, it is necessary to examine what reinvestment opportunities are available and to consider what funds could be accumulated by the firm to a common terminal date or horizon, which must be no sooner than the expiry of the longer project.

Choice of a reinvestment rate for such an analysis will depend on whether the firm is operating on a profit-maximizing basis or on a capital-rationing basis. If the former, the applicable reinvestment rate will be simply the firm's cost of capital since this is the rate it will be earning on marginal investments. If all the funds available on this basis can't be used, a portion of the firm's outstanding securities can be retired. If the firm is in a capital-rationing situation, the reinvestment rate will be a higher rate, dependent on the opportunity cost of funds in future periods.

The longer project will be chosen, despite its lower internal rate of return, if the estimated reinvestment rate is sufficiently low relative to the internal rate of return. This may be expected to happen quite frequently if the cost of capital is used as the reinvestment rate, if only because neither project will be regarded as acceptable if its internal rate of return is not greater than the cost of capital. Occasionally however, the expected reinvestment rate will be above the internal rate of return of the longer-lived project, because the cost of capital is expected to rise or because a capital rationing situation is expected to develop. In such a case the shorter project is to be preferred as its quicker cash throwoff makes funds available for reinvestment sooner.

While our example is in terms of longer and shorter projects having definite lives, it also appears in those cases where there is a marked difference in the time shape of the receipts stream, so that in one case, for example, half the investment is recovered in two years, while in the other it takes eight.

If the firm is pursuing a policy of maximizing long run profits and accepting all those projects for which the internal rate exceeds the cost of capital, it should, of course, accept both projects unless they are mutually exclusive, in which case a careful analysis of the reinvestment situation should be carried out. Where the firm is in a capital-rationing situation, a similar analysis may be necessary.

Use of the benefit-cost criterion will lead to appropriate rankings for projects of different lives, since free funds can be reinvested at the discounting rate. A partial exception arises in the capital rationing case. Here projects may be displaced, or postponed, and it may be desirable to use the cutoff rate as a measure of the opportunity cost for calculating benefit-cost ratios and as an implicit reinvestment rate.

4.9   Avoid Double Counting

This warning should be unnecessary. Unfortunately, there are some fairly subtle traps into which the analyst may fall. It would be impossible to catalog all of the possible errors of this variety.

Perhaps the commonest is that of charging interest on the investment as an expense, then calculating an internal rate of return or benefit-cost ratio on the remaining profits. Such imputed interest is not a cash flow (if it is, the project and its financing are hopelessly scrambled up and should be separated), and its inclusion as an expense results in an understatement of the desirability of the project. The appropriate allowance for interest is included in the analysis when cost of capital is considered as part of the decision process. Putting it in anywhere else counts it twice.

Closely related is the practice of including interest during construction as part of the capital cost of a project. If all outlays are dated and appropriate discounting takes place, this item is automatically provided for. Where it is desired to treat outlays as if they took place at a single point in time, i.e., at the beginning of the receipt stream, earlier expenditures should be accumulated with an allowance for interest to this point. Where this is done, however, the appropriate interest rate to use is not the bond rate, which is frequently used for this purpose, but the cost of capital, if the benefit-cost criterion is being used, or the actual internal rate, where the internal rate criterion is being used. Ordinarily, the latter can most conveniently be found by dating all expenditures and discounting the entire stream at one step.

A similar practice is that of charging depreciation as an expense, then applying benefit-cost analysis or computing the internal rate of return. The internal rate criterion, as has been shown, calculates the return on the unrecovered capital invested in the project, and makes full provision for the recovery of capital in this way. Capital recovery in benefit-cost analysis is provided for by the requirement that the benefit-cost ratio exceed 1.0. Further depreciation charges are not only unnecessary but incorrect in either case.

There are other ways of counting the same tricks twice which should also be avoided. A project which improves the earning power of a service station increases its value to the company owning it. The increase in value is entirely the result of the increased earning power, and an analysis which takes into account both the increased earnings and the increased value is clearly wrong as it involves double counting. Where the residual value at time of planned disposition is affected (by an increase in earning power subsequent to the time of disposition) and earning power prior to disposition is increased, there is, of course, no double counting if both are included.

4.10 Replacement Situations

Another type of horizon problem arises when we come to consider replacement situations. For the most part, we have examined projects on the assumption that their lives were known beforehand. While this is true of certain types of assets, such as oil wells, peat bogs, and dams subject to silting at a predictable rate, it is an oversimplification in most cases. Machines do not simply fall apart at the end of their life span, instead they become more expensive to repair and more intermittent in the character of service which they render, and probably obsolescent as well. Determining the appropriate time for the replacement of an existing facility is a capital budgeting problem, while determining the economic life of an asset is a closely related one. Even if we can predict the economic service lives of various machines, these may differ for different alternatives, i.e., one machine may be more durable than the other. This is a special type of mutually exclusive project situation. To make a fair comparison between the more durable and less durable assets, it is necessary to place them on the same footing with respect to the period of analysis to be considered. If they are associated with a particular operation which has a known terminal date, discounted costs prior to that date should be minimized; where there is no terminal date, it is usually preferable to assume an infinite chain of replacements.

The simplest problem is one of determining the economic life of a single machine. More frequent replacement means more capital is tied up in the machine, while less frequent replacement means higher repair costs and out-of-service costs.

Further, resale price of the asset falls as its age increases, but the user cost of continuing to use it for an additional year normally drops from year to year. In practice, resale price can be deducted from the appropriate replacement cost when incurred, i.e., treated as a trade-in. As life increases, capital cost per period falls, while operating expenses per period increase. The optimum life is chosen at the point where the increase in operating expenses is equated with the decrease in capital cost. This problem is considered in the example below.

More difficult problems arise where the pace of technological change is considered. Here, the productivity of new machines increases, so that, presumably, subsequent machines will either cost less to buy or to operate. Where this situation exists, it will be a factor tending to postpone replacement slightly, in order to get a more productive replacement.

Some problems also involve planning for expanded capacity at the time of replacement. It is impossible to deal with all such problems here, for a comprehensive treatment of them would be mathematically involved and would require more space than that at our disposal.

It should be noted that the calculated economic life at the time of installation does not determine the appropriate time of replacement.

The former was a forecast, and was undoubtedly subject to forecasting errors. The search for investment proposals should involve a systematic review of the performance of equipment, beginning some time well in advance of its originally forecast retirement age, and a search for possible replacements.

As soon as the best potential replacement offers a benefit-cost ratio in excess of 1.0, taking into account the savings it offers over existing equipment, replacement should take place, if profits are to be maximized. Postponing replacement until the gains produce a higher benefit-cost ratio normally leads to higher costs over a period of time and is suboptimal. Of course, if the firm is in a capital rationing situation, analysis of the postponability of otherwise acceptable projects along the lines suggested in Chapter 9 will frequently select certain replacement projects as the best candidates for postponement. This is because replacement becomes more urgent and more profitable the longer it is delayed, whereas other projects may not "improve with age."

Example: Life of a Truck[14]

A trucking company has the following estimates of data on the cost of running a truck costing $5,000:

Year	Operating expenses	Trade-in value at end of year
1	1,000	3,000
2	1,100	1,800
3	1,250	1,000
4	1,500	700
5	1,900	500
6	2,500	300
7	3,500	200

If its cost of capital is 10 percent, at what age should it replace the truck?

Costs *per replacement cycle*, which we will consider first, consist of the capital outlay made at the beginning of the cycle, less any trade-in received, plus operating expenses during the cycle. For convenience

---

[14]For a more comprehensive treatment, see G. Terborgh, *Dynamic Equipment Policy* (New York: McGraw-Hill, 1949); M. Sasieni, A. Yaspan, and L. Friedman, *Operations Research* (New York: Wiley, 1959), Chap. 5; P. Massé, *Optimal Investment Decisions* (Englewood Cliffs, N. J.: Prentice-Hall, 1962), Chap. 2.

in the analysis, these can be regarded as occurring at the beginning of the cycle if we take their present values at that point. As a first step in our calculation, therefore, calculate the present value of operating expenses for the various possible lives:

Year	Operating expenses	Present value at 10%	Cumulative P.V. from year 1
1	1,000	909	909
2	1,100	910	1,819
3	1,250	938	2,757
4	1,500	1,025	3,782
5	1,900	1,180	4,962
6	2,500	1,410	6,372
7	3,500	1,790	8,162

Cost of a one year replacement cycle is the present value of operating costs, $909, plus the capital outlay of $5,000 for the initial cycle and $2,000 for subsequent cycles, after deducting the trade-in of $3,000. Cost of a two year replacement cycle is $1,819 in present value of operating costs plus $5,000 for the initial cycle and $3,200 for subsequent cycles, crediting the trade-in from the previous cycle against the cost of the replacement. Costs calculated in similar fashion for replacement cycles of greater length are as follows:

Life	First cycle cost (initial year)	Subsequent cycle cost (beginning of cycle)
1	5,909	2,909
2	6,819	5,019
3	7,757	6,757
4	8,752	8,082
5	9,962	9,462
6	11,372	11,072
7	13,162	12,962

Providing the service indefinitely with a one year replacement cycle will require an initial outlay worth $5,909, and subsequent annual outlays of $2,909 in perpetuity. Replacing every second year will require an initial outlay of $6,819, with a further equivalent outlay of $5,019 every *second* year and so on.

The present value of the cost of each alternative can be regarded as the sum of the initial cycle cost and the present value of a perpetuity of the amount of the subsequent cycle costs incurred at appropriate intervals, at the cost of capital rate. Factors for this can be calculated simply from the formula

$$\frac{1}{k\,n}$$

where

> k = the annual discount rate
> n = number of years in the replacement cycle.

Substituting in the formula, the present value factor to be applied to subsequent cycle costs is, for a one year cycle, 1/0.10 or 10.00, for a two year cycle, 1/2(.10) or 5.00, and so on.

Using these factors, we can calculate the present value of costs for alternative replacement cycle lengths, as in Table 4-5. To find the economic life of the truck, we choose the replacement cycle which minimizes the present value of costs.

TABLE 4-5
LEAST COST SOLUTION TO TRUCK REPLACEMENT PROBLEM

Life	Cost/subsequent cycle	Present value factor	Cost of future cycles	Initial cycle	Total cost
1	$ 2,909	10.00	$29,090	$ 5,909	$34,999
2	5,019	5.00	25,095	6,819	31,914
3	6,757	3.33	22,501	7,757	30,258
4	8,082	2.50	20,205	8,752	28,957
5	9,462	2.00	18,924	9,962	28,886
6	11,072	1.67	18,453	11,372	29,825
7	12,962	1.43	18,536	13,162	31,798

The economic life of the truck, i.e., the age at which it should be replaced, is 5 years in this case.

4.11 The Treatment of Price Level Changes

An increasing amount of attention has been focused on the problem of price level changes, particularly inflation, in recent years. That these produce distortions in reported incomes, using conventional accounting standards, is reasonably clear.[15] Unless care is taken, they

---

[15] The most complete treatment of this problem is E. O. Edwards and P. Bell, *The Theory and Measurement of Business Income* (Berkeley: University of California, 1961).

may also distort the decision-making process and lead to inappropriate choices.

It should be noted that we have no clear way of forecasting price changes accurately. This does not mean we may ignore them. It may mean we should hedge against them by appropriate capital structure adjustments.[16] Merely to assume a continuation of the present price level is to forecast no change, and is no "sounder" than making an explicit forecast (unless we are hedged against it). In the following we will assume that the decision maker has an explicit forecast and desires to incorporate it into his analysis. Before examining how this might be done we should note that the fact that practically everybody anticipates inflation is not a particularly good reason for following the crowd in this regard. In the past, such virtual unanimity has often been followed by a reversal in the trend, often lasting a number of years. There may be more substantial reasons for expecting inflation in the current situation, however. Because of the forecasting difficulty, a conservative policy would seem to dictate examination of the consequences of alternative changes in the price level and an attempt to hedge against them. This is a matter of overall financial policy and is beyond the scope of this book.

Since it is current dollars which are being committed, it is perhaps most natural, as well as convenient, to carry out the analysis in terms of current dollars, i.e., units of purchasing power equivalent to today's dollar. The basic feature of an analysis which attempts to take account of expected future price level changes is to distinguish between two types of benefits and costs:

(a) "Real Value" benefits and costs, which will rise and fall in monetary amount with changes in the price level.
(b) "Fixed Dollar" benefits and costs which will remain constant, in monetary units despite changes in the price level.

In the simplest type of analysis, which we will consider in the example below, no attempt is made to draw finer distinctions. On the average, real value benefits and real value costs may be expected to increase in monetary value with an increase in the price level at about the same rate as prices generally. Since they are expressed, presumably, at current price levels, there is no need to make any adjustment for future changes in prices. Alternatively, they may be expressed in future prices then deflated. Not all prices and not all costs go up at

---

[16]J. F. Weston, *Managerial Finance* (New York: Holt, Rinehart & Winston, 1962), pp. 257-60.

the same rate, however. The increase in wage rates has exceeded the increase in price levels, for example, as man-hour productivity has increased. A more sophisticated approach is one which separates real-value benefits and costs into different groups, subject to different rates of change in prices, projects benefits and costs in terms of future price levels, then deflates the totals by the anticipated general price index to derive an estimate in current dollars. Costs which are growing more rapidly than others will carry an increased weight in such a calculation.

In either type of calculation, future fixed dollar benefits and costs must be deflated by the expected price index, to convert them into dollars of present day purchasing power. If I lend you $100 today and get back $100 in 5 years time, while the retail price index has risen from 100 to 125, I'm only getting back the purchasing power equivalent of $80.

Example—Simple Corrections

Firm *A* can sign a contract for 5 year's supply of a particular part at the present price of $5.00, with an option for a 5 year renewal at the price prevailing in 5 years time. Current consumption is 1000 units per year, and is expected to increase by 100 units each year. As an alternative, it can buy a machine costing $20,000, with operating expense of $2.00 per unit at current price levels. Life of the machine is 10 years, its scrap value nil. The income tax rate is 50 percent, the depreciation rate for tax purposes 10 percent straight line.

Price levels, currently 100, are expected to increase by 2 points per year to 102, 104, and so on. Tax calculations are shown in Table 4-6

TABLE 4-6
TAX CALCULATIONS: MAKE OR BUY PROBLEM
(Future Dollars)

Year	Price level	Units	Price/ unit	Purchases saved	Expense/ unit	Operating expense	Depr'n.	Taxable income	Income tax
1 . . .	100	1000	5.00	5,000	2.00	2,000	1,000	2,000	1,000
2 . . .	102	1100	5.00	5,500	2.04	2,244	1,000	2,256	1,128
3 . . .	104	1200	5.00	6,000	2.08	2,496	1,000	2,504	1,252
4 . . .	106	1300	5.00	6,500	2.12	2,756	1,000	2,744	1,372
5 . . .	108	1400	5.00	7,000	2.16	3,004	1,000	2,996	1,498
6 . . .	110	1500	5.50	8,250	2.20	3,300	1,000	3,950	1,975
7 . . .	112	1600	5.50	8,800	2.24	3,584	1,000	4,216	2,108
8 . . .	114	1700	5.50	9,350	2.28	3,876	1,000	4,474	2,237
9 . . .	116	1800	5.50	9,900	2.32	4,176	1,000	4,724	2,362
10 . . .	118	1900	5.50	10,450	2.36	4,484	1,000	4,966	2,883

which is in future dollars, reflecting the anticipated increase in operating expenses owing to the rising price level and the anticipated higher price at which the purchase contract can be renewed. Depreciation allowances are based on original cost of the asset in current dollars, though they are fixed-dollar benefits which can only be deducted as future dollars of lower value.

It is usually necessary to calculate benefits and costs in future dollars to calculate the tax liability, as this will depend on savings actually made less expenses actually incurred in future-year dollars. Since we have these estimates in future-year dollars, it is necessary to adjust for purchasing power before calculating the benefit-cost ratio. The schedule of benefits and costs is shown in Table 4-7.

TABLE 4-7
ADJUSTED SCHEDULE OF BENEFITS AND COSTS

Year	Price level	Benefits (Purchases saved) Future $	Current $	Costs Future $ Cap. & opg.	Tax	Total	Current $
Initial . . 100		—	—	20,000	—	20,000	20,000
1 . . 100		5,000	5,000	2,000	1,000	3,000	3,000
2 . . 102		5,500	5,400	2,244	1,128	3,372	3,300
3 . . 104		6,000	5,870	2,496	1,252	3,748	3,600
4 . . 106		6,500	6,130	2,756	1,372	4,128	3,900
5 . . 108		7,000	6,480	3,004	1,498	4,502	4,170
6 . . 110		8,250	7,500	3,300	1,975	5,275	4,800
7 . . 112		8,800	7,850	3,584	2,108	5,692	5,080
8 . . 114		9,350	8,220	3,876	2,237	6,113	5,360
9 . . 116		9,900	8,530	4,176	2,362	6,538	5,630
10 . . 118		10,450	8,850	4,484	2,883	7,367	6,240

The company's cost of capital is 10 percent. It can calculate its benefit-cost ratio for "make" rather than "buy" in three ways.

(a) Using current year prices and costs (not shown). This yields a benefit-cost ratio of 0.91.

(b) Using unadjusted future year benefits and costs. This is a completely undesirable figure, equivalent to adding gallons (present dollars) to quarts (future dollars) without converting to a common unit.

(c) Using future year benefits and costs, adjusted to a current price level basis. This benefit-cost ratio is only 0.88. It is lower than (a). As price levels rise, costs will rise with them under the "make" alternative, but prices under the "buy" alternative are pegged for 5 year periods by the terms of the contract. Under such conditions "buy" is a more favorable alternative than it would be under a stable price level [the implicit assumption of (a)].

PROBLEMS

1. A cabinet committee has been appointed to decide between two proposed plans for the development of the Purple River. Plan A calls for the construction of two dams. The larger of the two will cost $3 million, and produce benefits of $400,000 per year. The smaller dam will cost $2 million. It will produce direct benefits of $150,000 annually but will increase the benefits from the first dam by an additional $150,000. Plan B calls for the construction of a single larger dam costing $10 million. This dam would be located at the same site as the larger dam in plan A and would flood out the smaller damsite as well. It would produce annual benefits of $900,000. The life of all dams is expected to exceed 100 years.

(a) If the opportunity cost of capital to society is 8 percent on a before tax basis, which plan of development should be chosen?

(b) Over what range of costs of capital is Plan A preferable? Plan B?

2. The permanent federal dam subcommittee is reviewing a proposal to dam the Blank River. Total federal cost is estimated at $60 million for the construction of the dam. The state government will have to spend another $10 million to reroute a freeway which currently passes near the damsite. Annual benefits from the project are expected to include power generated, worth $5.9 million, improved recreation, $400,000, improved navigation, $240,000, and flood control, worth $820,000. The project's share of departmental overhead is estimated at $100,000 per year. In addition to the average annual gain from prevention of flood damage, elimination of the flood threat is expected to increase the value of farm lands in the valley below the dam by $10 million.

The present freeway is heavily used. The rerouted freeway will be slightly longer, and is expected to increase the cost of transportation to motorists using it, by $1 million per year.

Assuming a life of 50 years and cost of capital of 8 percent,

(a) What goes into the numerator of the benefit-cost ratio?

(b) Into the denominator?

(c) Should the dam be built?

3. The cost of planting a particular variety of rubber trees is $600 per acre. Yields from an acre of rubber trees of this type follow the following pattern:

Age, years	Annual yield, lbs.
0–5	0
6–10	1,000
11–15	2,000
16–20	3,000
21–25	2,500
26–30	1,500
31–40	1,000

Estimated harvesting costs are $100 per acre per year. Planting costs are deductible, for tax purposes, in the year in which they are incurred.

(a) Assuming a rubber price of $0.20 per lb., an income tax rate of 50 percent, and a cost of capital of 10 percent, at what age should rubber trees be replaced?

(b) What is the effect of changes in

(i) rubber prices (ii) harvesting costs (iii) income tax rates (iv) the cost of capital, on the optimum age for replacement?

(c) If we assume that rubber prices will increase at 2 percent per annum, that harvesting costs will increase at 5 percent per annum, and that an annual improvement of 1 percent in productivity is available through improved planting stock, what happens to the optimum age for replanting?

CHAPTER 5

The Evaluation Process:
Costs of Capital from Specific Sources

5.1 Why Consider Cost of Capital?

The cost-of-capital concept is one of the fundamental cornerstones of the theory of finance. While there is fairly general agreement concerning the usefulness of the concept and how it should be applied, there has been a fundamental lack of agreement on exactly what it is or how it should be measured. So long as this remains so, any estimate of the cost of capital requires, at some point, the exercise of informed judgment. The contribution of theory, in its present state, is to narrow the range of possible estimates within which judgment must be exercised.

As we saw in Chapter 3, an estimate of the cost of capital is necessary in the application of the more sophisticated and satisfactory measures of desirability, including discounted benefit-cost ratios and the internal rate of return. We have also seen that it is necessary to consider the cost of capital at the project design stage. These are the primary reasons for its consideration here. In addition it may be useful to management in making decisions between alternative financing proposals. Here, however, cost may not be the deciding factor, as questions of retaining control, or of avoiding risk, may be paramount.[1]

We must tread warily, however, for there are a number of different concepts of the cost of capital, some of which may be more appropriate in certain situations than others.

5.2 Which Cost of Capital to Consider

For decision-making purposes in general, it is *future* costs, and

---

[1] See P. Hunt, C. M. Williams, and G. Donaldson, *Basic Business Finance*, (3d ed.; Homewood, Ill.: Irwin, 1966), Chaps. 18, 19, for a balanced discussion of the issues relevant to financing decisions.

not historical ones which are relevant. Capital expenditure decisions, involving the weighing of future benefits against present outlays, are no exception to this rule; indeed extra care should be taken to apply this standard.

The most intuitively appealing concept of cost of capital is simply the cost associated with the use of a particular block of funds raised from a single source, either by a single security issue or a package of securities. This certainly is one kind of cost of capital and one that has certain uses. In this study, this concept will be referred to as the *specific cost* of capital (from a specified source).[2] However, no firm, except perhaps one that is at the point of being born, relies exclusively on funds from a single source. As a result, generally speaking, the specific cost of funds from a particular source is not the same as the *inclusive cost* of funds from all sources.

The observed inclusive cost at any time is merely a single point on a schedule which reflects the amounts of funds which would be available to the firm at that time at different prices. This schedule will be referred to as the *average cost of funds* schedule. Related to it, in the usual manner, is the marginal cost of funds schedule. For capital budgeting purposes, and for most financing decisions, we need to have an estimate of the *marginal cost of funds*. As we shall see in the next chapter, it is also possible to distinguish between short-run and long-run costs and a variety of shades in between.

As in many cases, the use of funds from one source alters the terms on which they are available from other sources, it is generally incorrect to associate the marginal costs of funds *to the firm* with the marginal cost of funds *from a specific source*. The former is an inclusive concept of cost, the latter specific, in the terminology employed here. The appropriate cost concept for all expenditure decisions and most financing decisions is the inclusive concept,[3] and it is only in financing decisions which involve two alternatives which do not affect the firm's capital structure (e.g., in choosing between two alternative bond issues of similar size) that it is appropriate to use specific costs as a criterion for decision-making purposes.

We may also distinguish between *spot* costs, i.e., those prevailing in the market at any given moment and *normalized* costs, those that reflect, by some averaging process, an estimate of costs from which

---

[2]The term "out of pocket" cost might be preferable in certain cases, but in others, as we shall see, there may be no actual outlay of funds associated with this cost.

[3]The question of whether the short-run or long-run variety is to be employed is discussed further in Chapter 6.

the cyclical element, i.e., the variation attributable to the fluctuation in interest rates and security prices over the business cycle, has been abstracted. We shall argue in Chapter 6 that, while spot costs only should be considered in financing decisions, the normalized cost figure should be used for expenditure decisions. In this chapter, however, we shall be concerned with the estimation of spot costs only.

5.3   The Relationship of Capital Cost to Valuation

The notion of capital cost is intimately related to the problem of valuation, and it is the absence of a fully satisfactory theory of the valuation of the firm that is responsible for the generally unsatisfactory state of capital-cost theory. As we shall see, a meaningful notion of profit maximization requires that present stockholders' funds be employed within the firm only if they are worth as much to the stockholders within the firm as they would be if handed over to them in cash, and outside funds should be used only to the extent that they do not detract from the market value of the stockholders' holdings. The (inclusive) marginal cost of capital is simply the amount of earnings that extra funds must produce to justify their use within the firm in the light of this profit maximization concept. If we knew exactly how the market was going to value additional earnings, we would know exactly how much earnings would have to be produced to justify any given increase in the volume of funds used by the firm, i.e., the cost of capital. Unfortunately, we don't, so we must rely, at some point, on judgment rather than arithmetic.

The concept of cost of capital used for investment decision purposes is thus an opportunity cost concept. As it is the rate of return which must be earned on assets to justify their acquisition, it might be more appropriate to refer to it as the "required rate of return," but the term "cost of capital" has become entrenched in the literature, and will be retained here.

It is possible to attempt to measure inclusive costs directly or to attempt to synthesize an estimate of inclusive costs from estimates of specific costs. The latter approach, while less direct, has the merit of bringing out certain important interrelationships and will be followed here. Estimates of the specific costs of certain types of funds are necessary in any event for the analysis of those financing decisions in which they are appropriate.

5.4   Specific Costs: The General Case

The most general formula for specific costs is similar to the formula for the internal rate of return. It can be found by solving the following expression for k:

$$Q_0 - \sum_{t=1}^{n} \frac{C_t}{(1+k)^t} = 0 \tag{1}$$

where Q_0 is the sum received, net of all underwriting costs, and the C_t represent the cash earnings necessary to pay interest, dividends, sinking fund contributions etc., in subsequent periods, after deduction of the appropriate tax credits. It will sometimes be convenient to use the continuous form

$$Q_0 - \int_0^\infty C(t)e^{-kt}\, dt = 0 \tag{1a}$$

The formal relationship between the cost of capital and the internal rate of return has already been discussed and the present value profile associated with a typical source of funds was shown in Fig. 3-5. Use of the formula is shown in the example below. There are, however, conventional formulas for calculating costs of capital from different sources which are more convenient for hand calculation and produce close approximations to the value of k.

It should be remembered that we are concerned with the anticipated future cost of capital and not the historical cost. Thus it is important to use the estimated receipts from a new issue of the security in question in calculating costs of capital for funds from this particular source. This is no problem when a new issue is being prepared and the issue price and underwriting costs are known, but there is a problem, for example, in computing the cost of debt when no new issue of debt is being contemplated. Historical costs have no relevance in such a circumstance, and the cost calculation must be based on what the issue could be sold for now. This may most easily be calculated from the present market price less estimated underwriting costs.

Examples Using General Formula

XYZ Manufacturing Co. 5 percent bonds of 1972 may be sold for a net price to the issuer in 1962 of $95.00. It is required to calculate the cost of an issue of $1,000,000 (par value) of these bonds, bearing a sinking fund commitment of $80,000 annually for the first five years and $120,000 annually for the last five. The marginal tax rate is 50 percent. The first step is to calculate the annual cash outlay. This is comprised of three elements:

(a) the interest payments, plus
(b) the sinking fund payments, minus
(c) the tax credit on the interest payments and the amortization of discount, which for this example will be taken on a straight line basis.

Table 5-1 shows the calculations.

TABLE 5-1
CASH FLOW FOR DEBT SERVICE, XYZ MANUFACTURING CO.

Year	Sinking fund payment	Interest payment	Less: tax credit (50%)		
			Interest	Amortization	Cash flow
1963	80,000	50,000	25,000	2,500	102,500
1964	80,000	46,000	23,000	2,500	100,500
1965	80,000	42,000	21,000	2,500	98,500
1966	80,000	38,000	19,000	2,500	96,500
1967	80,000	34,000	17,000	2,500	94,500
1968	120,000	30,000	15,000	2,500	132,500
1969	120,000	24,000	12,000	2,500	129,500
1970	120,000	18,000	9,000	2,500	126,500
1971	120,000	12,000	6,000	2,500	123,500
1972	120,000	6,000	3,000	2,500	120,500

The next step is to find the present value at varying rates of discount and sketch the present value profile. Table 5-2 shows the necessary calculations, while Fig. 5-1 shows the resulting part of the present value profile. The cost of capital is found at the intersection of $V - C$ curve with the x-axis. By extrapolation, the cost is 3.04 percent.

FIGURE 5-1

TABLE 5-2
CALCULATIONS: PRESENT VALUE OF DEBT SERVICE CHARGES
XYZ MANUFACTURING CO.

Year	Variable	Cash flow	Present value at:		
			2½%	2¾%	3%
1963	C_1	102,500	99,999	99,753	99,517
1964	C_2	100,500	45,656	95,194	94,731
1965	C_3	98,500	91,467	90,797	90,137
1966	C_4	96,500	87,419	86,580	85,740
1967	C_5	94,500	83,529	82,517	81,516
1968	C_6	132,500	114,255	112,598	110,296
1969	C_7	129,500	108,935	107,097	105,296
1970	C_8	126,500	103,819	101,820	99,859
1971	C_9	123,500	98,886	96,750	94,650
1972	C_{10}	120,500	94,135	91,869	89,664
$-\sum_t C_t$		−1,125,000	−978,100	964,975	952,079
	Q_0	950,000	950,000	950,000	950,000
	$V-C$	−175,000	−28,100	−14,975	−2,079

5.5 Specific Costs: Bonds or Notes

In the case of borrowing, where the borrower receives the full face value of the bonds or notes, the cost is simply the interest rate, adjusted for the tax deductibility of interest, or

$$k = (1 - T)R \tag{2}$$

where T is the marginal tax rate and R is the nominal or coupon rate of return.

Most frequently, however, bonds are sold at a price differing from the par value at which they must be repaid. The approximate cost of bonds sold at a discount or premium is given by[4]

$$k = \frac{(1-T)\left[R + \frac{1}{n}(P - Q_0)\right]}{\frac{1}{2}(Q_0 + P)} \tag{3}$$

---

[4]Formula (3) implicitly assumes that issue expense and the amortization of premium or discount is taxable or deductible, respectively, as it is under U. S. tax law. If the latter are not deductible, as is the case in Canada, the formula must be modified as follows:

$$k = \frac{(1-T)\left[R + \frac{1}{n}(W - Q_0)\right] + \frac{1}{n}(P - W)}{\frac{1}{2}(Q_0 + P)} \tag{3a}$$

where W is the price received before deducting issue expenses.

where P is the par value of the bond and n is the number of years to maturity, the other terms having the definitions already given.

The second half of the term in brackets in the numerator represents the amortization of premium or discount and is negative in the case of an issue sold at a premium. The denominator reflects the average amount outstanding during the life of the loan. The principal drawback of the formula is that it takes no account of differences in the size and timing of sinking fund payments, which may be crucial factors in some cases.

In the case of perpetual bonds, Formula (3) simplifies to

$$k = \frac{(1-T)R}{Q_0} \tag{4}$$

Example

The above formula may be used to calculate an approximate cost of capital for the XYZ bond issue described in Sec. 5.4 above. Substituting in Formula (3), the cost is

$$k = \frac{(1-0.50)\left[5.00 + \dfrac{1}{10}(100.00 - 95.00)\right]}{\frac{1}{2}(95.00 + 100.00)}$$

$$= \frac{2.75}{97.50}$$

$$= 2.82\%$$

This approximation understates the true rate calculated from Formula (1) because it does not take account of the specific period-by-period timing of the outlays for sinking fund payments nor of the annual compounding implicit in Formula (1).

5.6 Specific Costs: Preferred Stock

It is perhaps necessary to explain why the dividend on preferred stock must be regarded as a cost. One may take a legalistic position and claim that such dividends represent a distribution of earnings to "owners," or the view of some accountants that because there is no binding legal obligation to pay dividends on preferred, the dividends do not constitute a "cost."[5] Such quibbles merely beg the question.

From the point of view of the common stockholders, preferred stock represents an alternative source of senior funds having many of the characteristics of debt but certain advantages in particular circumstances.[6] Dividends on preferred, even though they are not legal obligations to the same extent as debt servicing charges, are a cost to the common stockholder. Few corporations would issue preferred without the intention of paying regular dividends and the consequences of failure to do so can be extremely serious. Frequently preferred issues gain voting rights when the dividend is passed, often they gain control. Worse, perhaps, than the danger of loss of control is the damage done to the company's credit standing. Its preferred issues, even its bonds, may cease to be eligible for trustee investment, and the accumulation of arrearages adversely affects the likelihood of being able to pay dividends on the common. As a consequence, the firm may find difficulty in raising funds on reasonable terms except by the sale of well-secured senior bonds. If its borrowing capacity in this direction is fully utilized, it may not be able to raise funds through regular channels at all, and may be driven to use expensive "back-door" sources of credit.

For these reasons, the decision to pass a preferred dividend will not be taken lightly. If there is no distributable surplus or the dividend would render the company insolvent, there may be little choice. While the obligation to pay is a moral one, rather than a legal one, the cost is economically relevant.

The cost of a straight preferred issue, like that of a debt issue, is most accurately calculated by using Formula (1), particularly when there is a sinking fund involved or when it is planned to call parts of the issue at specified dates. The conventional approximation treats preferred as a perpetual obligation and the dividend as an interest payment which is not tax-deductible, giving the formula

---

[5] As expressed for example by Martin W. Davenport in his discussion of D. Durand "Costs of Debt and Equity Funds for Business: Trends and problems of Measurement," in *Conference on Research in Business Finance* (New York: National Bureau of Economic Research, 1952), p. 254 [reprinted in E. Solomon (ed.), *The Management of Corporate Capital* (Glencoe: The Free Press, 1959), p. 121].

[6] See G. Donaldson, "In Defense of Preferred Stock," *Harvard Business Review*, Vol. 40 (July-August, 1962), pp. 123-36. The point is elaborated further in the same author's *Corporate Debt Capacity* (Boston: Harvard Business School, 1962). See also J. F. Childs, *Long Term Financing* (Englewood Cliffs, N. J.: Prentice-Hall, 1961), pp.28-31.

$$k = \frac{D}{Q_0} \tag{5}$$

where D is the annual dividend.

Formula (5) is applicable as it stands only to straight preferred issues. For convertible or participating issues, a more sophisticated approach is required. This will be discussed in Sec. 5.11. As Q_0 will be dependent on the market price of the company's outstanding preferred stock, or other companies' issues of comparable risk, k is in part influenced by the extent of prior claims and the earnings coverage available for the payment of dividends. It is thus *not* independent of capital structure as the formula might appear to suggest.

5.7 The Cost of Equity Capital: Common Stock

The objections mentioned in connection with our attempt to measure the cost of funds raised by issuing preferred are apt to be raised again, with more vehemence, when it is proposed to measure the "cost" of equity funds. However, management is, at any given point in time, responsible only to the existing common stockholders, and is, by implication, concerned with maximizing their long run profits. As already noted further investment in the firm is worthwhile if, and only if, it is expected to leave them at least as well off, in terms of prospective income and the market value of their holdings, as they were before. Let us confine ourselves for the moment to examining a firm which is constrained, for some reason, to use common stock financing exclusively.

Issuing new common stock may do several things:

(1) It entitles the holders of the new shares to all future dividends on an equal basis with the holders of existing shares.
(2) It entitles the new shareholders to a pro rata share in the undistributed profits of the company, and, more generally, to a pro rata share in the assets in the event of winding up.
(3) It may as a consequence result in lower earnings per share or a reduction in book value as far as the existing stockholders are concerned, and may reduce market value.

Unless the earnings from a new investment requiring a new stock issue are expected to be sufficiently great to prevent dilution and a consequent worsening in the income from or market value of their stock, the new stock should not be sold and the investment should not be undertaken. The required rate of return on the new investment is the implicit cost of funds. What is this required rate of return?

The interrelationships between capital structure and the cost of equity funds are complex and uncertain and will be discussed in Chapter 6. For the moment we shall retain the assumption that the company has an all-equity capital structure.

Even under these restrictive assumptions, a number of measurement proposals have been put forward. Of these, only two are worthy of serious consideration.

The first of these uses the earnings-price ratio, or, more specifically, the expected earnings-price ratio as the cost of capital. If E_A is the expected average earnings per share, and Q_0^* is the amount which would be received from the sale of a single share, cost is expressed by[7]

$$k = \frac{E_A}{Q_0^*} \tag{6}$$

This proposed measure implicitly assumes that the only factor influencing market price is earnings per share and that if the new investment produces earnings per share for the new shares equal to that which would have been earned on existing shares in its absence, market price will be unaffected, and present shareholders protected against dilution.

The second measurement proposal is somewhat more sophisticated, and regards the market price as dependent on the dividend being paid and the rate of growth in the dividend. The cost element is the dividend. Its growth is dependent on retained earnings. A fraction b of the earnings per share E_t are invested each period at an expected rate of return *on book value* of r^*. The expected dividend in period t is

$$D_t = (1-b)E_t \tag{7}$$

while income per share at time t is

$$E_t = E_{t-1} + r^* b\, E_{t-1} \tag{8}$$

i.e., E_t grows at the rate $g = br^*$, so that

$$E_t = E_0 e^{gt} \tag{9}$$

---

[7]For a defense of this view see Ezra Solomon, "Measuring a Company's Cost of Capital," *Journal of Business* (October, 1955), reprinted in E. Solomon (ed.), *op. cit.*, pp. 128-40. See also J. F. Childs, *op. cit.*, p. 322.

and

$$D_t = D_0 e^{gt}$$

Substituting in equation 1a yields

$$Q_0 = \int_0^\infty D_0 e^{-t(k-g)} dt$$

integrating (if $k > g$)

$$Q_0 = \frac{D_0}{k-g} \tag{10}$$

whence

(11)

$$k = \frac{D_0}{Q_0} + g$$

The cost of equity capital, using this formula, is simply the current dividend yield plus the average growth rate (adjusted for issue costs).[8]

The two expressions come to the same thing if E_0 is a normalized earnings estimate equal to E_A when all earnings are paid out (the trivial case in which $g = b = 0$ and $D_0 = E_0$), or when book value is identical to market value,[9] a circumstance which is likely to be unusual.

Other formulas have been suggested by various authors. One of these is simply the dividend-price ratio.[10] Besides carrying with it the unwarranted implication that the cost of capital can be reduced to zero by cutting the dividend, this formula is undesirable because it ignores entirely the participation of new shareholders in the future growth of the company and in its assets.

Both (6) and (11) are suitable only as approximations. Both implicitly assume no borrowing, and (11) assumes in addition that there

---

[8]M. J. Gordon and E. Shapiro, "Capital Equipment Analysis: The Required Rate of Profit," *Management Science*, Vol. 3 (October, 1956), pp. 102-10, reprinted in E. Solomon (ed.), *op. cit.*, pp. 141-49. See also H. Bierman and S. Smidt, *The Capital Budgeting Decision* (New York: Macmillan, 1960), pp. 141-55.

[9]Gordon and Shapiro, in Solomon, *op. cit.*, pp. 145-46.

[10]This figure is used, for example, by the Federal Power Commission in setting rates of return for utility companies under its jurisdiction.

is no outside financing and that b and r are constants.[11] However, they are often used as an approximation under other conditions.[12]

The two give an equivalent measure when book value and market value are identical. When the former is greater, (11) gives an estimate below that of (6), and conversely. Their relationship to the "correct" cost allowing for leverage, and the possibility of continued outside financing is somewhat more complex. As we do not have a generally accepted "correct" valuation model, we do not have a generally accepted "correct" cost. The models presented by Gordon are perhaps the most satisfactory developed to date. For most conceivable values of the variables, these suggest that (11) is, if anything, an underestimate of the value of k.[13]

5.8   The Special Case of Rights Offerings

When stock is not offered to the public at large, but is offered to existing stockholders through the medium of a privileged subscription or rights offering, shares are usually sold at a price lower than the existing market. Use of the offering price in calculating the specific cost associated with a rights offering would indicate that this method of raising funds was more expensive than a straight public offering. That this is an incorrect conclusion is demonstrated by consideration of the results which would occur if the issue were to be taken up entirely by the stockholders. Each stockholder's prorata share in the company would be unchanged, though his investment will have increased by the amount subscribed. All that is needed to insure that he is as well off after the issue as he was before is for the market value of the firm to increase by the amount of cash subscribed under the offering. This requires that the earnings from the use of the new funds must be sufficient, when capitalized, to increase the market value by the amount of the new funds. The appropriate specific cost estimate is exactly the same as that derived above for the general common stock case.

This conclusion is not altered if the stockholders do not subscribe to the issue, but sell their rights. Here they are parting with a portion of their equity, for a consideration, while the integrity of their re-

---

[11]M. J. Gordon, *op. cit.* (1962), p. 44.

[12]Bierman and Smidt, for example, present no alternative to Formula 11.

[13]See, e.g., Gordon, *op. cit.* (1962), p. 52, Eq. 4.11, p. 112, Eq. 8.31, and p. 169. See also J. Linter, "The Cost of Capital and Optimal Financing of Corporate Growth," *Journal of Finance*, Vol. XVIII (May, 1963), pp. 292-310.

maining equity is maintained by meeting the earnings standard specified.

5.9 The Cost of Retained Earnings

There are two ways of approaching the problem of estimating the cost of retained earnings. They can be regarded as the equivalent of a fully subscribed rights offering, with certain tax advantages, or the problem can be approached on an "opportunity cost" basis.

If we choose to approach the evaluation of retained earnings cost by the rights approach, we note, first of all, that there are no underwriting costs, so there is no need to make a deduction from the market price in the denominator if Formulas (6) or (11) are to be adopted. If, however, earnings were paid as dividends and a simultaneous rights offering made, stockholders would be subject to tax on the dividends and would only be able to subscribe an amount equal to $(1 - T)D_0$ where T is the marginal tax rate applicable to the individual stockholder. To be as well off as he would be under the rights offering, it is only sufficient that the value of his shares rise by an amount which, after making due provision for any tax on capital gains, is equal to the net dividend he would have received after tax.

Without growth from reinvested earnings, Formula (11) reduces to

$$P = \frac{D}{k} \tag{12}$$

whence

$$\Delta P = \frac{\Delta D}{k} \tag{12a}$$

Making appropriate deductions for both taxes, at rates Tc for capital gains tax and Ty for the income taxes (5.12a), the condition stated above yields

$$(1 - Tc)\Delta P = \frac{(1 - Ty)\Delta D}{k} \tag{13}$$

whence

$$k = \frac{(1 - Ty)D}{(1 - Tc)P} \tag{14}$$

If the corporation is paying dividends of 1.00, and shares are selling to yield 6.25 percent at a price of 16, then the required rate of return, for a stockholder in the 75 percent tax bracket subject to a capital gains tax rate of 25 percent, is

$$k = \frac{(1-0.75)\ 1.00}{(1-0.25)16.00} = 2.08\%$$

However, for a stockholder in the 40 percent marginal tax bracket, subject to a capital gain tax of only 20 percent, the required return is

$$k = \frac{(1-0.40)\ 1.00}{(1-0.20)16.00}$$
$$k = \ 4.69\%$$

For the nontaxable stockholder, the minimum required return is the full 6.25 percent.

If this standard is to be used, there is no apparent way for management to resolve the conflict of interest between the high-tax-bracket stockholders and the tax-exempt stockholders. However, there is no need to give up quite so easily. These are minimum requirements. If the company meets the minimum return requirements of its tax-exempt stockholders on all the funds reinvested, it will exceed the requirements of the taxable stockholders, so we will have a situation where none of the stockholders will be made worse off, and some will be made better off, with the result a clear gain. This will only be possible, of course, if there is an infinitely elastic supply of investment opportunities available offering prospective rates of return near the tax-free stockholder's required rate. Fortunately, such a reservoir of projects is available through the security markets. There will ordinarily be stock available in a number of companies offering yields similar to those required by the tax-exempt stockholders, with roughly comparable risk. In many cases, the company can buy its own stock. These alternative investment opportunities provide a floor below which no project should be accepted. To the extent that intercompany dividends are taxable, the acceptable yield on marginal projects may be reduced slightly, but caution should be exercised here. The possibility of acquiring a sufficiently large interest in other companies to permit filing a consolidated return may reduce the impact of taxes, or it may be possible to find situations in which most of the expected "yield" is in the form of capital gains. Normally, the market rates of return on investments in other companies with similar risk characteristics should be adopted as a minimum required rate of return for reinvested earnings.

It must be noted at this point that all this standard does is provide us with a "cutoff" rate for capital budgeting purposes. It does not tell us whether we should reinvest funds nor, if so, how much. Some comments on this problem follow.

5.10 Some Comments on Dividend Policy

While it is possible for management to resolve the problem of what minimum rate of return to require on retained earnings, management is faced with a dilemma in resolving the conflicting interests of different groups of stockholders in the actual decision of how much to reinvest. Available investment opportunities, if market investments are taken into account, are apt to be much larger than earnings for most corporations.

Nor does it do much good to state that reinvestment should be carried to the point where it maximizes the price of the stock, for this is merely to restate the problem. Unfortunately, we don't know what the relationship between dividend payout rates and stock valuation is, in the market place as opposed to theory, and we are unlikely to find out much because the high correlation between dividends and earnings makes it extremely difficult to unscramble the omelet even using refined statistical analysis.

Theories are many and varied, and space limitations preclude a complete review here.[14] One of the difficulties in resolving the theoretical problem lies in the fact that the supply of funds to the firm is not independent of the prospects for growth implicit in the demand for funds within the firm, a point which has already been noted.

As a practical matter, however, we would suggest that funds be retained only if internal investment opportunities offer a clearly higher rate of return than the market capitalization rate for the firm as a whole (see Chapter 6). If enough projects are available to use up the

---

[14]See, for example, J. E. Walter, "Dividend Policies and Common Stock Prices," *Journal of Finance*, Vol. XI (March, 1956), pp. 29-41; F. Modigliani and M. H. Miller, "Dividend Policy, Growth and the Valuation of Shares," *Journal of Business*, Vol. 34 (October, 1961), pp. 411-33; J. E. Walter, "Dividend Policy: Its Influence on the Value of the Enterprise," *Journal of Finance*, Vol. XVIII (May, 1963), pp. 280-91; J. Lintner, "Dividends, Earnings, Leverage, Stock Prices and the Supply of Capital to Corporations," *Review of Economics and Statistics*, Vol. XLIV (August, 1962), pp. 243-70, I. Friend and M. Puckett, "Dividends and Stock Prices," *American Economic Review*, Vol. LIV (September, 1964), pp. 656-82.

entire depreciation accruals and earnings stream on this basis, then the entire earnings stream should be retained. If this only uses a fraction of the available earnings, the balance should be paid out. If no projects meet these requirements, all earnings should be paid as dividends or stock repurchased. This will probably give an estimate of the cutoff rate which errs on the low side but the added complications of a "correct" calculation may not be worthwhile in most practical situations.[15]

While the market investments opportunity was noted above, this should be resorted to with caution. Operating management has, in most cases, no clear mandate to turn the firm into an investment trust. The individual stockholders are probably as capable of selecting their own portfolio investments with their own money. There may be a case for it on a temporary basis, e.g., if projects meeting the retention standard are likely to be available in the next budget period. This does not apply, of course, to investments undertaken with a view to obtaining control or ultimate merger.

To the extent, if any, that dividend policy does not maximize stock prices, all our estimates of equity costs will be overstated. Our formulas apply, strictly, only when dividend policy is optimal in this sense.[16] Since, however, substantial deviations in dividend payout do not appear to have any clearly demonstrated effect on valuation, any error introduced is likely to be slight.

5.11   Depreciation Accruals

It is an even more common, but equally fallacious, practice to regard funds released by earned depreciation and similar accruals as free. Depreciation, if earned, represents the conversion of fixed assets into cash which should not be reinvested in less liquid assets unless the effect of reinvestment is to maintain the value of the company. If it will not, there is always the alternative of reducing debt or giving the cash back to stockholders either by purchasing shares on the market or, where this is not permitted by law, by a formal reduction in capital. Cost should therefore be taken as a minimum, as the cost of the debt which could otherwise be retired. For most purposes,

---

[15]See M. J. Gordon, *op. cit.* (1962), pp. 46-54; E. M. Lerner and W. T. Carleton, "Capital Budgeting and Stock Valuation," *American Economic Review*, Vol. LIV (September, 1964), pp. 683-702.

[16]More strictly, the capital budget, the optimum dividend, and the financing plan are interdependent and should be simultaneously determined. For the practical objections to this approach, see Sec. 2.6 above.

however, as reduction in total capital employed (in one form or another) is the alternative to reinvesting such accruals, the appropriate imputed cost is, again, the marginal cost of funds to the firm, to be discussed in Chapter 6.

5.12 Convertible Preferreds and Debentures

These types of securities are usually issued by a firm as an alternative to common stock issues at a time when the market is believed to be abnormally depressed so that sale of common would unduly dilute the holdings of existing shareholders. Compared with regular preferred issues or debentures, they probably sell on a lower yield basis, owing to the existence of the conversion feature. It would be a mistake, however, to regard the funds thus raised as cheap. The reason for this is that if the fortunes of the company, or the state of the market, improves to that point where the common stock is selling above the conversion price, the holders of the convertible issue can exchange it for common and enjoy all the advantages of common stock ownership. Such issues, then, contain built-in future dilution (for the common stock) as an intrinsic feature, and are best regarded as an indirect way of selling common stock above the present market. Their cost should be evaluated as the higher of:

(a) their cost calculated on the assumption that conversion does not take place and they remain as senior obligations in their original form, or
(b) their cost when considered as if they were common stock, calculated from the formula for common stock cost, but substituting in the denominator the effective issue price on a common stock basis, i.e., the proceeds from each share divided by the number of common shares into which it may be converted.

While the cost calculated under (b) will normally be higher, conservatism dictates that (a) be considered and substituted if it is higher, which will be the case only when the possibility of reaching the conversion price appears to be remote. If in fact it is never reached, there is little likelihood that the shares will be converted and the cost calculated under (a) will then be the relevant one.

In many cases the scheduled conversion price increases through time, so that a series of subsequent prices must be considered. In this case, we may use

$$k = \frac{D_o(1+g)^t}{P_t} + g \qquad\qquad (11a)$$

where P_t is the scheduled future conversion price per share of common stock. If there are a series of such rates, the highest should be taken.

5.13   Participating Issues

Like convertibles, participating issues have a dual nature. Although the possibility of conversion does not exist, they may share in earnings just as if they had been converted. From the common stockholder's point of view they are even less attractive, for if subsequent difficulties develop, their preferred status reemerges to claim priority in dividends. Their cost should be calculated in a similar manner to that for convertible issues, except that the denominator in the *(b)* part of the calculation is calculated on the basis of their right to participate in dividends. If this is on a share-for-share basis, the selling price in terms of common share equivalents is the price of one share. If they are entitled to receive ten times the dividend, as, for example, in the case where common shares are $10 par and the participating preferred $100 par, the price in common stock equivalent is one-tenth the price of one share.

5.14   Specific Costs and Marginal Costs

One of the commonest fallacies in the analysis of capital budgeting decisions is to regard the cost of debt as identical to the marginal cost of capital. The confusion has arisen because traditional capital theory (e.g., Bohm-Bawerk, Fisher) speaks of investment being carried to the point where the marginal productivity of capital equals the market rate of interest as the condition of equilibrium in the capital market. Careful examination of the theory will usually indicate that it is based on several assumptions, either explicit or implicit:

(a) That the economy is one in which all capital is raised by borrowing.
(b) That there is only one type of credit instrument.
(c) That there is perfect knowledge and an absence of risk.

The theory is perfectly valid, granted these assumptions; the fallacy arises in attempting to apply it, without alteration, in a world where the assumptions are contrary to fact. Doing so can lead to absurd results, as the following example will illustrate.

Firm A had in three successive years the same set of investment opportunities given in Table 5-3. All projects are equal in risk. It began Year 1 with a 100 percent equity capital structure. The treasurer, a persuasive man who had just heard of marginal cost, indicated to the management that they could raise $900,000 by issuing debentures at 5½ percent, and convinced his colleagues that the whole "package" should be approved.

TABLE 5-3
INVESTMENT OPPORTUNITIES: FIRM A

Year 1		Year 2		Year 3	
Amount of investment	Rate of return	Amount of investment	Rate of return	Amount of investment	Rate of return
100,000 20		100,000 20		100,000 20	
200,000 15		200,000 15		200,000 15	
200,000 10		200,000 10		200,000 10	
200,000 8		200,000 8		200,000 8	
200,000 6		200,000 6		200,000 6	

The second year, convinced of his wisdom, the management accepted the first four projects when he told them that he could borrow a further $700,000 at 7½ percent or $800,000 at 9 percent, rejecting the fifth as promising a yield below the marginal cost of capital.

When budget time came around the third year, the treasurer was somewhat mystified to learn that the firm's investment bankers refused to issue more debt for him, suggesting that he issue equity, at an estimated cost of 19 percent. He has beaten the bushes carefully in an effort to find more debt money, but so far had only been able to come up with a possible finance company loan of $100,000 at 18 percent. It seemed that the marginal cost of funds had risen to 18 percent, so he recommended that the budget be cut back sharply and only the first project be adopted. He had not made up his mind about the financing but was inclined to go along with the finance company loan as it was cheaper, although there were certain onerous conditions attached by the finance company which he was not happy with.

Confronted with this presentation at the budget meeting, the production manager got out an envelope and began figuring. He noted that the average return on the investments made over the three years, if the current budget were adopted, would be 12 percent, whereas the same amount could have been invested to earn an average of 13.3 percent, if they had not been in such a hurry to commit funds in the first year. (His calculations are shown in Table 5-4.) Furthermore, he had noted that several trade creditors had refused to lengthen their credit lines and one or two friends had kidded him about A being overextended. He said that he thought the treasurer owed them all an explanation of how this new system had gone wrong.

What the treasurer overlooked was that debt capacity is a function of earning power and the equity base provided by the stockholders. Unless the base is enlarged, a firm will sooner or later exhaust its borrowing capacity and be forced into the equity market. Even if the financing is done in blocks consisting of debt or equity, using the debt rate as a marginal cost leads to the preemption of the available capital supply by low-yielding projects, forcing higher-yielding ones out, unless some provision in the calculations is made for the equity financing which will eventually have to be done to preserve borrowing power.

It also means that budgets are larger than they should be, and if financed by debt, more debt is incurred than would be desirable if a more conservative policy were followed, increasing risk unnecessarily. Had *A* followed a policy which took explicit account of the need for further equity, they would not only have been able to increase their profitability, but would have had debt of only $1,000,000 at the beginning of Year 3 instead of $1,600,000.

TABLE 5-4
PROSPECTIVE RETURN ON INVESTMENT: FIRM *A*

	Actual budgets			Production manager's alternative	
	Spent	%		Spent	%
Year 1	100,000	20	Year 1	100,000	20
	200,000	15		200,000	15
	200,000	10		200,000	10
	200,000	8	Year 2	100,000	20
	200,000	6		200,000	15
Year 2	100,000	20		200,000	10
	200,000	15	Year 3	100,000	20
	200,000	10		200,000	15
	200,000	8		200,000	10
Year 3	100,000	20		200,000	8
			Totals	300,000	20
Totals	300,000	20		600,000	15
	400,000	15		600,000	10
	400,000	10		200,000	8
	400,000	8		1,700,000	13.3
	200,000	6			
	1,700,000	12.0			

When the capital structure is changed by an issue of debt, the relevant cost is not only the out-of-pocket cost of the debt itself, but includes the increase in the cost of equity resulting from the higher risk premium attached to the shares as a result of the debt.

For example, consider a firm with an income of $100,000 after taxes and a current market value of $1,000,000. If the firm issues $200,000 in 6 percent debentures and as a result the price-earnings multiplier drops to 8.0, the additional earnings which must be obtained to maintain the value of shareholders' investment are as follows:

Net income required for stockholders	
($1,000,000 ÷ 8)	125,000
Interest on debt	12,000
Less tax credit	6,000
Required earnings	131,000
Present level of earnings	100,000
Required increase	31,000

The required rate of return on $200,000 investment is 15.5 percent, ($31,000 ÷ $200,000) not the 3 percent out-of-pocket cost of the new funds. Unfortunately, this rule is not simple to apply in practice because of the difficulty of knowing beforehand what effect a change in debt will have on the capitalization rate which the market will apply. If we had a reliable valuation model, the answer would be easily calculated. As we do not, we shall have to approach the problem by a more circuitous route. Before doing so, we shall examine some special cases where specific costs must be calculated with great care.

5.15   Special Problems in Analyzing the Cost of Capital

Installment purchases and the acquisition of assets by leasing pose some problems in the estimation of cost of capital. In cases of this kind it is easy to get the asset acquisition part of the transaction mixed up with the funds-acquisition part, violating the rule given in Sec. 4.6. There may also be some charges other than interest which are properly considered part of the cost of the funds. For example, when insurance is part of the transaction, the insurance costs may be omitted only if the insurance is required anyway and the premiums are no greater than those which would have to be paid through other channels in any event. Where the insurance is not required but is accepted merely as one of the conditions of obtaining the loan, the premiums should be included as one of the costs of the loan. So should any excess of premium over the normal commercial premium for similar risks. Service charges should be included in the cost. An additional reason for the use of great caution in accepting the stated interest rate is that it is often stated in a misleading fashion and is charged on the full face amount of the loan for the full period, though the average amount outstanding is only one-half of this amount.

In the installment loan case, because of the way the loan is amortized, the interest portion of the payments will be tax deductible while the balance will not. Because the timing of the reduction in tax liability and the inclusion of service charges and so on, there will usually result an irregular payments stream. It is preferable to use the iterative procedure of the general case (Sec. 5.4), particularly when one proposed installment purchase is being compared with another or with leasing, especially if accuracy is desired.

Because an installment purchase usually involves the acquisition of an asset, care should be taken to separate the financial side of the transaction from the asset side. Usually purchase for cash is an available alternative (funds coming from general corporate sources) so that there are really two decisions to be made, viz., whether to acquire the asset and whether to finance it by installment purchase. Failure to follow this rule results in the use of "net" cash flow estimates which almost invariably overstate the desirability of the acquisition, as indicated in Sec. 4.6 above and the following example:

Example

ABC Ltd., a Canadian corporation, is considering the acquisition of a fork-lift truck to improve materials handling in their warehouse. It is estimated that the truck will save $5,000 per year in labor costs and $1,000 in inventory carrying costs. The estimated life of the truck is six years. Scrap value is assumed to be nil. Maximum rate of depreciation for income tax purposes is 33⅓ percent on a declining balance basis. The truck can be bought for $10,000 cash or for a down payment of $3,000 with the balance payable in 16 quarterly installments of $437.50 plus interest at 3 percent per quarter on the unpaid balance.

The wrong way of examining this proposed purchase is to lump the whole transaction together as has been done in Table 5-5.

The correct approach is to separate the asset-acquisition and fund-raising parts of the transaction, as is done in Tables 5-6 and 5-7. Table 5-6 indicates that the true rate of return on the acquisition of the asset is not the spectacular 75 percent shown by the calculation in Table 5-5, though it remains a respectable 32 percent. This is the rate of return from acquiring the asset, irrespective of the way it is financed, so that if it can be financed more cheaply than through the installment purchases, there is a clear gain. Whether the asset should be acquired is a decision that should be taken on its own merits. If

TABLE 5-5
ANALYSIS OF FORK-LIFT ACQUISITION, ABC LTD. (INCORRECT)

Year	Cash savings	Cash outlays			Net cash flow
		Principal	Interest	Taxes	
1	6,000	1,750	761	953	2,536
2	6,000	1,750	551	1,613	2,085
3	6,000	1,750	341	2,089	1,820
4	6,000	1,750	131	2,441	1,678
5	6,000	–	–	2,671	3,329
6	6,000	–	–	2,781	3,219

Initial outlay $3,000
Rate of return 75 percent

this decision is favorable, consideration can then be given to how acquisition is to be financed. If the installment loan is the financing alternative which leads to the lowest cost of capital, then it should be bought on the installment plan. If not, it should be bought for cash and alternative sources of funds used. Table 5-7 indicates that the installment loan will provide $7,000 in debt financing at an after-tax cost of 5 percent.

TABLE 5-6
ANALYSIS OF FORK-LIFT ACQUISITION, ABC LTD. (CORRECT)

Year	Cash savings	Tax	Net cash savings
1	6,000	1,333	4,667
2	6,000	1,889	4,111
3	6,000	2,259	3,740
4	6,000	2,506	3,494
5	6,000	2,670	3,329
6	6,000	2,780	3,219

Initial outlay $10,000
Rate of return   32 percent

TABLE 5-7
ANALYSIS OF INSTALLMENT LOAN, ABC LTD. (CORRECT)

Year	Payment	Tax saving on interest	Net outlay
1	2,511	381	2,130
2	2,301	275	2,026
3	2,091	170	1,921
4	1,881	66	1,815

Amount received $7,000
Cost of capital   5 percent

It is desirable to regard the leasing of equipment or plant as an alternative form of debt. True, it is the physical asset which is borrowed rather than the money to buy it, but this distinction is legalistic and is of importance only insofar as the repayment may be made in kind, so that if for some reason the value of the asset falls, either as a result of a general depression or because a new invention has rendered the original asset obsolete, the risk is borne by the "lender," i.e., the lessor, rather than the lessee. This may be an important consideration in an industry where rapid technical change is the rule, but in most cases the lessor will expect to be compensated for bearing this risk.

Leasing has been quite fashionable in recent years, and is, at least superficially, attractive for a number of reasons. First of all, it provides "off the balance sheet" financing. The leasehold liability does not show on the balance sheet, although it may be noted in the annual report depending on the company's reporting practice. Thus it provides a means of obtaining what is essentially debt financing while still satisfying prejudices against having debt appear on the balance sheet. The resulting understatement of leverage isn't likely to fool prospective creditors, unless they are very naive, as they can and will find out about lease obligations directly. The only people left in the dark are likely to be the public stockholders.

A more appealing attraction, for many small firms in particular, is that leasing is a means of borrowing the entire cost of an asset, while most lenders will normally only lend a percentage of the cost of an asset against that asset as security. If the firm is severely limited, because of its size, in avenues of access to the capital market, and can raise the required funds in no other way, this argument is an acceptable one, but it must be remembered that the lessor is assuming an additional risk for which he will expect to be paid. It is important to know precisely what the extra funds cost. Making this calculation will in all cases be revealing and may drive management to find alternative sources of funds which were formerly dismissed as too costly. If the extra funds are not needed, it doesn't make too much sense to pay for them.

The final appeal in leasing contracts lies in their supposed tax advantages. Much of the recent popularity of leasing stems from its use in the United States as a means of tax avoidance. The law, however, is constantly being changed to close "loopholes," particularly in respect to leasing. The first requirement in assessing an asset-leasing proposal is to obtain adequate tax counsel. Even this may be no guarantee, for the law may be changed ("clarified") subsequent to the making of the contract. Leases containing options to purchase are particularly suspect. The major advantages of leases from a tax standpoint seem to be

(1) If lease payments may be deducted as an expense, leasing may effectively be used to obtain a higher rate of writeoff than the permitted depreciation rate. With new methods of depreciation, this advantage is minimized.
(2) Leasing real estate effectively allows the writeoff of land costs, but only at the price of having any residual value, or increment therein, accrue to the lessor.

In calculating the cost of capital implicit in a leasing contract, it is desirable to follow the same routine as that outlined for installment purchase. Care must be taken that all differences in tax treatment are taken into account in the cost of capital calculation.

Example

While the directors of ABC Ltd. were still mulling over the proposed acquisition of their fork-lift truck, the finance company offered to lease them the truck for $200 a month, on a six-year lease which provided that ABC Ltd. would assume all repair and maintenance costs. The rental payments would be deductible in full for tax purposes but they would no longer be able to claim depreciation. The resulting calculation of capital costs is shown in Table 5-8.

TABLE 5–8
ANALYSIS OF LEASING COST, ABC LTD.

Year	Rental	Tax saving on rental	Tax loss on depreciation	Net tax effect on lease status	Cash outlay
1	2,400	1,200	1,667	+467	2,867
2	2,400	1,200	1,111	− 89	2,311
3	2,400	1,200	741	−459	1,941
4	2,400	1,200	494	−706	1,694
5	2,400	1,200	329	−871	1,529
6	2,400	1,200	220	−980	1,420
					11,762

Amount received $10,000
Cost of capital   5.5 percent

This cost seemed quite reasonable, and in view of the company's need for funds, it was felt that it was more desirable to raise $10,000 at a cost of 5.5 percent than to raise $7,000 at a cost of 5 percent. The treasurer demurred, however, stating that the additional $3,000 was costing the company a lot more than 5.5 percent, and that other sources of the funds ought to be investigated. The meeting was adjourned for 15 minutes to enable him to calculate the *incremental* cost of raising the extra $3,000 by adopting the leasing proposal. The result of his calculations is shown in Table 5-9.

TABLE 5-9
INCREMENTAL COST OF EXTRA FUNDS RAISED BY LEASING, ABC LTD.

Year	Cash outlay, installment loan	Cash outlay, leasing	Incremental outlay
1	2,130	2,867	737
2	2,026	2,311	285
3	1,921	1,941	20
4	1,815	1,694	(121)
5	—	1,529	1,529
6	—	1,420	1,420
	Extra Funds Received $3,000		
	Cost of Capital	6 percent	

PROBLEMS

1. What is the cost of borrowing funds for a firm in the 50 percent tax bracket contemplating the following bond issues?

	Offering price	Net to issuer	Coupon rate	Maturity
(a)	98.00	96.00	4.50	20
(b)	97.50	95.00	5.00	10
(c)	103.00	100.00	3.75	15
(d)	105.00	102.00	3.50	10

2. What is the cost of equity capital for the following firms?

	(a)		(b)		(c)	
Year	Earnings per share	Dividends per share	Earnings per share	Dividends per share	Earnings per share	Dividends per share
1	1.17	0.60	2.57	1.23	1.48	0.85
2	0.31	0.60	2.65	1.40	1.49	0.90
3	0.33	0.45	3.07	1.40	1.56	0.95
4	0.45	0.40	3.18	1.60	1.71	1.00
5	0.24	0.40	3.62	1.60	1.81	1.10
Price, latest	$14.38		84.00		34.00	

3. *(a)* Burroughs Corp. Convertible Subordinated Debenture 4½ percent of 1981 are convertible into 26.72 common shares per $1,000 par value at any time. The debentures sell for $128.00, the shares at $43.00. Debentures are callable at $102.375.

Earnings and dividends on the common have been as follows:

	Earned per share	Dividends per share
1961 . . . . . . 1.58		1.00
1962 . . . . . . 1.42		1.00
1963 . . . . . . 1.15		1.00
1964 . . . . . . 1.38		1.00
1965 . . . . . . 1.17 (9 mos.)		1.00

What is the cost of the funds represented by these convertible debentures?

4. A firm is contemplating the installation of a packaging machine which will save $6,000 per year in labor, reduced damage to goods, and in packaging materials after deducting all operating costs. Life of the machine is estimated at six years, at the end of which time net scrap value is nil, after taking account of removal costs. The firm uses sum-of-the years' digits depreciation.

The machine may be purchased for $10,000 cash or monthly installments totaling $1,930 per year, of which the interest component is $460, 390, 310, 230, 140 and 50 in the first through sixth years. Alternatively, it may be rented for $2,400 per year.

(a) What is the rate of return on the machine?
(b) What is the cost of capital raised under the installment loan?
(c) What is the cost of leasing the asset?
(d) If the firm's cost of capital is 10 percent, which action would you recommend? Why?

CHAPTER 6

The Evaluation Process:
Cost of Capital to the Firm

6.1 Alternative Methods of Combining

The selection of projects for inclusion in the market value-maximizing budget requires that all projects having discounted benefit-cost ratios in excess of 1.0 be accepted, when the discount rate used is the marginal cost of capital to the firm. We have seen (Sec. 5.14) that it is not appropriate to use the specific cost of debt as the marginal cost of capital, even if only debt financing is currently contemplated, because of the existence of debt limits and the danger of using up borrowing capacity. More generally, increasing the relative level of debt may increase the market capitalization rate on the common shares, and this additional cost on the equity component of the existing capital structure should be imputed as part of the cost of debt.[1] While most students of the problem agree this far, disagreement breaks out at the next step, i.e., making the actual imputations or presenting alternative methods of calculating marginal costs.

One alternative to using specific contractual costs of debt as a marginal cost is to impose an earnings coverage requirement similar to that used by investment analysts in rating bonds. Thus if the minimum earnings coverage acceptable is 4 times interest charges, then if the (before tax) cost of debt is 5 percent, the coverage cost, i.e., earnings necessary to provide the desired coverage is 20 percent (also before taxes).[2] This approach certainly has practical merit in that it will prevent the more naive errors of the type discussed in Sec. 5.14.

---

[1]See R. Lindsay and A. W. Sametz, *Financial Management: An Analytical Approach* (Homewood, Ill.: Irwin, 1963), pp. 148-52, for an elaboration of this point.

[2]The concept is introduced and discussed by P. Hunt, C. M. Williams, and G. Donaldson, *Basic Business Finance* (3d ed.; Homewood, Ill.: Irwin, 1966), pp. 440-41.

However, it does not explicitly consider the effect of altered debt levels on the equity capitalization rate and, as such, is neither the appropriate imputed cost of debt nor an accurate measure of the marginal cost of funds (except by accident).

Some of the approaches do not specifically attempt to measure marginal cost or at any rate are not claimed to do so by their proponents. Thus an average of specific costs, weighted by their respective shares in the total capital structure, has been advocated by Childs, who proposes book value weights, and by Bierman and Smidt, who use current market values as weights.[3] Weston, who also uses current market value weights, claims that it is a good approximation to marginal costs,[4] but the others make no such claim. The validity of this approach will be examined below.

An alternative weighting scheme uses as weights the anticipated additions to capital over some (not specified) horizon.[5] Costs of these incremental funds are not identified as marginal costs, however.

Solomon has rejected weighted averages of this type and has proposed what amounts to a separately weighted average for each project, with the debt component weighted by the imputed borrowing power of the project in question. This is to be considered in relation to a rising supply curve for equity funds in determining the budget. Solomon has suggested that the debt charges should be netted against the cash flows from the project, to give a rate of return on equity. Equity requirements will be determined by the projects included in the budget, debt requirements by the imputed borrowing power. So the process determines both the capital budget and the plan for financing it. While it is possible to apply this approach consistently, to do so requires considerable sophistication both on the part of the analyst and the management who must use it. Borrowing power is, of course, a function of risk and this scheme will alter the capital structure in response to changes in the commercial risk of the operation. The drawback is that it scrambles together and confuses the analysis of projects and that of their financing, which we have sought to avoid, and is apt to lead to the adoption of projects on the basis of

---

[3]J. F. Childs, *Long Term Financing* (Englewood Cliffs, N. J.: Prentice-Hall, 1961), p. 378; H. Bierman and S. Smidt, *The Capital Budgeting Decision* (New York: Macmillan, 1960), p. 135.

[4]J. F. Weston, *Managerial Finance* (New York: Holt, Rinehart and Winston, 1962), p. 232.

[5]J. Dean, *Capital Budgeting* (New York: Columbia, 1951), p. 50; R. W. Johnson, *Financial Management* (2d ed., Boston: Allyn and Bacon), p. 216.

the financing available as part of the package and to excessive use of high cost debt, through leasing and installment purchases, unless a standard of debt capacity other than that of the lenders is applied.[6] It is possible to preserve the useful features of this approach in other ways, as we shall see in Chapter 11. Solomon has since suggested a weighted average approach, based on market value weights,[7] as an approximation to the marginal cost we are seeking.

Lindsay and Sametz have suggested an alternative approach based on a segmented supply curve having successive components of debt, depreciation accruals, retained earnings, and new equity, with additional chunks of debt thrown in at appropriate intervals to balance the capital structure, which they have named "sequential marginal costing."[8] This implies that the firm faces a rising supply curve of funds and that there is an optimum capital structure for the firm.

Faced with this range of suggested approaches, the would-be analyst is apt to be at least bewildered. There are two major points of difference between the different schools of thought. The first relates to the shape of the cost function facing the firm. Does cost rise as a function of the volume of funds raised, as suggested by Solomon (1955) and by Lindsay and Sametz, or is it flat, or nearly so, as is implicit in the average costing approach? A second, and slightly more subtle question is also involved: is cost of capital dependent on the capital structure or not? If it is, and if there is an optimal capital structure, then average costing will give incorrect results unless the company is at this point, and then only if the proposed increment is also optimal in structure and cost is independent of the amount raised.

These are essentially questions of valuation. How will additional earnings be valued? How does capital structure affect value? We shall examine the latter problem first as it has been the source of a great deal of confusion and has generated, in the words of one recent critic, "more passion than reason."[9]

6.2   The Notion of an Optimal Capital Structure

The traditional view of the effect of leverage on capital structure

---

[6]E. Solomon, "Measuring a Company's Cost of Capital," *Journal of Business* (October, 1955), reprinted in E. Solomon (ed.), *The Management of Corporate Capital* (Glencoe: The Free Press, 1959), pp. 128-40 (referred to henceforth as Solomon, 1959).

[7]E. Solomon, *The Theory of Financial Management* (New York: Columbia, 1963), p. 88.

[8]Lindsay and Sametz, *op. cit.*, Chaps. 8, 9.

[9]A. J. Boness, "A Pedagogic Note on the Cost of Capital," *Journal of Finance*, Vol. XIX (March, 1964), p. 99.

has been that certain amounts of debt can be raised at a cost below the cost of equity, either at constant cost or at a cost increasing slightly as the debt-equity ratio rises. It is further claimed that small amounts of debt do not affect the earnings-price ratio, or capitalization rate applied to the equity share of earnings, so that overall costs can be reduced by using some debt. Beyond a certain debt-equity ratio, costs of both debt and equity rise owing to the increasing riskiness of each, so that eventually the rising cost of debt raises the average cost of capital for the two sources combined. At some point, average cost is at a minimum. The location of this point indicates the optimum debt-equity mix for the firm.[10]

This is equivalent to another proposition to the effect that the market value of the firm is maximized at the same debt-equity ratio.

The propositions are shown graphically in Fig. 6-1.

FIGURE 6–1
TRADITIONAL VIEWS OF OPTIMUM CAPITAL STRUCTURE

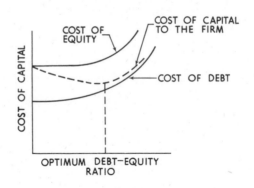

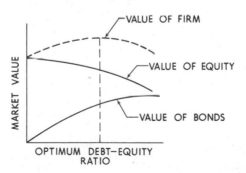

---

[10]Among the many references may be cited B. Graham and D. L. Dodd, *Security Analysis* (2nd ed.; New York: McGraw-Hill, 1941), pp. 541-42.

6.3   The Modigliani-Miller Hypothesis

In an article published in 1958, Modigliani and Miller suggested that the traditional view is incorrect, offering theoretical arguments as well as empirical evidence against it.[11]

The Modigliani-Miller position is that, irrespective of the effect of the debt-equity ratio on interest rates, the capitalization rate on equity will rise by an amount just sufficient to offset any possible saving, so that cost of capital, and the value of the firm as a whole are independent of the leverage employed. The relationship is illustrated graphically in Fig. 6-2.

FIGURE 6-2
THE MODIGLIANI-MILLER HYPOTHESIS

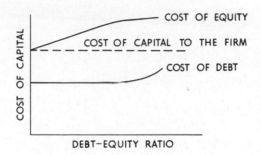

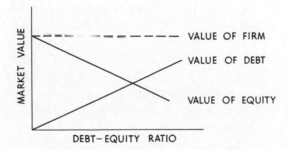

The way in which this adjustment is brought about is as follows:
Suppose we have two firms, with identical risk characteristics. Expected operating income of the two firms is identical at $1,000,000

---

[11]F. Modigliani and M. H. Miller, "The Cost of Capital, Corporation Finance and the Theory of Investment," *American Economic Review*, Vol. XLV (June, 1958), pp. 261-97, reprinted in Solomon (1959), pp. 150-81.

per year, Suppose further that there is no income tax and that all profits are paid as dividends. The only difference between the two firms is in their capital structure. Firm A is entirely financed by equity, and has one million common shares. Firm B has $5,000,000 in 6 percent debentures and 500,000 common shares. Suppose that the market value of shares in A is $10, so that the market value of firm A is $10,000,000. The optimum capital structure theory asserts that B's value (the market value of all claims on B's income) will be greater than that of A (unless the debt is so excessive that it is lower).

Partial income statements and per share dividends are shown in Table 6-1.

TABLE 6-1
INCOME STATEMENTS, A AND B

	A	B
Operating income	1,000,000	1,000,000
Interest	–	300,000
Earnings & dividends	1,000,000	700,000
Shares outstanding	1,000,000	500,000
Dividends per share	1.00	1.40

Suppose first of all that the value of B were higher, say $11,000,000. (Per share earnings of B have higher risk because of the existence of leverage and will sell at a lower price-earnings ratio.) Suppose for simplicity's sake that the debentures sell at par, so that the fraction of the value attributable to the common shares is $6,000,000 or $12 per share.

Now examine the case of an investor who holds 1,000 shares of B. His annual dividend income is $1,400 and he must bear 1/500 of the risk of fluctuations in B's income. He can sell his holdings for $12,000, buy 20,000 worth of shares in A, borrowing $8,000 on private account. His income would become:

Dividends		$2,000
Less:	Interest	480
	Net	$1,520

He would own 1/500 of the shares of A, so that his risk would be unchanged, but he can increase his income if he makes the switch. It will pay him to sell B and buy A. The selling pressure will drive the price of B's shares down and A's shares up, and the opportunity for profit which leads to this selling pressure will continue as long as B is valued at a price above A.

Suppose, on the contrary, that the value of B was below the value of A, say $9,000,000, so that the price of B's shares was only $8.00. The investor holding 1,000 shares in A could sell these for $10,000, buy 500 shares of B, leaving the variability of his income unchanged, and buy $6,000 worth of bonds. His income will be increased from $1,000 to

Dividends	$ 700
Interest	360
	$1,060

Again switches of this type will be profitable as long as B is valued below A. Thus, in equilibrium the value of the two companies must be equal, their costs of capital equal, and the cost of capital independent of capital structure.

Several criticisms of the Modigliani-Miller hypothesis have been advanced on theoretical grounds. Durand has argued that personal leverage is not equivalent to corporate leverage because corporate leverage is typically in long term form and is held at arm's length by the investor through the medium of limited liability, whereas personal leverage (buying on margin) is typically in the form of demand loans subject to margin calls, and carries full personal liability. Further, all investors are subject to limits on the amount of margin commitments and many institutional investors are not permitted to buy on margin at all. It is thus questionable whether there is enough arbitrage of the sort described to provide for value equalization.[12] Attainment of the results is thus not certain, but is dependent on the risk preferences and aversions of individual investors as well as institutional constraints on their behavior. Leverage at the portfolio level can, of course, be increased by more sophisticated methods than margin borrowing. Selling bonds out of portfolio holdings and using the proceeds to buy shares can be just as effective as the "sale" of newly created claims, and can have the same arbitrage effects. It still remains a question of fact whether, in the real world, enough investors do so to bring about the predicted results.

Before looking at the empirical evidence, it should be noted that the predicted result is, strictly speaking, applicable only in a world where there are no taxes on corporate incomes, or at least where there is no double taxation of earnings on equity. Where interest is tax

---

[12]D. Durand, "The Cost of Capital in an Imperfect Market; A Reply to Modigliani and Miller," *American Economic Review*, Vol. XLVI (June, 1959), reprinted in Solomon (1959), pp. 182-97.

deductible but dividends are not, the model predicts a slight decrease in cost of capital, resulting solely from the tax deductibility of interest and not from its lower specific cost. If debt were interest free, there would be no advantage in using it. The optimal capital structure then, is one incorporating the maximum amount of debt obtainable or otherwise acceptable. The predicted downward slope is, however, slight, and can probably be ignored for practical purposes.

The empirical evidence available to date is, unfortunately, conflicting. Modigliani and Miller, in their original article, present two empirical studies, dealing with a cross section of oil companies in 1953 and of electrical utilities in 1947-48, results of both of which tend to support the hypothesis. Durand, in his reply, presents data on banks for 1953 and public utilities for 1955 which tend to refute it. Barges, in a more recent study, has pointed out possible biases in the statistical techniques used by Modigliani and Miller and has investigated data for railroads, department stores and cement companies, all of which tend to support the traditional view.[13] The empirical evidence so far adduced by either side is far from conclusive, and more data need to be examined. One of the difficulties, however, is that the Modigliani-Miller proposition relates to cost of capital in long-run (complete) equilibrium. While economic theorists are usually in equilibrium, markets are not, so no amount of evidence can refute the contention that this would happen in equilibrium. If the market is tending towards equilibrium but is always out of it, firms can, in principle, exploit the current state of the market by appropriate choices of debt and equity, as the traditional model contends. Differences in costs would be capitalized in the move toward equilibrium to the advantage of the initial shareholders. Whether the deviations from long-run equilibrium are large enough to be worth pursuing, or whether they last long enough to allow firms to take advantage of them, are important empirical questions. It is possible to specify theoretical models incorporating institutional or behavioral constraints which prevent the attainment of Modigliani-Miller equilibrium. Durand's model in which all investors have a strong aversion to personal leverage is one such although it is not very convincing in the light of available alternatives. In the following sections we propose to examine another model in which various kinds of equilibrium are attained and examine the effects on the cost of capital.

---

[13]A. Barges, *The Effect of Capital Structure on the Cost of Capital,* (Englewood Cliffs, N. J.: Prentice-Hall, 1964).

6.4   Cost of Capital in the Short Run

We can examine a number of supply curves of capital to the firm, depending on the flexibility of the options open to the company and the extent to which adjustments in market capitalization rates take place. The firm, at any point in time, is at a point on or above all supply schedules, which relate not to the funds to be added to those at its disposal, but to the total funds at its actual or potential disposal.

In the short run, we assume that the firm is limited in additional financing to the funds it can raise from privately negotiated short term or term loans on the debt side and to retained earnings on the equity side. It can reduce the funds at its disposal by prepayment or purchase of outstanding debt in the open market to the extent that cash is generated from operations during the period, but equity cannot be reduced. The only short run information about these activities generally available in the market is any change in the dividend rate, and this is, accordingly, the only factor capable of affecting the capitalization rate on the common shares. New investments made do not affect earnings expectations immediately.

Under these conditions, we can draw a set of cost curves, one for each level of equity investment, showing the cost of debt for various levels of debt *at the given level of equity*. These will have the shape shown in Fig. 6-3, with the following characteristic features:

(a) a vertical portion at the left, representing the minimum level to which debt may be reduced by devoting all available cash flows to debt retirement.

(b) a fairly flat portion to the right of the lower limit, showing the average cost of various quantities of debt. This portion will rise, slowly at first, then more steeply as debt capacity is approached, the credit position of the borrower impaired, and the firm driven to seek borrowed funds from more expensive sources.

(c) another vertical portion at the right, representing the nonavailability of further credit at the existing level of equity.

FIGURE 6–3

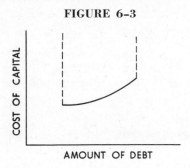

AMOUNT OF DEBT

For each level of equity, cost of equity is not affected in the short run by the increase in debt, so that the average cost of capital, obtained by weighting the respective costs by the proportions of debt and equity in the capital structure, behaves as indicated in Fig. 6-4 because debt, initially, is cheaper than equity and increasing the amount of debt in the debt-equity mix lowers cost. As the proportion of debt rises, so does the cost of debt, and the average cost of capital eventually turns upward.

FIGURE 6-4

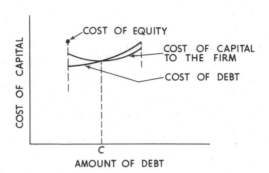

Under these conditions there is an optimum capital structure at point C, where the average cost of capital is lowest.

We can show the short-run cost of capital for the firm in a three-dimensional figure, as a function of debt and equity. To do so, draw a curve similar to that of Fig. 6-4 for each attainable level of equity. (Equity cannot be reduced in the short run and cannot be increased beyond a limit imposed by 100 percent retention of earnings.) Imagine that the curves for each level of equity have been cut out and placed in an appropriate position sketched in Fig. 6-5. If we keep adding sections parallel to the debt axis in this fashion until we have filled in the spaces for every attainable equity level, we will have the short run cost of capital represented by a surface in a three-dimensional figure.

A cross section through this surface parallel to the y (debt) plane gives us Fig. 6-4, as is obvious from the manner of construction. A cross section parallel to the x (equity) axis gives us the alternative profile of Fig. 6-6.

Equity investment in the short run can be increased only by increas-

FIGURE 6-5

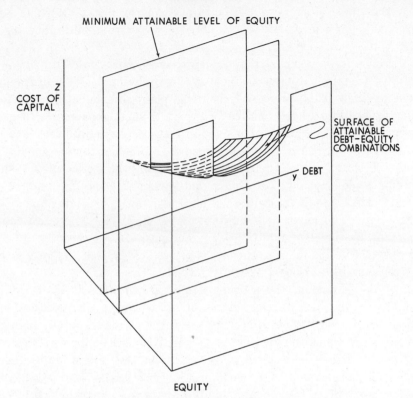

ing the portion of earnings retained. Other things being equal, this will reduce the price-earnings ratio, or increase the cost of equity capital, so that we have, for each level of debt, a curve similar to EE'

FIGURE 6-6

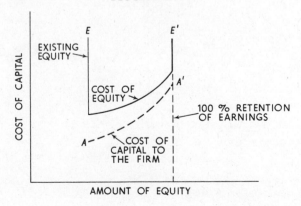

in Fig. 6-6 showing the cost of equity capital and a curve similar to
AA' showing the average cost of capital for the firm as a whole. (At
extremely high levels of debt, where debt costs exceed equity costs,
AA' will lie above EE'.)

Because it is rather clumsy to try to work with three-dimensional
figures, we can map the surface on a two-dimensional figure using
contour lines to indicate the locus of all points on the surface having
identical capital costs. This construction is analogous to the use of
isoquants to map a production surface or the use of indifference curves
in price theory. Such a two-dimensional representation is shown in
Fig. 6-7, the amount of debt is measured along the y-axis, the amount
of equity along the x-axis. Upper and lower limits on the amount of
equity attainable in the period are shown as lines perpendicular to the
axis. Upper and lower debt limits are also shown, but these are functions of the level of equity so are not perpendicular to the y-axis.
Within these boundaries, the average cost of capital is represented
by contour lines. (isocost lines).

On this diagram, the various combinations of debt and equity
which give the firm a fixed volume of funds can be represented by a
45° line, such as AA', intersecting the respective axes at the amount
fixed. We can pick the lowest-cost combination for financing a desired
volume of funds by selecting the point on the lowest indifference
curve tangent to a 45° line such as AA'. This can be connected with
lowest cost points for other amounts to give the expansion path PP',

FIGURE 6-7

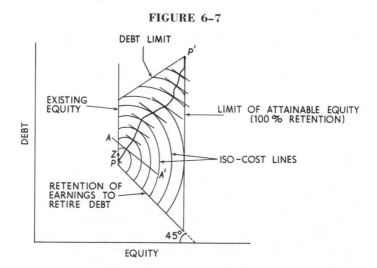

which must pass through the upper right hand corner point P' but is not otherwise constrained. This expansion path connects all the points for which capital costs are at a minimum for the respective supply of funds and can in turn be used to construct the short run average cost of capital curve in Fig. 6-8.

FIGURE 6-8

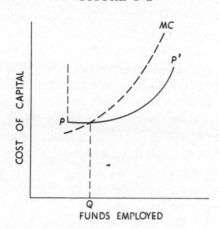

The curve may be U-shaped, with a minimum point like Q, or costs of capital may increase from the outset. We can draw a marginal cost curve MC corresponding to the average cost of funds PP' in Fig. 6-8.

Referring back to Fig. 6-7, the existing capital structure of the firm may be represented by a point Z somewhere on the diagram. It must lie on the lower equity limit but may not coincide with point P. If it does not, it will pay the firm to alter its capital structure by changing its short-term debt level until P is reached.

6.5 The Cost of Capital in the Intermediate Run

In the intermediate run, the range of financing options is increased. Long term debt and equity securities may be issued. As these will be public knowledge, the market's capitalization rates will adjust to reflect prospective earnings from the new investment. The new investment will not have been fully "digested" by the firm, and its exact effect on earnings will be unknown, so that complete revaluation of the new situation will not have taken place. The possibilities of reducing capital employed in either form or in total are also broadened, as equity may be increased to refund debt, or what is less common, but equally feasible in many cases, debt increased to obtain the funds to effect either a formal reduction in capital or, in legal jurisdictions where it is permissible, to buy back the company's shares on the open market.

We may sketch cost curves for the various types of capital as was done in the short-run case. The resulting curves will lie either on or below the short-run curves. (They cannot be above, as the short-run options remain available.) There is now an upper limit on debt, but no lower limit, owing to the refunding possibility, and the upper limit will be somewhat higher, since funding a portion of the debt will reduce the risk associated with any given level of debt.

There is no theoretical upper limit on equity and no lower limit except that resulting from the borrowing limit. (In theory, in Canada, the United Kingdom, and certain other Commonwealth countries, a company could convert itself into a company limited by guarantee and eliminate equity entirely.) As equity is increased, the dilution effect is likely to swamp the earnings anticipation effect and result in increasing costs of equity.

Without drawing the curves for individual security types, which are similar to those in Fig. 6-3–6-6, we can proceed to sketch the overall function, which is shown in Fig. 6-9.

FIGURE 6-9

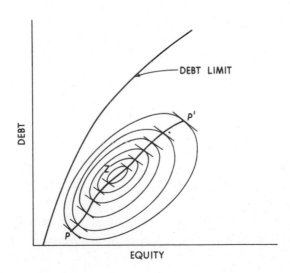

Once more we can derive the expansion path *PP'*, to which corresponds the intermediate run cost of funds curve shown in Fig. 6-10. This curve will lie at all points on or below the short run cost curve of Fig. 6-8, shown dotted in Fig. 6-10. *MCI* is the relevant marginal cost curve.

FIGURE 6-10

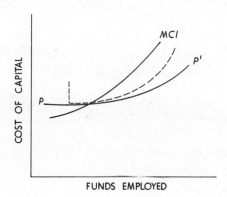

As before, the existing position of the firm will be somewhere in Fig. 6-9. If it is not on the expansion path *PP'*, it will pay the firm to alter its capital structure.

6.6 The Cost of Capital in the Long Run

In the long run, no further financing options become available, but the effects of financing on the size and stability of earnings becomes widely known and the market completes its adjustment to revised earnings expectations and to the revised risk characteristics of the firm which has completed financing.

To the extent that the financing was justified to acquire earning assets, this has become reflected in earnings expectations, so the dilution effect disappears. As a result, the cost of capital becomes independent of the volume of funds employed, being determined by the market capitalization rates applicable to earnings of the appropriate risk category.

At least for a given capital structure, the long run cost of capital curve is flat as in Fig. 6-11, and the marginal cost curve is coincident with it.

FIGURE 6-11

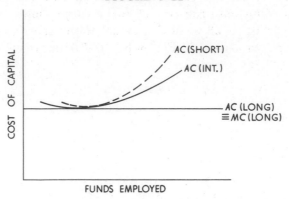

FUNDS EMPLOYED

But capital structure affects the risk of fluctuating earnings as far as the common shareholder is concerned, and it is necessary to consider whether there is an optimum capital structure in the long run. If there is, the marginal cost of capital in the long run, which is the relevant criterion for investment decision purposes, is the weighted average cost of capital at the optimum capital structure, which we may or may not know with any degree of confidence. If there is not, then the weighted average cost of capital in the long run will be the same, irrespective of what the capital structure is. Further, in the long run, the firm does not face a rising supply curve of funds. The empirical evidence for this is the experience of a relatively large number of Canadian mining and oil firms which have increased the capital at their disposal several times over at no apparent increase in cost. As Gordon has asserted, cost of capital is in part a function of the prospective rate of return on funds used in the firm, and where a firm has evidence that it can profitably employ several times its existing capital, it can usually be raised. Cross section studies do not indicate that the average cost of capital for large firms is above that of small; if anything they indicate the opposite. The barriers to corporate growth are not to be sought in a rising supply curve of funds, except in the short or intermediate run, but in inability to generate sufficiently attractive investment proposals and/or to build an organization capable of carrying them out at a sufficient rate.

Even if we grant that, in the long run, knowledge of the prospective profitability of added investment may make the supply of funds schedule horizontal with respect to the amount raised, this does not necessarily imply that there is no optimal capital structure. The isocost lines might, for example, take the form sketched in Fig. 6-12.

FIGURE 6-12

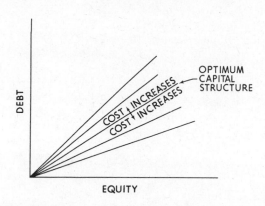

However, the equalization process envisaged by Modigliani and Miller is, in our view, more likely to be effective in the long run than the short, and in our judgment, it is likely to take place, though it may not show up in statistical analyses. If so, it is safe to use the weighted average cost of capital, at the existing capital structure, as a measure of the long-run cost of capital. This does not mean that the firm cannot or should not seek to finance in a way that takes advantage of a temporary disequilibrium in the market. It does suggest, however, that any gains thus made will be capitalized relatively quickly and will accrue to the shareholders as capital gains rather than from the ability of the firm to undertake marginal projects which its less financially astute competitors might reject.

Does anything remain of the optimum capital structure notion? Yes, but in the short and intermediate run only.

The sequential marginal cost curve of Linsay and Sametz may be derived from the expansion path in the intermediate run case, as shown in Fig. 6-13.

For practical reasons of cost, it is essential that financing be done in blocks of debt or equity or, less frequently, both together.

As a consequence the expansion path actually followed will not be the smooth idealized expansion path AA' but will be the stair-shaped path, $ABCDEFGA'$. AB, CD, EF, and GA' represent additions to equity; BC and FG additions to debt; while DE is a simultaneous offering of debt and equity. The extent of the rising cost as funds increase will depend on the extent to which the market takes account of the profit prospects of the company.

FIGURE 6-13

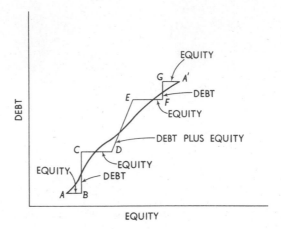

6.7   Estimating the Marginal Cost of Funds

As was argued above, the firm which successfully exploits the departures of the market from long-run equilibrium can expect to have any resulting savings capitalized rather quickly, so that they are realized at once, rather than over an indefinite future. If this is so, the applicable marginal cost of funds for investment decision purposes is the long-run marginal cost which, in the model we have examined, is equal to the long-run average cost.

This must be measured by using the weights of the existing capital structure at market values, which reflect opportunity costs, rather than at book values, which reflect historical costs and are irrelevant for decision making purposes. Use of the structure of intended financing cannot be supported; if this will change the overall structure, specific costs of debt, preferred and equity, will all shift to produce the long-run cost equal to that resulting from using the weights implicit in the present structure.

Some adjustments are necessary, however. Leasehold obligations should be capitalized at the implicit specific rate calculated in Sec. 5.15 and added to the other outstanding long term obligations at market value. In using this standard, equity is valued at market price times number of shares; this figure replaces the capital and surplus item in the balance sheet. The common share specific cost is used for all, while the specific costs for depreciation and retained earnings do not enter the picture.

The following example will illustrate the calculations involved.

Example

Argus Corporation Limited had the following capital structure as of October, 1965.

	Shares or amount outstanding	Market price
5½% Notes, Series *C*, due 1975	$10,000,000	100.00 est.
Class *A* Preference shares		
$2.50 series.	136,565 shs.	51.375
$2.60 series.	200,000 shs.	51.00
Class *B* Preference shares		
$2.70 dividend	300,000 shs.	50.50
Class *C* (participating)		
Preferred shares	6,770,944 shs.	12.375
Common shares	1,692,736 shs.	20.500

Class *C* preferred are entitled to a preferred dividend of $0.30 per share and are entitled to participate pari passu with the common after dividends of $0.30 have been paid on the common shares. The 1965 dividends on both Class *C* and common totaled $0.39, but the current rate is $0.42. The estimated rate of growth in earnings is 15 percent per annum.

What is Argus' cost of capital?

The notes are estimated to be selling at par, so their effective after tax cost is 2.75 percent. Class *A* and *B* preference shares are straight preferred issues, and their cost is easily calculated:

Class *A*	2.50 series	$2.50/51.375 = 0.0488$
	2.60 series	$2.60/51.000 = 0.0510$
Class *B*		$2.70/50.500 = 0.0535$

Class *C* shares are now participating in dividends at the common share rate, and their dividend may be expected to grow at the same rate as that on the common shares. Consequently, they will be evaluated as if they were common shares:

$$k = \frac{0.42}{12.375} + 0.15 = 0.184$$

As the market price of common is somewhat higher, common share funds are a bit cheaper.

$$k = \frac{0.42}{20.50} + 0.15 = 0.1705$$

These various components of the capital structure are then given weights which correspond to their respective market values. The weights are multiplied by the respective costs and the weighted average cost of capital determined.

	(1) Shares	(2) Price	(3) Market value ($000) (1)×(2)	(4) Cost	(3)×(4)
Notes	—	—	10,000	0.0275	275
Class A 2.50 .	136,565	51.375	7,020	0.0488	341
2.60 .	200,000	51.000	10,200	0.0510	520
Class B	300,000	50.500	15,150	0.0535	810
Class C	6,770,944	12.375	83,800	0.1840	15,400
Common . . .	1,692,736	20.500	34,700	0.1705	4,910
			160,870		23,256

$$\text{Weighted Average Cost of Capital} = \frac{23,256}{160,870} = 14.5 \text{ percent}$$

The cost of capital figure which results from these calculations is a long-run cost in the Marshallian sense, i.e., after making allowance for all the expected market adjustments. It is, however, a spot cost, corresponding to a particular moment in time. There are a number of general factors affecting the level of spot costs generally though not the spot costs of any particular company. These include shifts in saving habits and the demand for funds arising from the business cycle and countercyclical policies of the government.

Though the point has been ignored for the sake of simplicity in exposition, the discounting procedures discussed in Chapter 4 are formally correct only when the appropriate spot (though long-run) rate is used for individual time periods in the future. In general it is quite sufficient to use an average of expected spot rates. However, the existing spot rate may not fill the bill in this regard as it may be unduly influenced by cyclical factors. It may be felt that an average of historical spot rates ought to be used. This can be merely an average of rates experienced over the past five or ten years, or a more sophisticated exponential smoothing scheme may be employed. Both are illustrated in the following example:

Example

Corporation *A*'s debt cost, dividend yield and growth rate are shown on an annual average basis together with capital structure at average market prices and annual estimates of the weighted average cost of capital in the following table:

	Debt		Equity				Weighted
Year	% of M.V.	Cost	% of Mkt. value	Div. yield	Annual growth rate	Cost	average cost
1 30	30	0.030	70	0.05	0.03	0.08	0.065
2 35	35	0.028	65	0.06	0.01	0.07	0.055
3 37	37	0.027	63	0.07	0	0.07	0.054
4 32	32	0.031	68	0.05	0.03	0.08	0.064
5 29	29	0.033	71	0.04	0.05	0.09	0.074
6 31	31	0.032	69	0.05	0.05	0.10	0.079
7 34	34	0.029	66	0.06	0.02	0.08	0.063
8 33	33	0.032	67	0.06	0.02	0.08	0.064
9 28	28	0.037	72	0.04	0.08	0.12	0.097
10 30	30	0.030	70	0.03	0.07	0.10	0.079

As will be seen from Fig. 6-14, besides the cyclical pattern of changes in cost of capital, there is an apparent upward trend.

FIGURE 6–14
LONG RUN COSTS OF CAPITAL: CORPORATION *A*

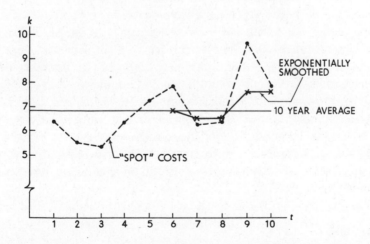

The analyst in year 10 may decide to use the current spot rate as his best estimate of future costs, or he may use the 10-year average of 6.9 percent shown in the solid line in Fig. 6-14, or he may decide to use exponential smoothing, which is an averaging process giving more weight to recent years and perhaps more indicative of the trend. The basic formula is

$$K_t = Wk_t + (1-w)K_{t-1} \tag{1}$$

where K_t is the normalized value, k_t, the observed value in year t and w has a weight between 0 and 1.

Using $w = 0.4$, and setting K_5 equal to the average of the first five years (to get started on some basis—its influence is measured by $(1-w)^t$, where t is measured from the starting point so no great accuracy is necessary) we get the following results for years 6-10:

Year	k_t	K_{t-1}	$K_t = 0.4k_t + 0.6K_{t-1}$
6	0.079	0.0624	0.069
7	0.063	0.0688	0.066
8	0.064	0.0664	0.065
9	0.097	0.0654	0.078
10	0.079	0.0780	0.078

In this case the results do not differ appreciably from the spot figure for year 10, but year 10 appears to be part of the way down from a cyclical peak and this would probably be a fairly good estimate for the next few years. The long term average is probably less suitable if there really is a trend. Other weights can be used, of course, and will give different results. Despite the apparent precision of the above calculation, it must be remembered that it is only an estimate and is to be used with discretion. While it would be appropriate for corporation A to use a discount rate of 8 percent in calculating benefit-cost ratios, management must be prepared to scrutinize carefully those projects with a discounted benefit-cost ratio only slightly in excess of 1.0. Should the appropriate rate turn out to have been 9 percent instead of 8, some of these marginal profit prospects will have turned into losses.

PROBLEMS

1. Using the following data, calculate the cost of capital for Amalgamated Tree Farms, Inc.

Amalgamated Tree Farms, Inc.
Capital Structure

	$000
5¼ First Mortgage Bonds, due 1983	
(market price 98.00)	18,500
5¾% Debentures, due 1978	
(market price 97.50)	57,000
Common Stock, no par value	
10,400,000 shares	

Amalgamated Tree Farms, Inc.
Selected Financial Data

Year	Earned per share	Dividends per share	Common stock price range
1960 . . . . 2.26		1.50	29–38
1961 . . . . 2.36		1.50	26–36
1962 . . . . 2.64		1.50	31–38
1963 . . . . 3.46		1.50	33–42
1964 . . . . 3.52		2.00	37–53
1965 . . . . 3.98		2.00	52–73

Latest price $53.00

2. Using data from *Moody's*, or *Standard and Poor's*, and current quotations, calculate costs of capital for the following companies:

(a) United States Steel Corporation

(b) Federated Department Stores, Inc.

(c) Home Oil Company, Limited

(d) General Dynamics Corp.

(e) Xerox Corporation

3. Estimated cost of capital for Federated Inkwells, Ltd. is as follows:

1956 . . . . . . 6.8%		1961 . . . . . . 6.9%
1957 . . . . . . 7.2%		1962 . . . . . . 7.2%
1958 . . . . . . 7.8%		1963 . . . . . . 6.8%
1959 . . . . . . 8.3%		1964 . . . . . . 7.6%
1960 . . . . . . 7.5%		1965 . . . . . . 8.1%

(a) Calculate the exponentially smoothed series using 0.2, 0.4, 0.6, 0.8 as values of w.

(b) What is the effect of changing the value of w?

4. How would you determine what cost of capital to use in setting capital budgets for a firm which had no publicly held securities?

CHAPTER 7

The Evaluation Process:
Cost of Capital in the Public Sector

7.1   The Role of Cost of Capital in the Evaluation of
Public Sector Investments

The cost of capital plays the same formal role in the evaluation of public sector investment projects that it does in the private sector, i.e., it is the rate of discount to be used in calculating benefit-cost ratios or to be compared with the internal rate of return, although the latter criterion is less commonly used by government bodies.

The rationale for its use is somewhat different. In the private sector, it is used because it leads directly to the private sector goal of profit maximization. In the public sector, its basic function is similar, in that it should lead to a maximization of social benefits, providing these have been appropriately measured. It will play a key role in determining the scale and capital intensity of projects in the public sector. In this capacity, it will determine how available funds may best be allocated among competing projects.

A more controversial application is also possible, in which it is used not only to ration funds among projects, but to determine the magnitude of the public budget. Constitutionally, the various levels of government have certain responsibilities and powers. These require the use of resources. Other resource-using activities which are not forbidden are left to the private sector. If social welfare is to be maximized, it is clear, at least in principle, that the marginal product of a dollar's worth of resources used as input for one government activity must be the same as that for another government activity or for the private sector.[1]

---

[1]Present national income accounting practices beg this question by valuing government output at input cost, making no allowance for the excess of benefits that may be

147

The bulk of government expenditures are not allocated on economic criteria, though economic analysis is used to a considerable extent for certain types of expenditures, i.e., water resource development,[2] highways,[3] and more recently (and controversially) in the national defense establishment. Many types of expenditures continue to be allocated on a purely political logrolling basis or on some sort of "requirements" basis. The latter implies that the job to be done is specified, that the requirements are known and that the appropriate level of expenditure is that "required" to do the job. This latter approach has many sincere exponents and while we have rejected its private sector counterpart, the "urgency" criterion, it should be reexamined in relation to the problems of the public sector. Much of the criticism of the widely publicized efforts of U. S. Defense Secretary McNamara to control defense expenditures comes from interested parties and can be regarded as special pleading. A substantial amount, including much of that coming from within the services, comes from people who sincerely think that national security is an absolute, i.e., that it is possible to determine what is needed to provide complete security and that it is the clear responsibility of the federal government to provide it, whatever the cost. This has wide emotional appeal and would be acceptable if supported by the facts. The opposing view, on which the program is based, is that absolute security doesn't exist. Instead, varying levels of security can be provided with budgets of various sizes, and the defense budget must allocate resources efficiently within the department to obtain the highest level of security for given defense expenditures. An appropriate amount of resources must be left free for other "absolute essentials" such as food, housing, clothing and, within the government sector, law enforcement, education, and national

---

created, while the benefits generated in the form of profit in the private sector are counted. The net effect of this is uncertain, for while the benefits of certain government activities outweigh their costs considerably, the reverse is undoubtedly true of others. This is only one of many factors that make use of national accounting data questionable as a measure of welfare, and not necessarily the most important, nor is this the place to propose solutions.

[2]See, J. V. Krutilla and O. Eckstein, *Multiple Purpose River Development* (Baltimore: Johns Hopkins, 1958); O. Eckstein, *Water Resource Development* (Cambridge: Harvard, 1961); J. Hirshleifer, J. C. De Haven and J. W. Milliman, *Water Supply: Economics, Technology and Policy* (Chicago: University of Chicago, 1960) and R. N. McKeen, *Efficiency in Government Through Systems Analysis* (New York: Wiley, 1958).

[3]See Committee on Planning and Design Policies, *Informational Report on Road User Benefit Analyses for Highway Improvements* (Washington: Am. Assoc. of State Highway Officials, 1960); H. D. Mohring and M. Harwitz, *Highway Benefits, An Analytical Approach* (Evanston: Northwestern, 1962).

parks. An attempt to provide maximum security, with no constraints, would require that all resources to be devoted to defense (including such essential supporting activities as the provision of a subsistence diet and housing for those fit to bear arms or work in defense industries). While something of this nature may be required in wartime and was perhaps approached in Britain during World War II, it is not a valid policy in peacetime, as in the long run there will be nothing left worth defending. While judgment must play a large part in the estimation of benefits from an activity of this type, and one may disagree with some or even all of the actual evaluations made, there can be little doubt that the underlying principles of such a policy are the only ones consistent with rational behavior.

Another area where the "requirements" basis is frequently invoked is in law enforcement. It is held by some to be a moral imperative that no crime or other violation should go undetected or unpunished. While we may have certain reservations about the theological validity of this proposition, let us entertain it for a moment as a guide to policy, and examine the progress of law enforcement in the mythical town of Frontiersville, which had a lurid beginning as a mining community somewhere in the West. Crime was rampant, until the town was incorporated and a sheriff hired. Losses due to crime in the last year before the sheriff arrived were $175,000. After he was hired, at an annual cost of $6,000, a few badmen were run out of town, and while thievery continued at a reduced pace, some of the loot was recovered, and losses dropped to $100,000. The sheriff complained that he was unable to keep up with the wrongdoing singlehanded, so the town fathers raised his pay to $7,000 and hired a deputy for $5,000, and the next year losses dropped to $75,000. In subsequent years the law enforcement payroll grew and the town got cleaner and cleaner, but not lily white. The policing budget grew, and losses from crime dwindled as follows:

Year	Budget ($000)	Losses due to Crime ($000)
0 (no sheriff)	0	175
1	6	100
2	12	75
3	18	60
4	24	48
5	30	38
6	36	28
7	42	20
8	48	14
9	54	10
10	60	8

At the end of ten years, the policing budget was ten times its original size, but crime had not been wiped out. Burglary insurance rates had reached a new low, such insurance having been unobtainable ten years earlier. Examining the changes in rates over the past couple of years, an enterprising lad, formerly the cashier in a gambling den but now the town clerk and tax collector, observed that had everyone in town carried such insurance the premium reductions in the past two years would have produced total savings of only $6,000, while taxes had gone up by $12,000 to pay for two new deputies and a spare horse for the sheriff. He proposed that the size of the sheriff's department be cut, pointing out the possible savings to the townspeople. There was great indignation at this suggestion, the sheriff pointed out the clerk's former underworld connections and he was fired forthwith. Ten years later, the law enforcement budget was $600,000 and only $1,000 was stolen in Frontiersville, which by this time had the highest tax rate in the state, had lost half its population, and still had no water supply.

While the sheriff was away on a speaking tour of the East, the mine owners, who had had nothing left for themselves after paying taxes the past few years, closed the mine. The former clerk, who had sought his fortune in Wall Street after being run out of town, bought it, along with much of the real estate, for a song. Concealing his identity from the town fathers by wearing a false handlebar mustache, he offered, on behalf of "undisclosed Eastern interests" to reopen the mine if the sheriff's budget was cut to $60,000. After much complaining about the Eastern "money trust" this was done and Frontiersville thrived.

Revealing his identity, our hero was asked why he had only cut the budget to $60,000 instead of $48,000 as he had proposed earlier. He noted that with the budget of $48,000, the marginal productivity of the sheriff's office, in terms of losses from crime avoided, was $6,000 and equal to marginal cost. However, there were other intangible benefits from having the larger force, which were not included in the measure of benefits he had used, so that this was probably a bit below the optimum level. Extending the budget to $60,000 was in recognition of this, and a gesture in the direction of the popular view that crime must be stamped out at all costs.

7.2   Traditional Views

Contemporary discussions in the traditionally oriented literature of public finance accept the notion that the optimal budget is one in which the marginal utility of the last dollar spent in satisfying public wants is equal to that of the last dollar spent in satisfying private wants,[4] but do not go very far in specifying how, in concrete cases, this is to be determined. As we shall see, this is really a threefold problem, where capital expenditures are involved. It is, in the first instance, a problem of measuring benefits and costs, often under conditions where no market yardstick is available, even for a starting point. This has received relatively scant attention in the literature generally.

Secondly, it is a problem of identifying and appropriately weighting the incidence of benefits on individuals to arrive at an estimate of social benefits. This problem, which raises a number of theoretical issues concerning the possibility of meaningful interpersonal comparisons of utility and the construction of social welfare functions has been a central topic of discussion among economic theorists for many years, but remains unsolved in any generally accepted sense.

Finally, there is the problem of selecting the appropriate discount rate to convert future benefits into present value terms.

Discussion of the first two problems will be deferred to Chapter 8. For the present we will assume that the problems of measurement and weighting have been resolved and concern ourselves with the third problem only. Again, this is one which the classical literature on public finance has ignored, except inferentially. Musgrave has indicated that pay-as-you-go finance, which he regards as efficient, assesses the out-of-pocket interest cost of projects as a cost, which would imply that benefits should exceed costs when discounted at the prevailing government borrowing rate.[5] Elsewhere, however, he indicates that the difference between the yield of benefits from public projects and that of the private projects foregone as a result of the shift of capital from the private sector through government borrowing is one of the elements in the burden of the national debt.[6] This suggests the use of the marginal efficiency of capital, or internal rate of return in the private sector, as an appropriate measure of the cost of capital to the public sector. Exponents of both of these views, as well as others, may be found. It should be noted that much of the classical literature has assumed the problem away, since with perfect markets throughout and an absence of risk there will be one interest rate in

---

[4]R. A. Musgrave, *The Theory of Public Finance* (New York: McGraw-Hill, 1959), pp. 55-57.

[5]*Ibid.*, p. 560.

[6]*Ibid.*, p. 578.

the economy, for both the government and the private sector, and the marginal efficiency of capital in the latter will equal the rate of interest. Unfortunately, in the real world, some choice has to be made.

Because the problem has not been dealt with in any great detail, it is perhaps incorrect to identify any one viewpoint as the "traditional" viewpoint. If any view is deserving of this label it is the view which identifies the cost of capital to the public sector with the interest rate on government debt. This is the practice recommended and used by a number of agencies of the federal government.[7]

As Eckstein has pointed out,[8] this approach must be rejected on two grounds. In the first place, the government bond rate does not contain within it any allowance for the riskiness of the project. Since the government possesses taxing powers and the power to print money, the risk of default is negligible regardless of the merits of the project. Secondly, in a full employment economy (which it is appropriate to assume because full employment can be maintained without any individual project), resources must be diverted to the project in question from other uses and financed either by taxation or inflation. A more accurate measure of the social cost of the capital committed to the project is the marginal productivity of capital in the sector from which it is withdrawn, as it is the yield from these projects which must be foregone in order to obtain the benefits of the public project. If it does not produce an equivalent return there is a clear loss to society from its adoption. There are a number of variants of this opportunity cost approach, however.

7.3   Opportunity Costs to the Economy

One basic method of estimating the opportunity cost to the economy is that developed by Krutilla and Eckstein.[9] If the capital market were perfect, there would be only one interest rate, as the government and private borrowers would borrow on similar terms. The existence of different rates in different sectors of the economy reflects market imperfections. To assess the marginal cost to the economy of the

---

[7]Federal Inter-Agency River Basin Committee, Subcommittee on Benefits and Costs, *Proposed Practices for Economic Analysis of River Basin Projects* (1950) (hereafter cited as Green Book), pp. 24, 78; U. S., Bureau of the Budget, Circular A-47 (December 31, 1952), cited by Eckstein, *op. cit.*, pp. 94-95.

[8]*Ibid.*, p. 96.

[9]J. V. Krutilla and O. Eckstein, *op. cit.*, Ch. IV.

capital used in the project it is necessary to identify the sectors from which the funds will be drawn and construct a "weighted average marginal cost" of funds.

This requires an examination of the tax structure to determine which portions of revenues are derived from specific taxes. An analysis of the extent of tax shifting must then be made to determine the incidence of the tax on specific sectors. Estimates of opportunity costs of funds by sectors are then multiplied by the proportion of the total tax revenues provided by each sector to derive an estimate of opportunity costs for the economy as a whole.

Suppose, for example, that the Slobbovian government derives 50 percent of its revenue from a tax on alcohol, 25 percent from a tax on food, and 25 percent from a tax on land. Suppose further that the tax on alcohol is shifted 100 percent to alcoholics, that 50 percent of the tax on food is shifted to consumers, and 50 percent borne by landlords and that the land tax cannot be shifted. Finally, assume that 50 percent of the consuming population are alcoholics. We can derive weights reflecting the incidence of taxes on the various sectors as shown in Table 7-1.

TABLE 7-1
CALCULATION OF WEIGHTED AVERAGE MARGINAL
COST OF FUNDS IN SLOBBOVIA

Tax	Portion of budget	Incidence Alcoholics	Incidence Teetotallers	Incidence Landlords	Weighted average
Alcohol	0.50	0.5000	–	–	
Food	0.25	0.0625	0.0625	0.125	
Land	0.25	–	–	0.250	
Weights		0.5625	0.0625	0.375	
Sector Opportunity Cost. .		0.24	0.08	0.12	
		0.135	0.005	0.045	0.185

This approach has a strong logical appeal, but some objections should be noted. In the first place, not enough is known about tax incidence to make possible any great degree of precision in the estimates of weights. Estimates of opportunity costs by sectors can be estimated a bit more accurately from market data. Care should be taken to avoid the trap of identifying bond interest rates with the marginal cost of funds to firms in the business sector, for reasons which have been discussed in Chapters 5 and 6. Care should also be taken to convert costs of capital for the private sectors to a before-tax basis consistent with the rate to be used in the public sector.

This approach seems to assume that all the funds for the project are raised by taxation; this has led to attempts to derive estimates on the basis of postulated borrowing patterns in cases where the project will be financed by borrowing.[10] It is, however, inappropriate to single out a single project or group of projects as being financed by borrowing and treat the rest of the budget as being financed by taxation, even if the projects are being financed by revenue bonds on a self-liquidating basis. The latter may only be a device chosen for fiscal convenience. Decisions concerning the level of taxation and borrowing at any one time are apt to be affected by considerations of fiscal policy, rather than the level of expenditures as such.

If following Musgrave, we conceive of the budget as having three separate components, capital expenditure decisions must be regarded as part of the allocation budget, considered to be kept in balance, while the stabilization budget provides for planned deficits or surpluses as required for economic stabilization. If this is the case, then it is preferable to regard the funds for all projects as raised by taxation. However, adoption of the Musgrave framework in its entirety is not consistent with using the actual pattern of tax receipts to determine weights. The third component of the Musgrave budgetary framework consists of taxes and subsidies imposed to redistribute income. The actual pattern of tax receipts reflects not only the opportunity cost of the funds for the project but is influenced by the costs of redistribution. The amount of error is probably slight however.

An alternative is to use, as the opportunity cost, the marginal rate of return in the most productive sector, irrespective of where the funds come form. The argument for this approach is that the funds *could* be devoted to this use and that this would be the most efficient use to make of them unless the proposed project offers a higher rate of return.[11] This is perhaps the most suitable of the simple opportunity cost approaches we have been discussing. The fact that a portion of the funds are derived from a sector in which they are relatively unproductive is not sufficient justification for utilizing them to carry out slightly better projects when more worthwhile uses for the funds are available.

---

[10]G. L. Reuber and R. J. Wonnacott, *The Cost of Capital in Canada with Special Reference to Public Development of the Columbia River* (Washington: Resources for the Future, Inc., 1961).

[11]To maximize output, funds *should* be devoted to this use until the return therein is reduced to a competitive level.

A more sophisticated approach to the opportunity cost problem is to attempt to fit an aggregate production function to time series data for the entire economy.[12] While promising, neither the data nor the techniques are sufficiently reliable at the present time.

7.4 Rejection of Market-Determined Time Preference

In economic theory, the rate of interest plays the role of equating the marginal rate of time preference with the marginal productivity of capital, as these are expressed in the supply and demand schedules for loanable funds. Our opportunity cost analysis has been concerned with productivity only, but it is clear that, when markets are in or near full employment equilibrium, the cost thus developed, minus risk premiums, is a tolerably accurate measure of the preference of those in the market for enjoyment of present benefits versus future benefits. What is less clear, however, is whether consumers' sovereignty, expressed in market prices, is a suitable guide to public policy when different intertemporal distributions of benefits are being considered. If not, it might be appropriate to consider some alternative discount rate.

One basis for such rejection of market rates as a measure of social time preference is the neoclassical notion that individuals tend to over-discount the future. The state should, presumably, correct for this excessive discounting in its role as guardian of the general welfare and must not favor one generation over another. It is not a great step from this view to the Marxist proposition that consumers' preferences in this regard are exceptionally suspect and should be rejected out of hand and some other criterion substituted.[13] At its extreme, this leads to the view that the state should use a marginal rate of time preference of zero if it is not to discriminate between generations, i.e., that undiscounted benefit cost ratios are an appropriate criterion.

A somewhat more sophisticated approach within the neoclassical tradition is that of Baumol who argues that individuals may have two distinct time preferences, one for their voluntary decisions, the other for collective decisions to which others are forced to contribute via the tax mechanism.[14] This latter rate is expressed through the

---

[12]This approach is examined, using a simple Cobb-Douglas production function, in Reuber and Wonnacott, *op. cit.*, Appendix A.

[13]M. H. Dobb, *On Economic Theory and Socialism* (London: Routledge, 1955), pp. 244, 258-60.

[14]W. J. Baumol, *Welfare Economics and the Theory of the State* (Cambridge: Harvard, 1952), pp. 91-93. See also Eckstein, *op. cit.*, pp. 99-100.

political process rather than the market place. Hence market evidence may be irrelevant.

The argument for a different (usually lower) rate than that given by the market is, really, an argument that benefits to future generations must be accorded more weight than the market rate is ready to do. Even if we accept this proposition, however, it is not clear that accepting projects with lower rates of discount is the appropriate way to do it.

Consider the following example which is oversimplified but indicates the nature of the objection to this approach. The investment opportunity schedule for the private sector offers the following opportunities for net new investment in each time period:

Amount	Rate of return
$1,000,000	15%
1,000,000	10%
1,000,000	5%

In addition to this, capital recoveries through depreciation, and other sources, can be reinvested to earn the same amount as was earned in the initial project. In other words, $1,000,000 net investment in the private sector creates a perpetual increase in income of $150,000 per year, while $2,000,000 creates an increase of $250,000. If the marginal propensity to save out of the new income is zero, effects of subsequent years are additive, so that a net investment level of $2,000,000 will produce an annual increase of $250,000 in income originating in the private sector.

A similar set of opportunities exists in the public sector. The present level of saving is $4,000,000 per year. Our criterion that investment in both sectors be carried to the point where marginal productivities are equal requires us to invest $2,000,000 in each sector, producing additional income in subsequent years as follows:

Alternative A

	First year	Fifth year	Tenth year
Private sector	250,000	1,250,000	2,500,000
Public sector	250,000	1,250,000	2,500,000
Total increase in income	500,000	2,500,000	5,000,000

Suppose, instead of following this rule, investment in the public sector is carried to the point of accepting projects yielding 5 percent, in order to do equity to future generations. With given savings, it then becomes necessary for the private sector to reduce its investment to $1,000,000 so that we get the following result:

Alternative B

	First year	Fifth year	Tenth year
Private sector	150,000	750,000	1,500,000
Public sector	300,000	1,500,000	3,000,000
Total increase in income	450,000	2,250,000	4,500,000

The total increase in income is reduced, although the increase in income (benefits) in the public sector is greater than in the equal marginal productivity case. This choice implies that society attached a higher relative value to public sector benefits than to those in the private sector; in this case it is willing to give up one dollar in private benefits for fifty cents in public benefits. Even if we accept this value judgment, however, we are not maximizing social welfare by such a choice, for we can use the tax mechanism to effect the following redistribution of the income generated under alternative *A*:

Alternative A Plus Redistribution

	First year	Fifth year	Tenth year
Private sector income	250,000	1,250,000	2,500,000
Less taxes	100,000	500,000	1,000,000
Private sector net	150,000	750,000	1,500,000
Public sector income	250,000	1,250,000	2,500,000
Plus taxes	100,000	500,000	1,000,000
	350,000	1,750,000	3,500,000

By an appropriate tax policy and an efficient investment policy it is possible to leave the private sector as well off and make the public sector better off than it would be under an inefficient investment policy chosen for distributional reasons. It is also possible to leave the public sector as well off and make the private sector better off, of course, or make both better off. The assumption of a zero marginal propensity to save is unreal; by dropping it we introduce compound growth which makes the comparison even more unfavorable to alternative *B*.

This example depends for its neatness on the assumption of fixed savings; the proposition which it is designed to illustrate does not. We must, in general, reject policies that attempt to redistribute benefits in favor of future generations by lowering the cutoff rate for investments in the public sector, since the desired levels of benefits can be at least equaled by a policy of efficient investment (requiring equal marginal productivities in both sectors) plus redistribution.

This is not an argument in favor of a smaller public sector, but against inefficient resource allocation in either sector. The same results would follow if private investment were expanded at the expense of more productive opportunities in the public sector. Profitability requirements in the private sector tend to impose a constraint on such expansion however. There undoubtedly are projects in the public sector being passed over although they offer opportunities for more productive employment of capital than are generally available in the private sector. At the same time, many projects with inferior productivity are being undertaken. More careful evaluation procedures should lead to greater efficiency within the public sector, at which point the question of whether it should be expanded or not will be easier to answer.

There may be exceptions to the universal applicability of this efficiency criterion within government, for example where a particular project produces a desired redistribution which would be particularly difficult to effect otherwise. We should be cautious about allowing this exception, however, since "difficult" in this context may merely mean politically embarrassing. The opportunities to use this device to subsidize, in a fashion obscure to the public at large, special interests in whose favor an open redistribution would be totally unacceptable are substantial and may be difficult to detect. In general, it would probably be safer to simply rule out the exceptions. Any subsidy which cannot be defended in the legislature should probably not be paid.

7.5 Some Further Complications

Professor Eckstein has argued that the government borrowing rate is inappropriate and that an opportunity cost standard is relevant. However, for peculiar reasons, he recommends use of the government borrowing rate for evaluation purposes, and presumably for design purposes as well, coupled with the requirement that the benefit-cost ratio exceed 1.0 by a sufficient margin so that the benefit-cost ratio at the opportunity cost rate exceed 1.0.[15] This is really equivalent to requiring that the project's capital intensity or durability be carried

---

[15]Eckstein, *op. cit.*, pp. 101-3.

to the point where the marginal productivity of capital invested in the project is equal to the borrowing rate or the average productivity is equal to the opportunity cost rate, whichever occurs first. This is in our view clearly undesirable and is likely in practice to lead to the construction of too few projects which are too grandiose in scale.

The procedure is not justified on the basis of its own rationality but as an antidote to other irrationalities in the capital allocation process. The first argument is that capital should be allocated rationally in the private sector since systematic provision is made, through depreciation, for capital recovery and reinvestment. Present practice in the public sector makes no provision for such recovery, and the proposal is aimed at producing durable projects where the rate of attrition due to this factor is reduced. This should be rejected on two grounds. First of all, capital intensity is not the equivalent of durability, despite the unfortunate confusion arising from the "period of production" concept which appears to persist. Second, even if it were, it would be preferable to rationalize the budgetary process along the lines suggested by Musgrave and make provision in the allocation budgets for capital recovery,[16] rather than introduce a countervailing irrationality of dubious effectiveness.

The second argument is that the private sector uses decision criteria which are biased toward short-lived projects. Payback is specifically cited as such a criterion. Providing one substitutes "noncapital intensive" for "short-lived" (period of production once more), this is a justifiable criticism of payback, which has been criticized above for a number of reasons. To the extent that payback is replaced by more sophisticated criteria, however, there is no such bias and no reason to introduce a possibly compensating bias in the public sector.

---

[16]Musgrave, *op. cit.*, p. 560.

CHAPTER 8

Other Problems of Evaluation in the Public Sector

8.1 Public and Private Benefits: Standards for Social Evaluation

In the private sector, where a firm is attempting to decide whether or not to undertake a particular project, the benefits which it must take into account are relatively well defined; they are the benefits that accrue to it as an entity, usually in the form of cash receipts or savings. In the public sector, however, things are not this neat. While there are cases where all of the benefits accrue to the public treasury and neither costs nor benefits are imposed on other parties as the result of a project's adoption, these are in the minority. Most public projects will ordinarily result in:

(a) Direct benefits which accrue to taxpayers in general, in the form of cost savings for particular services which the government is already committed to provide, and/or

(b) Indirect benefits accruing to individuals or groups in the community as a result of the project. They may or may not pay for these services, and whether they do is, in principle, irrelevant in determining whether the project should be undertaken.

The sum of these two classes of benefit is the total social benefit generated by the project. The components may be weighted to reflect the social evaluation of benefits accruing to particular identifiable groups.

Public benefits are obtained only through utilizing resources, costs of which are the costs of the project. Costs incurred to obtain public benefits are also of two types:

(c) Direct public costs, borne by the Treasury.

(d) Associated private costs, borne by individuals or groups within the community.

Total social cost is the appropriately weighted sum of these costs. Note that all projects, public and private, create social benefits and costs. Private projects create benefits and costs in the same manner as public projects. Social evaluations of private projects are also possible. These will ordinarily be the same as private evaluations except when:

(1) The distribution of benefits differs from the distribution of costs and the parts of the population on which the benefits and costs fall are differently weighted in the social welfare function, or

(2) There are external economies or diseconomies, so that benefits are created which do not accrue to the owners of the project or associated costs are imposed elsewhere in the economy which are not charged to the owners.

Where there are serious discrepancies between the social evaluations and private evaluations of private projects, there are economic grounds for government intervention leading to regulation or transfer of the activity in question to the public sector. The analysis of such situations is the primary subject of classical welfare economics.[1] The object of such regulation or transfer is to insure that projects are considered and selected throughout the economy, and not just in the public sector, in such a way as to maximize the excess of social benefits over social costs. Government is not a profit maximizer as are business firms, but is, or should be, a social welfare maximizer, and it is for this reason that the analytical techniques of the private sector may be utilized by the government with appropriate modifications.

Because government is concerned with social welfare maximization, it goes without saying that it should consider social benefits and social costs only. In many cases it is impossible to construct a measure of benefits and costs comparable in scope to the measures used by private firms. Because we have tended to allocate to government those activities where discrepancies between private and social evaluations are particularly great, any attempt to use such a measure is apt to be seriously misleading. Such attempts are often made, however, most frequently perhaps at the municipal level, where the persistence of the corporate legal form and inappropriately limited fiscal powers has tended to cause identification of the public interest with that of the owners of real property. Even where this identification is not made, the private firm outlook tends to persist at this level. An example of this is given by the almost universal practice in North American cities of using common salt for snow and ice removal from streets. This

---

[1] A. C. Pigou, *The Economics of Welfare* (4th ed.; London: Macmillan, 1932).

practice poses, for automobile owners, the alternatives of having their vehicles undercoated at substantial initial cost or of incurring greater maintenance costs through corrosion of fenders, doors, etc. Alternative noncorrosive melting agents are available at somewhat higher cost than salt, but at a total social cost that is probably substantially below that imposed on car owners by its use. This is an example in which the application of inappropriate standards of economy leads to social waste on a large scale. It may be that attainment of optimum levels of activity in the public sector is dependent on the reform of fiscal arrangements; we must ignore this question here, however, and concern ourselves with the expenditure side of the budget only.

The analysis of public expenditures should attempt to identify all benefits and costs related to the project in question, should measure them as accurately as possible, and should identify their incidence on specific groups. In Chapter 4 we examined some of the problems involved in measuring benefits and costs which arise in any context; in this chapter we look at some of the problems which are peculiarly acute in the public sector.

8.2 Measuring Unmarketed Benefits

Where the stream of goods and services produced by a project is sold or where a voluntary user tax is imposed, and where there are no important indirect effects, the problem of measuring benefits is conceptually simple. They are simply the market value of the services produced and sold. Since the sale will occur in the future, there is still a substantial market research problem involved in forecasting sales, but this is of a practical rather than conceptual nature. It is no accident that the application of benefit-cost analysis has been carried farthest in those activities of government which have marketable output, such as electric power generation and highway construction (financed by user taxes). Yet such activities constitute a relatively small fraction of total government capital spending. Where the investment results in a reduction in outlays, e.g., for rent of offices, the problem is similarly straightforward.

National income accounting has sidestepped the question of evaluating benefits by equating the value of government services with the costs of providing them. This assumes that all projects have a benefit-cost ratio of 1.0, thus assuming away the problem of determining whether the projects are worthwhile or not. While this procedure may be justified at the national income accountant's level by the assumption that the expenditure would not have been approved if legislators had not thought it was worthwhile, it is of no use to us nor to the legislators who must make such decisions.

Where such direct market evidence of the value of benefits is not available, estimates must be constructed on some basis to measure what the benefits are worth. The most reliable concept in this regard is an estimate of what people would have been willing to pay for the service if they were required to, or of what they are paying for substitutes. Thus flood control benefits can be measured by calculating the effect on flood insurance premiums or by making an actuarial calculation of probable losses.[2] The former is a more satisfactory measurement, as it provides a market measure of the amount of protection the people involved are willing to pay for. Where costs of added flood protection exceed the reduction in premiums which would result from the provision of such protection, if would seem that insurance, rather than flood control, is the appropriate means of spreading the risk. It is true that insurance costs are borne mainly by those directly located in flood-prone areas, while flood control costs are not directly assessed against the users but are borne by the community at large. There is a strong argument for user charges in this type of situation to discourage excessive construction in flood-prone areas at the expense of the rest of the community.

Some services are provided on a collective basis in some communities, on a market basis in others. Where this is the case, market data from the one community may be used, with caution, to evaluate output which is distributed free in the other. There is, however, a fundamental problem here, in that where the service is marketed, it will ordinarily be consumed in varying quantities by different members of the community in accordance with their individual demand schedules. Where the service is free for the taking, consumption will ordinarily be greater if the demand schedules are identical. Yet it is not appropriate to value the extra-marginal units at the price established under market conditions because users would not be willing to pay that much for each of the units taken.

This situation is illustrated in Fig. 8-1. Suppose that the demand curve for the service is *MM'* and the service is marketed at a price

---

[2]See O. Eckstein, *Water Resource Development: The Economics of Project Evaluation* (Cambridge: Harvard, 1961), Ch. 5.

OP. Under these conditions the amount consumed is *OA.* If the service is now provided free, the amount consumed increases to *OB.* While *OACP* was an appropriate valuation for the output when it was marketed, using the same price for valuing the output when it becomes a free good is equivalent to valuing it at *OBDP,* which is clearly incorrect as the area *BCD* lies above the demand curve and could not be obtained as revenue even by a discriminating monopolist. In this example, the marginal unit (at *B*) is worth nothing, for this is what people would be willing to pay for it.

FIGURE 8-1

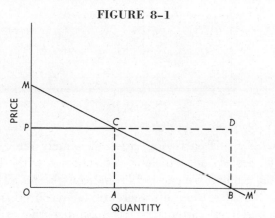

A somewhat similar problem arises in attempts to construct more elaborate indirect measures of value. The most commonly used measure of recreational benefits, to take fishing as an example, is to calculate the expenditures of fishermen on tackle, travel, and other expenses, incurred in the pursuit of their particular neurosis, reduce these to a per fisherman-day basis, and estimate the value of the recreational facility by forecasting the number of fisherman-days recreation it will provide. As Eckstein has pointed out, this is a question-begging approach to the problem.[3] Look at Fig. 8-2. Fishermen's expenditures total *OABT,* and we may be sure that the gross benefit is at least this great, so that the demand curve is somewhat higher. Even if we knew it to be *DD',* and knew gross benefits of fishing to be *OACP,* this is not a valid measure of the value of the fishing holes, which is only *TBCP,* as we have to *deduct* the value of the other inputs

---

[3] *Ibid.,* p. 41.

FIGURE 8–2

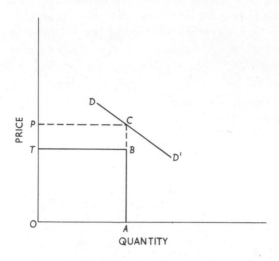

needed to satisfy this particular craving, namely the expenditures in tackle, travel, and so on, which we started out with. The only valid measure is the amount we can get from licenses; the way to be sure of maximizing benefits from this recreational resource is to direct the fisheries management authorities to maximize the excess of license revenues over the costs of improving fishing. This would of course require fishermen to pay for their fun, or be more economical in tackle expenditures, but would, after all, place them in the same position as circus-goers.[4]

There are serious difficulties in attempting to derive a value for benefits in many kinds of activities. However, ingenuity and resourcefulness, with which the analyst should be well supplied, will enable the construction of a variety of estimates which will at least indicate rough orders of magnitude. If these are all that is available, it is still better to utilize them on a rational basis than to throw rationality to the winds and proceed entirely on the basis of intuition or logrolling.

---

[4]This is not to be taken as a recommendation that fishermen be singled out for such treatment, which could equally be applied to duck hunters, picnickers, birdwatchers, and other groups who expect to be provided with their own equivalent of circuses at public expense. In other countries this list varies. Many European countries subsidize opera, ballet, and similar pursuits, while leaving fishermen to shift for themselves in a market system. The principle is the same, however.

Then there are instances where market criteria, because of imperfections in the market, provide an inaccurate estimate of benefits. For example, where alternative means of transportation are made feasible, it is possible to calculate savings to shippers on the basis of charges made by former carriers. Where these are in excess of marginal costs (e.g., on railroads, operating under conditions of decreasing cost), the net saving to the community is the cost avoided by the change in method of transportation. The saving to shippers should be offset against the loss in the contribution to railroad overhead resulting from the shift in traffic, whether the loss is borne by the railway or passed on to other users of "captive" traffic.[5] Benefits and costs accruing to these groups might be differently weighted; this is a problem we discuss in Sec. 8.4.

8.3 Measuring Indirect Benefits

The attainment of optimum levels of investment in activities which generate external economies or diseconomies requires that such economies or diseconomies be taken into account in measuring the productivity of the activity in question, even if they cannot be brought within its scope via the market mechanism or some sort of tax-subsidy arrangement. The problem of measuring external benefits is apt to be particularly acute in public sector calculations, since they are frequently responsible for the activity being allocated to the public sector in the first instance. It is impossible here to attempt to catalog external effects, though we shall give some examples.

Even where external benefits are marketable, they may not in fact be marketed for good reasons. Because of this there is a natural temptation for the proponents of a project to attribute to it all sorts of supposed external effects which will improve its chances of being carried out. For this reason it is an administrative necessity that the ultimate evaluation on which the accept-reject decision is based be performed somewhere other than in the agency from which the proposal originates. It is also, perhaps, more necessary to indicate what *does not* constitute an external benefit than what does.

Many projects are "justified" on the grounds that they will create employment and lead to growth in the community. There may be an external benefit of this kind, but it is limited in amount to the increase

---

[5]O. Eckstein, *op. cit.*, pp. 167-75.

in income earned by the factors of production in this particular employment over what they would have earned elsewhere in the economy, less the costs of moving. It is *not* equivalent to the size of the payroll attracted, and, from the point of view of the economy as a whole, is probably sufficiently small to be ignored. A partial exception may exist in underdeveloped countries where "infrastructure" investments are being considered. In this case the potential increase in factor incomes is the basic justification of the project. To avoid counting the same tricks twice, an evaluation should be made of the entire program including the infrastructure investment and the industrial undertakings it is designed to support, thus "internalizing" the benefits within the program. It is quite appropriate in cost analyses for projects of this type to use the effective wage rate in less industrialized sectors, even if the wage actually paid is higher after the acquisition of skills. This presupposes that training costs are included in the costs of the project. A portion of the net benefits thus created accrues directly to the labor force in the form of higher wages.

When a program of this sort is prepared it will ordinarily have a number of components having various degrees of interdependence. While "internalization" of the benefits can be accomplished by considering the program as a whole, some flexibility in the budget can be maintained by considering direct benefits and costs of all subsets of projects within the program, treated as mutually exclusive opportunities. This can be done in the usual fashion or by treating the budget as a linear programming problem.[6] This need not interfere with later implementation of some of the projects originally excluded from the program.

8.4   The Social Welfare Function and Problems of Weighting

In Sec. 1.6 the notion of a social welfare function was introduced briefly, as a means of weighting the benefits received by different individuals. The need for a social welfare function arises because, in general, there is not a unique solution to the problem of maximizing social welfare in an economy. Perfect competition of the textbook variety can be shown, in the absence of external effects, to lead to an optimum allocation of resources, given an income distribution.[7]

---

[6]H. M. Weingartner, *Mathematical Programming and the Analysis of Capital Budgeting Problems* (Englewood Cliffs, N. J.: Prentice-Hall, 1963), pp. 39-43, 147-52.

Such an allocation is referred to as Pareto-optimal in the jargon of the welfare economist. Unfortunately, there are an infinite number of Pareto-optimal states, one corresponding to each possible distribution of income.

Economic theorists have, in general, claimed that interpersonal comparisons of utility or welfare are fundamentally ascientific,[8] so that it is impossible to select a unique optimum without specifying an income distribution in advance.[9] Nor will this be enough. The resource allocation and constellation of prices determined by the exercise of consumers' sovereignty with a given distribution of income will itself generate a different distribution of income in the form of payments to the factors of production, so a system of taxes and subsidies will usually be required to maintain the desired distribution. A number of attempts have been made to get around the problem of specifying a social welfare function; these cannot be examined in detail here, nor have they been too successful.[10]

For practical purposes, the social welfare function consists of a set of weights to be used in evaluating the benefits and costs accruing to or incurred by various individuals (in practice, groups) and which represents the judgment of the government of the day. We will beg the question of how they are formed from individual preferences except to note that if the results are not satisfactory, the government will be replaced at the next election if not sooner.[11]

There are two ways in which such a function may be used. The weights may be attached to estimates of benefits and costs and used in evaluating projects. Thus we might have a project with the benefit and cost estimates presented in Table 8-1. The unadjusted benefit-cost

---

[7]K. E. Boulding, "Welfare Economics" in B. F. Haley (ed.), *A Survey of Contemporary Economics*, Vol. II (Homewood, Ill.: Irwin, 1952), p. 34.

[8]L. Robbins, *An Essay on The Nature and Significance of Economic Science* (London: Macmillan, 1935).

[9]A. Bergson, "A Reformulation of Certain Aspects of Welfare Economics," *Quarterly Journal of Economics*, Vol. 52, pp. 310-34.

[10]For a fuller discussion see J. Rothenberg, *The Measurement of Social Welfare* (Englewood Cliffs, N. J.: Prentice-Hall, 1961), Chaps. 3-5 and the literature cited therein.

[11]It should be noted that this model, in which all states of nature, with the exception of who is to form the government, are ordered by the politicians, while majority rule decides which politician's set of preferences is to be imposed on society, is formally identical to that proposed by Blau as the exception to Arrow's Possibility Theorem. See J. Blau, "The Existence of Social Welfare Functions," *Econometrica*, Vol. 25 (April, 1957), pp. 302-13.

ratio is 0.89 so the project is not worth adopting. However, if a vege-tarian government weights the benefits and costs in accordance with the social welfare function given in Table 8–2, we can construct an adjusted benefit-cost ratio,[13] as shown in Table 8–3. Because of the

TABLE 8–1
UNWEIGHTED ESTIMATES OF BENEFITS AND COSTS

	Present value of	
Incidence[12]	Benefits	Costs
Vegetarians 100,000		50,000
Pensioners 100,000		100,000
Trade unionists 500,000		300,000
Bankers 100,000		450,000
Unadjusted totals: . . . 800,000		900,000
Benefit-cost ratio: 0.89		

TABLE 8–2
SOCIAL WELFARE FUNCTION

Incidence	Weight
Vegetarians 0.6	
Pensioners 1.0	
Trade unionists 1.5	
Bankers 0.1	

differential weighting of different groups, the adjusted benefit-cost ratio is 1.48, and the project is worthwhile.

TABLE 8–3
ADJUSTED BENEFIT-COST ESTIMATES

		Weighted present value of	
Incidence	Weights	Benefits	Costs
Vegetarians 0.6		60,000	30,000
Pensioners 1.0		100,000	100,000
Trade unionists 1.5		750,000	450,000
Bankers 0.1		10,000	45,000
Adjusted totals: 920,000			625,000
Adjusted benefit-cost ratio = 1.48			

[12]This example assumes incidence can be assigned to disjoint sets. In practice the problem can be resolved by specifying a sufficient number of groups to take care of vegetarians who are also trade unionists or by assigning individuals to groups on the basis of their assumed major interest.

[13]It will be noted that a relatively low weight is given to the party's hard-core sup-porters. This is normal in a two-party system since the party is dependent on uncommitted voters to retain office. Its own hard-core supporters have no real alternative and can be ignored most of the time, if the party is in office. This is one of the features tending to moderate both extremes in such a system and making for stability in it.

The alternative is to reject weighting on individual projects, but to proceed to an efficient allocation of resources using unweighted benefit-cost estimates, carrying out the redistribution by means of direct taxes and subsidies determined in accordance with the social welfare function. In principle this is more efficient and likely to lead to higher total output in the economy, for the reasons discussed in Sec. 7.4 where the same problem was examined in terms of equity between generations. In practice, the choice may not be nearly as clear cut. The only taxes which do not affect resource allocation are taxes on true economic rents and poll taxes. There are administrative difficulties involved in defining the former, while the latter have become a dirty word, largely owing to their use for reasons unconnected with fiscal equity. Outright subsidies also tend to be unpopular, and there are circumstances where governments, even of the most individualistic persuasion, have felt compelled to interfere in the exercise of free choice in spending patterns (e.g., by providing free, compulsory education). When these factors are taken into consideration, there are some cases in which optimal decisions are as likely to be approached in one way as in another. The only difficulty is that it is very hard to determine just what all the effects are.

8.5   Measuring Benefits and Costs with Underutilized Capacity

Benefit-cost analysis is an attempt to measure and compare benefits with costs, the latter reflecting the alternative benefits foregone. Market costs are a relatively good measure of opportunity cost in this sense under conditions where the economy is operating at a high level of employment. If we suppose, however, that there is substantial unemployment in the economy, the opportunity cost in terms of output foregone of employing workers who were heretofore unemployed is of course, nil.

This has led to proposals that, in periods of substantial unemployment, cost estimates be scaled down to reflect the "true" opportunity cost of otherwise unemployed labor. To apply this procedure consistently would require an analysis of the types of labor required for the project and the determination of prices for each type of labor which would just clear the market, since there may be shortages of certain types of labor while others are in excess supply.

This does not require explicit solution for the prices, since the problem can be resolved by solving the following linear programming problem:

$$\text{Maximize} \sum_i X_i(V_i - C_i)$$

Subject to n constraints of the form

$$\sum_i X_i d_{ij} \leq L_j$$

and

$$0 \leq X_i \leq 1$$

where V_i is the benefit and C_i the cost, exclusive of labor cost, invested in the ith project, X_i is the amount of project i undertaken and where d_{ij} is the labor input, of the ith project in man hours for the jth type of labor, while L_j is the estimated availability of this type of labor during the budgetary period. There is no need to make an explicit calculation of the wage rates, since these emerge as solutions to the dual to the above problem. We shall not go into the solution of this problem nor its interpretation here, since we do not believe it is a particularly fruitful line of attack.[14]

The reason why we reject this approach is that, in general, there is no reason to restrict its application to projects in the public sector which are of submarginal worth at current wage rates. It is quite conceivable that there are projects in the private sector which, while also less than marginally attractive at the current wage rate, are nevertheless socially preferable to some of the projects in the public sector which would be accepted using this criterion. Other projects in the public sector which are attractive at the current wage rate should perhaps be increased in scale, rather than adopting the projects in question. Adoption of submarginal projects in the public sector is a potentially effective means of eliminating unemployment. It is almost certain to be an inefficient means of doing so, since it leads to an inefficient allocation of resources when the full employment level has been reached. As other monetary and fiscal measures to attain full employment are available, it is our view that they should be used and all projects evaluated in terms of market prices (or any better estimates of full employment prices which are available). This should, in general, lead to more efficient resource allocation.[15]

---

[14]For other uses of linear programming models, see Chapter 9.

[15]What is being advocated here is an attempt to allocate society's *potential* savings at full employment in an efficient manner, rather than actual savings at a lower level of GNP.

A somewhat different problem arises in the case of projects in chronically depressed areas. These are areas which exhibit substantial unemployment and/or underemployment even in periods of substantially full employment for the economy as a whole. It is clear that in some cases frictional factors are such that the market mechanism is not operating to attract excess labor from such pockets quickly enough. While a full examination of depressed area policy is beyond our frame of reference here, there may well be instances in which the procedure described above can be applied to projects in such areas. It must be applied on a fairly detailed breakdown of labor inputs by types. An overall reduction of the labor cost component will not do since many projects will require skilled labor to be brought into the area, where local supplies are deficient, and their impact on employment of local unskilled labor may be minimal.

A good hard look at the technological requirements for the construction of the project and substitution possibilities should be taken. If the opportunity cost of unskilled labor is zero, it doesn't pay to use labor-saving techniques. However, as long as the contractor for the project must pay positive wages, the bidding system in vogue in most places will in fact encourage him to substitute capital for labor in order to minimize his costs and secure the contract. Bid evaluation and contract specification should take this factor into account. One solution would be to require contractors to bid on all aspects of the job other than the supply of local labor, the latter to be supplied free of charge to him in quantities limited only by the local supply, while the labor force is placed directly on the government payroll, or else paid by the contractor who is reimbursed without limit. While this procedure seems wasteful it is actually more efficient, in terms of real cost to the rest of the economy, than the conventional procedure which diverts scarce capital to the area to save redundant labor. It is assumed here that the inhabitants are to be provided with an income in one way or another.

PROBLEMS

1. The Economic Planning Department of Sarkhan is considering a proposal to build an 80-mile road from a provincial capital to a village which has hitherto only been accessible by river boat. The road will cost $2.4 million, annual maintenance charges will be approximately $100,000. The estimated cost of capital is 10 percent. The analysis sug-

gests that the following effects are likely to result from completion of the road:

(a) A saving of $50,000 per year on the cost of shipping agricultural produce from the village and its surrounding area.

(b) The opening up to development of an additional 50,000 acres of land. Development will cost $300 per acre, and produce, after 5 years, crops worth $100 per acre per year. The land will be settled by smallholders, who will move from other employment where their earnings average $150 per year. An estimated 8000 smallholdings will be provided. Land clearing and drainage costs will be borne by the government, and each settler will recieve a grant of $500 to assist him in meeting relocation costs. Prior to the time the main crop becomes established, catch crops yielding $20 per acre per year can be grown.

(c) The value of land on the present developed agricultural areas is expected to increase by $500,000, while the land in the new development will be worth $38 million, an increase of $30 million from its value as timber land.

(d) Tax revenue from the area will be increased by $100,000 per year.

(e) Value of timber output will be increased by $2 million in the first year, while land is being cleared, but will be reduced by $400,000 per year after clearing has taken place.

(f) The income of boat operators on the river will be reduced by $50,000 per year. Boats costing $300,000 and scheduled for replacement in 5 years will not be replaced, and the labor displaced will be absorbed elsewhere at equivalent wages.

Which of the effects listed above should be taken into account in the benefit cost analysis? Should the road be built?

2. A hydroelectric dam in an underdeveloped country will cost $50 million, of which $35 million will be for local materials and labor and $15 million for imported equipment. Estimated annual benefits are $4.5 million, for at least 75 years.

(a) If the opportunity cost of capital is 10 percent in the local economy, should the dam be built with public funds?

(b) If the imported equipment can be paid for with a 30 year 4 percent loan from an international agency, repayable in local currency, should this alter the decision. Why?

3. What variables would you take into account in an analysis of the desirability of expanding the state college system in your state?

CHAPTER 9

The Capital Rationing Problem

9.1 Origins of the Problem

Capital rationing situations in the firm arise when the firm must operate within a fixed budget, rather than accepting all projects which increase the present value of the firm according to the decision rules outlined in Sec. 3.9. They also occur in the public sector, when an over-all constraint is imposed on the size of the budget, so that it is not possible to accommodate all projects showing an excess of social benefits over costs.

Within the private sector, the constraints which lead to a decision to hold capital expenditures to a fixed sum may arise due to market conditions, or may be entirely self-imposed. Market constraints may be effective because, while the long-run supply curve of capital to the firm may be perfectly elastic, the short- or intermediate-run curve will ordinarily slope upward. Beyond limits, it may become perfectly inelastic. The rising supply price is probably the result of market imperfections and the information lag discussed in Chapter 6, but is none the less real for a firm which is attempting to add assets at a rate faster than the market is capitalizing its earnings prospects. A firm is this position could, presumably, finance temporarily with some of the more expensive forms of short-term debt, replacing this source with lower-cost permanent funds once the market capitalizes the augmented earning power. There is a limit to the profitability of this type of financing, and it is not without risk for any firm. It is particularly dangerous for a firm which expects to maintain a high rate of asset growth for the indefinite future, since it is likely to find itself in a situation in which it is forced to depend almost continuously on such treacherous sources of funds. Many firms in this type of growth situation are apt to restrict budgets to the amount they believe they can raise from "reasonably priced" sources, which do not lead to "excessive" leverage and resulting high levels of risk. For such firms, there is an "optimum" capital structure, not dependent on the cost of capital situation but determined by the maximum probability of default on debt which is acceptable to management or stockholders.

A somewhat less defensible capital rationing policy is one imposed by a decision to restrict investment to the funds available from depreciation accruals plus current earnings less dividends, i.e., to "cash flow" generated from operations. Such a policy may reflect extreme risk aversion on the part of the management. If so, it overlooks the possibility of financing greater expansion with equity raised by way of a rights offering, or the judicious use of long term debt, and/or convertible senior issues. It is more likely that such a policy originates from a combination of risk aversion with a concern for retaining control on the part of an insider group who, for reasons of their own, do not wish to increase their own investment. They may have more profitable opportunities elsewhere. Whatever the reason, they may be quite willing to sacrifice not only their own extra profits from the firm, but those of other stockholders, in order to retain control.

Capital rationing may, of course, be adopted as a temporary measure in any given year if a firm is normally able to handle all profitable projects from internal sources, expects to do so in the future, and wishes to maintain the dividend rate by postponing a few projects until next year. There is certainly a prima facie case for borrowing under these conditions, however. If investment opportunities are so limited, one might wish to scrutinize management's research and development activities and their ability to generate profitable projects in general.

The need for capital rationing may also arise where there is no effective funds constraint, but where the rate of growth must be restrained because of managerial "indigestion," or shortages of skilled personnel or critical materials. While this type of bottleneck problem can be handled by imposing an overall expenditure constraint, this will ordinarily prove to be an inefficient way to do so. The inputs of scarce materials and talents will not, ordinarily, be proportional to project cost. Some projects, such as electronic data processing systems, may find their primary justification in the way in which they enable the firm to economize on scarce managerial talents. Problems of this type, particularly those in which there is more than one scarce factor, are most satisfactorily handled by the use of linear programming models of the type to be discussed in Sec. 9.9.

Governments may wish to impose a limit on the size of their budget for reasons similar to those used by private firms. They may have manpower constraints or be faced with debt limits, imposed either by the market or by constitutional requirements. Central governments, with control over the money supply, will seldom face market imposed constraints, because they can create all the credit they need or want. They may wish to constrain expenditures for fiscal policy reasons, however, to reduce inflationary pressures or to improve the balance of payments. In developing countries there may be a need to consider foreign exchange requirements explicitly, along with other scarce factors such as managerial skills, in a linear programming budget model.

9.2 The Single Period Case-Ranking Problems

The simplest capital rationing situation, which we will examine in this section and the next, is one in which the expenditure constraint lasts for a single period only. It is necessary to study this case to indicate some of the properties of the solution of the more general case. This case is of practical as well as theoretical interest, however, because many (if not most) firms do not have sufficient knowledge of their future investment opportunities to apply the more sophisticated models to be discussed later in this chapter.

The easiest way of selecting projects, assuming they are of similar risk, for inclusion in a limited budget is to rank them in descending order of attractiveness, then to accept projects from the top of the list and work down until the funds are exhausted. Mutually exclusive projects are handled by breaking into a basic project and supplementary projects, in the manner illustrated in Sec. 4.7.

However, as we saw in Chapter 3, there are a number of ways of ranking projects, and these do not always give the same results. Consider, for example, a firm which seeks to select a set of projects costing no more than $500,000 from among the opportunities listed in Table 9.1. Note that project C is a multiple rate of return project, having a benefit-cost ratio below 1.0 (negative net benefits) at rates of discount below 11 percent or above 16 percent, but a ratio above 1.0 at discount rates in between these values.

Suppose that the firm's cost of capital, calculated according to the criteria established in Chapter 6, is 10 percent. If it ranks projects in order of benefit-cost ratios calculated at 10 percent (or, since costs of all projects in the example are equal, in order of the present value of net benefits) it will select projects in the following order:

TABLE 9–1

	Cost	*Benefit-Cost Ratio When Discounted At*						*Internal rate of return*
		20%	18%	16%	14%	12%	10%	
A . .	100,000	0.9	1.0	1.1	1.3	1.5	1.7	18%
B . .	100,000	1.0	1.1	1.2	1.3	1.4	1.5	20%
C. . .	100,000	0.8	0.9	1.0	1.1	1.1	0.9	11%, 16%
D . .	100,000	0.8	0.9	1.0	1.1	1.2	1.3	16%
E . .	100,000	0.5	0.7	0.9	1.0	1.1	1.2	14%
F . .	100,000	0.1	0.2	0.5	0.7	1.0	1.4	12%
G . .	100,000	0.3	0.5	0.7	0.9	1.1	1.2	13%

TABLE 9–2
SELECTION USING BENEFIT-COST RATIOS (10%)

Project	Benefit-cost ratio
A	1.7
B	1.5
F	1.4
D	1.3
E or G	1.2

If, on the other hand, it selects in order of descending internal rates of return, it will select in the following order

TABLE 9–3
SELECTION USING INTERNAL RATE OF RETURN

Project	Internal rate of return
B	20%
A	18%
C and D	16%
E	14%

Differences in the ranking, and in the set of projects selected, are obvious. Using the internal rate of return criterion leads to the adoption of project *C*, which was not only rejected on the basis of benefit-cost ratio rankings, but would be rejected if the firm adopted a profit maximizing strategy and carried investment to the point where the marginal rate of return was equal to the cost of capital, since it would be removed when the discount rate fell below 11 percent. When we have a constraint, however, we have an implicit opportunity cost of funds, which is associated with the constraint. The implicit opportunity cost is equal to the rate of return on the best project *excluded* from the final budget, i.e., the return which can be earned on funds in their best alternative use. In nearly all cases this will be higher than the firm's cost of capital calculated in the usual way. In this case, it is 13 percent, the rate of return on project G. Using the internal rate criterion for ranking is equivalent to selecting projects on the basis of their benefit-cost ratios, calculated at the opportunity cost rate, rather than on the regular cost of capital basis. In the example we have used, project C has a benefit-cost ratio in excess of 1.0 at the opportunity cost rate of 13 percent and is therefore in the adopted budget.

If we select projects initially on the basis of benefit-cost ratios (Table 9-2), we must recognize that there is an opportunity cost here also. Depending on whether we reject G or E, which have identical benefit-cost ratio rankings, the implicit opportunity cost is either 13 percent or 14 percent. If we recalculate benefit-cost ratios at the former rate, we get the ranking shown in Table 9-4.

TABLE 9-4
SELECTION USING BENEFIT-COST RATIOS (13%)

Project	Benefit-cost ratio
A	1.40
B	1.35
D	1.15
C	1.10+
E	1.05

Project F, included in the initial selection, has been deleted because its benefit-cost ratio falls below 1.0 when discounted at 13 percent, while project C has been included. Although differences in ranking remain, the list of adopted projects is identical to that derived by ranking the projects by internal rates of return.

The changes in benefit-cost ratio ranking, as discount rates change, reflect crossing present value profiles in the case of "normal" investment projects (see Fig. 3-4) and the presence of a multiple rate project. (As a useful exercise, sketch the present value profiles of projects in Table 9-1.) These, of course, occur because of different time-shapes in the income streams of different projects. For "normal" projects, characterized by an initial outlay of funds followed by an inflow, one project (such as A) will have a higher benefit-cost ratio than another (such as B) at high discount rates and a lower ratio at low discount rates only if it has a relatively higher cash flow in earlier periods and lower cash flow in later periods. The most frequent type of multiple rate-of-return project is the income-acceleration project, which may not increase overall cash flow from a project at all but which results in it being earned more quickly. It is clear that using the higher rate biases the selection in favor of projects which produce a relatively greater immediate cash flow.

In the case where the budget constraint is temporary and market imposed, this is a desirable type of alteration in the adopted project set. It produces cash more rapidly, thus directly reducing the impact of any constraint in future periods. Because the resulting higher earnings[1] will be capitalized, and the higher apparent growth rate may have a favorable effect on investor expectations, the intermediate run funds supply schedule may shift more to the right, further easing the constraint and hastening the day when it will cease to be binding.

Even in cases where the budget constraint is not due to market factors but is self-imposed, so that the "opportunity cost" is merely a measure of self-imposed loss, its use will lead to a more rapid expansion in cash flow. In cases where the constraint is tied to reported earnings, their more rapid growth will diminish the impact of the constraint in subsequent periods. This is, we feel, a strong argument for ranking projects in order of descending rates of return in many capital rationing situations, allocating funds from the top of the list until exhausted. In the case of multiple rate of return projects, the listing should indicate not only the rates at which such projects enter the budget but the rates at which they should be deleted from it. Table 9-5 gives such a ranking for the projects listed in Table 9-1.

TABLE 9–5
SCHEDULE FOR PROJECT ADOPTION

If budget is:	Implicit opportunity cost is:	Projects added:	Projects deleted:	Projects in budget
100,000	20%	B	—	B
200,000	18	A	—	B, A
400,000	16	C, D	—	B, A, C, D
500,000	14	E	—	B, A, C, D, E
600,000	13	G	—	B, A, C, D, E, G
700,000	12	F	—	B, A, C, D, E, F, G
600,000	11	—	C	B, A, D, E, F, G

One difficulty with this approach is apparent from inspection of the table. There are two budgets which just exhaust an allocation of

---

[1] Perhaps exaggerated in impact by the conventions of depreciation accounting.

$600,000. This is a direct result of the multiple return project C, and similar results will emerge whenever there are not enough other projects which enter the budget at a rate at which a multiple return project leaves it. In actual practice such problems may not occur frequently since we would expect to find opportunities increasing in number and amount as we reach lower rates of return—it is, after all, only high return projects which are scarce. What should be done when it does occur and coincides with the budget constraint is less certain. Following the reasoning above, we would be inclined to work down the table until the constraint was encountered for the first time, but only if the constraint was completely inflexible. Such a situation should call for a careful reappraisal of the projects and, more important, of financing alternatives which may have been neglected in setting the constraint. Adoption of project C in this context is in a sense equivalent to borrowing at 11 percent to finance some of the projects, and if alternative financing is available below this rate, serious consideration should be given to changing the constraint.

9.3   The Single Period Case: Minimizing the Cost of the Constraint

The procedure outlined above does not maximize the present value, at the company's cost of capital, added to the firm as a result of this year's budget and has been criticized by some authors because it does not.[2] It is recommended here because it leads, through time, to a more rapidly growing cash flow and the relaxing of the constraint.

One alternative to this procedure, which maximizes the present value added by this year's budget, is simply to rank in order of descending benefit-cost ratios. To some extent this is an unsatisfactory solution, arising from considering the problem in a one-period setting. Many projects could be postponed until next year, for example, and postponing those with the lowest benefit-cost ratios may not be the most satisfactory way of resolving the problem.

We prefer to regard the acceptance of all projects having benefit-cost ratios in excess of 1.0 as the ideal which would be attained in the absence of the constraint, and to select for postponement those projects which cause the smallest possible reduction (in present value added) from this profit maximizing ideal.

---

[2]E.g., J. H. Lorie and L. J. Savage, "Three Problems in Rationing Capital," *Journal of Business*, Vol. 28 (October, 1955), pp. 229-39, reprinted in E. Solomon (ed.), *The Management of Corporate Capital* (Glencoe: The Free Press, 1959), pp. 56-66.

Projects to be postponed, using this criterion, need not be those at the bottom of the list. Although these contribute the least to the long run profitability, they may not be the most postponable. The profitability of some projects as measured by internal rates of return may be unaffected by postponement; some, such as projects to cash in on volatile fashions, may be entirely dissipated; others, such as replacement of machine tools, will ordinarily be enhanced.

If the profit maximizing budget exceeds the maximum attainable supply of funds, the implicit opportunity cost of the constraint should be evaluated as the internal rate of return of the best extra-marginal project. Next, the list of available but rejected projects should be combed for income-acceleration projects having multiple rates of return which will be profitable at this opportunity cost rate. These should be added to the budget to help increase the supply of funds in subsequent periods.

Next, an index of postponability should be constructed by comparing the net present value of each project in the original maximizing budget, on the assumption that it is constructed next year, with its value as constructed this year, evaluated at the cost of capital rate. Subtracting next year's value from this year's value gives a measure of the reduction in present value which will result from postponement of the project. This may be divided by the funds the project would require to obtain an index of present value of losses,[3] resulting from postponement, per dollar of funds freed by postponement. The projects may then be ranked in descending order, using this index, and projects selected for postponement by working from the top down until the budget has been reduced by a sufficient amount.

Where the benefit-cost ratios of projects are not sensitive to the timing of their adoption, this procedure will (except for the inclusion of multiple rate projects) give the same result as ranking by means of benefit-cost ratios. It does introduce another element into the calculation, however, in the presence of such sensitivity and operates to minimize the reduction in present worth from its maximum level which is necessary to meet the budget constraint.

Example

Suppose we have the group of projects listed in Table 9-6, and a budget constraint of $500,000.

---

[3] Some may be gains.

TABLE 9–6

Project	Initial cost $000	Benefit-cost ratio	Internal rate of return, %	P.V. now of net benefits if done This year	Next year
A 100		1.7	18%	100	91
B 100		1.5	20	90	87
C. 100		0.9	16, 11	−10	−9
D 100		1.3	16	75	60
E 100		1.2	14	30	26
F 100		1.4	12	50	55
G 100		1.2	13	30	10

We start off by ranking the projects in terms of their benefit-cost ratios. This gives us the following ranking:

	Benefit-cost ratio	Net P.V. this year
A 1.7		100
B 1.5		90
F 1.4		50
D 1.3		75
E 1.2		30
G 1.2		30
C. 0.9		−10

Taking the first five, we have a budget tentatively consisting of projects A, B, F, D, E. The internal rate of return on the marginal excluded project, G, is 13 percent. Since the dual rate project C has a positive present value at the 13 percent opportunity cost rate, we adopt it to ease the budget constraint next year.

We next proceed to calculate the losses resulting from postponement for the projects (excluding C which we have decided to adopt anyway). These are as follows:

	(a) P.V. this year	(b) P.V. next year	Loss by delay (a)−(b)÷cost
A 100		91	0.09
B 90		87	0.03
D 75		60	0.15
E 30		26	0.04
F 50		55	−0.05
G 30		10	0.20

Some of the projects don't change much as a result of postponement, merely showing a loss reflecting the one-year deferral of the income; some show less loss than this amount, while F shows a gain. Presumably it is a project which is just becoming profitable this year. G on the other hand shows a substantial loss as the result of deferral. In order to bring our budget down within the constraint, we must delete projects F and B, which leaves us with a budget consisting of A, C, D, E, and G as the final budget.

To see why this is preferable to the initially selected group, compare the present value of the latter, with G delayed till next year:

	Initial selection	Final selection
A	100	100
B	90	87*
C.	–	– 10
D	75	75
E	30	30
F	50	55
G	10*	30
	355	367

*Delayed a year

Next year, of course, the projects which have been deferred from this year's budget must compete with the other projects for the available funds. If other projects are better, they may be postponed for another year; they may in fact never be accepted, depending on what other opportunities become available. If we don't know what will be available next year, this is a rational method of making the allocations on a year-by-year basis.

Setting a fixed budget constraint is a poor way of approaching the capital budgeting problem. Even where it is forced on the firm by market conditions, it is apt to be rather an elastic barrier, which can be pushed back to some extent by squeezing funds out of working capital, either by reducing current asset accounts or by increasing current liabilities. Alternative forms of financing should be carefully examined; some assets may be leased and term loans may finance the acquisition of others. There are limits to all of these, but they are seldom rigid limits, and the firm which appears to have a capital rationing situation on its hands should explore carefully any avenues open to it which will make it possible to adopt as large a proportion of the projects which are acceptable out of the unconstrained profit maximizing budget.

The one-period constraint is in many cases unduly artificial. Some large projects take several years to complete, and expenditures may be rescheduled within wide limits between various years' budgets. In resolving the problem in a one year setting, we introduced implicit assumptions concerning future opportunities and constraints. To get away from these artificial restrictions it is possible to consider several periods at once using some of the more sophisticated models to be examined in the next section.

9.4 The Use of Linear Programming Models in the Capital Rationing Case

An interesting approach to the solution of a multiperiod capital rationing problem is that developed by Martin Weingartner.[4] This treats the problem as one in linear programming. In this section we shall examine the Weingartner model and certain extensions of it which may provide for greater realism.

The model seeks to maximize the present value, as of the current date, of the excess of present values over costs resulting from the adoption of a particular budget. This is expressed in the objective function which is to

$$\text{Maximize } B = \sum_j X_j b_j \tag{1}$$

where X_j is the fraction of the jth project undertaken and b_j is its net present value ($V - C$ in our earlier terminology) when discounted at the cost of capital (market capitalization rate).

Each project is expected to involve cash outlays having present values C_{jt} in one or more of the periods t under consideration. These are regarded as fixed and not subject to alteration, i.e., by rescheduling the project. There are fixed budget constraints C_t, the present value today of the actual constraint in the tth period. This gives us a set of budget constraint inequalities

$$\sum_j X_j C_{jt} \leq C_t \tag{2}$$

one for each period being considered.

---

[4]H. M. Weingartner, *Mathematical Programming and the Analysis of Capital Budgeting Problems* (Englewood Cliffs, N. J.: Prentice-Hall, 1963).

It is impossible to construct a negative project, or to construct it more than once, so we have a third set of constraints:

$$0 \leq X_j \leq 1 \tag{3}$$

This is the basic model. While we shall consider an example, we cannot devote space here to the basic theory of linear programming, computation of solutions, or geometric illustrations of simple cases, and the reader must be referred elsewhere.[5]

9.5   The Basic Model Applied

As an example, suppose we have the projects listed in Table 9-6. The cost of capital is 10 percent. Projects 1-7 correspond to projects

TABLE 9-6
PROJECTS AVAILABLE FOR 3-PERIOD CAPITAL BUDGETING PROBLEM

Project j	b_j	Present values of benefits and costs in $000				
		c_{j1}	c_{j2}	c_{j3}	Y_{j2}	Y_{j3}
1	70	100	0	0	20	20
2	50	100	0	0	30	25
3	−10	100	0	0	60	60
4	30	100	0	0	10	8
5	20	100	0	0	6	4
6	40	100	0	0	8	9
7	20	60	36	0	3	5
8	64	0	91	0	0	18
9	45	0	91	0	0	27
10	−9	0	91	0	0	54
11	27	0	91	0	0	9
12	18	0	91	0	0	5
13	36	0	91	0	0	9
14	18	0	54	33	0	2
15	158	0	0	183	0	0
16	141	0	0	183	0	0
17	25	0	0	83	0	0
18	18	0	0	83	0	0
19	15	0	0	83	0	0
20	14	0	0	83	0	0

$$C_1 = 380$$
$$C_2 = 345$$
$$C_3 = 314$$

---

[5]There are many references available which consider this matter in any desired degree of detail. Relatively simple, yet of interest here in that integer programming is considered, is the treatment by W. J. Baumol, *Economic Theory and Operations Analysis* (2nd ed.; Englewood Cliffs, N. J.: Prentice-Hall, 1965), Chaps. 5, 6, 8.

A-G in Table 9-1, while projects 8-14 are similar projects, deferred for one period. While they are similar, they are independent; adoption of project 1 does not preclude adoption of project 8. Projects 7 and 14 differ from *G* in that their expenditures are spread over two periods. Projects 15-20 are different projects which become available in the third period. The columns headed Y_{j2} and Y_{j3} may be ignored for the present example. Budget constraints are set at \$380,000 per period in this example, which is the amount of the earnings from other operations which will be left after paying the desired dividend. This constraint has present values of 380 and 345 and 314 for the respective periods.

Our problem, expressed in the linear programming format, is to maximize

$$B = 70X_1 + 50X_2 - 10X_3 + 30X_4 + 20X_5 + 40X_6 + 20X_7 + 64X_8 + 45X_9$$
$$- 9X_{10} + 27X_{11} + 18X_{12} + 36X_{13} + 18X_{14} + 158X_{15} + 141X_{16} + 25X_{17}$$
$$+ 18X_{18} + 15X_{19} + 14X_{20}$$

Subject to:

$$100X_1 + 100X_2 + 100X_3 + 100X_4 + 100X_5 + 100X_6 + 60X_7 \leq 380$$
$$36X_7 + 91X_8 + 91X_9 + 91X_{10} + 91X_{11} + 91X_{12} + 91X_{13} + 54X_{14} \leq 345 \qquad \text{(2a)}$$
$$33X_{14} + 183X_{15} + 183X_{16} + 83X_{17} + 83X_{18} + 83X_{19} + 83X_{20} \leq 314$$

and

$$0 \leq X_j \leq 1.0 \qquad \text{for } X_j = 1, 2, \ldots, 20 \qquad \text{(3a)}$$

The optimum solution for this problem is given by the following values of *X*'s:

$X_1 = 1.0$	$X_6 = 1.0$	$X_{11} = 0.791$	$X_{16} = 0.716$
$X_2 = 1.0$	$X_7 = 0$	$X_{12} = 0$	$X_{17} = 0$
$X_3 = 0$	$X_8 = 1.0$	$X_{13} = 1.0$	$X_{18} = 0$
$X_4 = 0.800$	$X_9 = 1.0$	$X_{14} = 0$	$X_{19} = 0$
$X_5 = 0$	$X_{10} = 0$	$X_{15} = 1.0$	$X_{20} = 0$

Added present value totals \$609,297.

There are fractional values of several variables in the solution. There will be only one fractional project per period in any solution. These can be interpreted as directions to try a smaller version of the same project or can be eliminated entirely by imposing a condition that the X's be in integers using one of the available techniques for integer programming.[6] A simple alternative would be to adjust the budget constraint to take the entire project into the budget.

Most of the projects in this example require expenditures in a single period only. This is only an accident of its construction; it is quite capable of dealing with projects requiring expenditures in every period.[7]

If we compare the projects selected for the first period's budget, we find that they agree with the results which would be obtained by ranking in order of benefit-cost ratios. This is hardly surprising since the b_j's are net present values. The method is, in fact, the equivalent of benefit-cost ratio ranking taking into account interperiod relationships (most of which have been suppressed in this example by the choice of data in order to bring the equivalence out more clearly).

9.6   Dual Variables in the Basic Model

Any linear programming problem has a dual problem which is closely related to it. The original problem may be referred to as the "primal" problem, and if the primal problem has a solution, so does the dual.

The dual of the capital rationing problem may be written:

$$\text{Minimize} \qquad \sum_t P_t C_t + \sum_j U_j \tag{4}$$

$$\text{subject to} \qquad \sum_t P_t C_{jt} + U_j \geq b_j \tag{5}$$

$$\text{and} \qquad P_t \geq 0 \qquad t = 1, 2 \dots T \tag{6}$$

$$\qquad\qquad\qquad U_j \geq 0 \qquad j = 1, 2 \dots n \tag{7}$$

P_t and U_j are new variables, called "dual variables," and the definition of the other variables remains unchanged. We may write the dual problem corresponding to the problem in our example as follows:

$$\text{Minimize} \qquad 380P_1 + 345P_2 + 314P_3 + \sum_{j=1}^{20} U_j \tag{4a}$$

---

[6]Cf. Weingartner, *op. cit.*, pp. 19-24, 57-112.
[7]Cf. Weingartner, *op. cit.*, pp. 17-18, for such an example.

Subject to

$$
\begin{array}{llll}
100P_1 & & +U_1 & \geq 70 \\
100P_1 & & +U_2 & \geq 50 \\
100P_1 & & +U_3 & \geq -10 \\
100P_1 & & +U_4 & \geq 30 \\
100P_1 & & +U_5 & \geq 20 \\
100P_1 & & +U_6 & \geq 40 \\
60P_1+ 36P_2 & & +U_7 & \geq 20 \\
91P_2 & & +U_8 & \geq 64 \\
91P_2 & & +U_9 & \geq 45 \\
91P_2 & & +U_{10} & \geq -9 \\
91P_2 & & +U_{11} & \geq 27 \\
91P_2 & & +U_{12} & \geq 18 \\
91P_2 & & +U_{13} & \geq 36 \\
54P_2+ 33P_3 & & +U_{14} & \geq 18 \\
183P_3 & & +U_{15} & \geq 158 \\
183P_3 & & +U_{16} & \geq 141 \\
83P_3 & & +U_{17} & \geq 25 \\
83P_3 & & +U_{18} & \geq 18 \\
83P_3 & & +U_{19} & \geq 15 \\
83P_3 & & +U_{20} & \geq 14 \\
\end{array}
$$

(5a)

$$P_t, \ U_j \geq 0$$

The values of the dual variables for the optimal solution to this problem are as follows:

$P_1 = 0.300$		$P_2 = 0.297$		$P_3 = 0.770$
$U_1 = 40.0$	$U_6 = 10.0$	$U_{11} = 0$	$U_{16} = 0$	
$U_2 = 20.0$	$U_7 = 0$	$U_{12} = 0$	$U_{17} = 0$	
$U_3 = 0$	$U_8 = 37.0$	$U_{13} = 9.0$	$U_{18} = 0$	
$U_4 = 0$	$U_9 = 18.0$	$U_{14} = 17.0$	$U_{19} = 0$	
$U_5 = 0$	$U_{10} = 0$	$U_{15} = 0$	$U_{20} = 0$	

These dual variables have several properties, which follow from the duality theorem in linear programming.

(1) Each is associated with a particular constraint in the primal problem. The P_t are associated with the C_t and the U_j with the X_j.
(2) The dual variables have nonzero values if, and only if, the corresponding constraint in the primal problem is binding, i.e., fulfilled as an equality, and have zero values otherwise.

Dual variables have a well-established economic interpretation as marginal productivities, opportunity costs, or "shadow prices." This interpretation can be extended to this problem. The P_t obtained in the dual solution are the opportunity costs associated with the budget constraints and are the amount by which present value could be increased if a given constraint were relaxed to permit the investment of an additional dollar in that period.[8] They are, of course, related to the marginal productivity of the project which is fractionally adopted in that period. As noted earlier, it is a condition of the model that only one project is fractionally adopted in each period.

The U_j are associated with the constraints on the X_j, specifically, with the requirement that $X_j = 1$, and are a measure of the marginal productivity of each project.

From (5) we derive

$$U_j \geq b_j - \sum_j P_t C_{tj} \tag{8}$$

For projects which are adopted, giving us the optimal values of U_j and P_t, U_j is a measure of the amount by which the net present value of the jth project exceeds the sum of the products of the outlays on it times the opportunity cost associated with outlays in the respective period.

The dual variables may be useful as evaluators in making adjustments in the budget. If P_2 exceeds P_1 by a substantial margin, it may pay to shift funds from period 1 to period 2 by not utilizing them fully in the first period. This procedure is not permissible in the model as outlined above but is incorporated in one of Weingartner's variants on the original model, which we shall examine below. On the other hand, if P_1 exceeds P_2, the firm may wish to reconsider its constraints and borrow in period 1, thus increasing C_1, for repayment in period 2, thus reducing C_2. Further, the firm may wish to examine projects with high U_j values with a view to increasing their scale. (This is relatively insignificant; these projects have the highest benefit-cost ratios and this factor alone should have led to a reevaluation without reference to U_j.)

This is the basic model. Its weaknesses are obvious, but many of these can be overcome by sufficiently ingenious adaptation.

---

[8] As such they are more akin to benefit-cost ratios (on a net basis) than to interest rates, contrary to Weingartner's assertion, *op. cit.*, p. 26.

9.7　Handling Mutually Exclusive Opportunities in the Basic Model

This may be done in two ways. One is by using the fictitious project approach which was outlined earlier, i.e., if projects 6 and 8 are mutually exclusive, we may replace project 8 by project 8* which has the following characteristics.

$$
\begin{aligned}
b_{8^*} &= 64 \\
C_{18^*} &= -100 \\
C_{28^*} &= 91 \\
C_{38^*} &= 0 \\
Y_{28^*} &= -8 \\
Y_{38^*} &= 9
\end{aligned}
$$

Substitution of the appropriate values in equations (1a) and (2a) will give the desired solution. Alternatively, it is possible to leave (1a) and (2a) unchanged, but replace

$$
\begin{aligned}
& 0 \le X_6 \le 1 \\
& 0 \le X_8 \le 1 \\
\text{with} \quad & X_6 + X_8 \le 1 \\
& X_6 \ge 0 \\
& X_8 \ge 0
\end{aligned}
$$

in the constraint set (3a). This ensures that only one project will be adopted. This can be generalized to any set J of mutually exclusive alternatives by using

$$
\sum_{j \varepsilon J} X_j \le 1
$$

and retaining the nonnegativity conditions.

The only problem that may arise is that the solution may suggest the adoption of fractions of two or more mutually exclusive projects. This is in fact useful as it may suggest an alternative, midway in capital intensity between several projects, which is preferable to any.

9.8　Handling Externalities with the Basic Model

If a project has one value contingent on the adoption of another project, and a lower value if the other is not adopted, we can handle this by setting up two projects m_1 and m_2, which can be treated as mutually exclusive, as before. If m_1 is the higher value contingent on the adoption of project n, we can add a further constraint

$$X_{m1} \leq X_n$$

which will ensure that it is not adopted unless n is also adopted.[9] Similar formulations can be developed for other types of interrelationship between projects.

9.9 Incorporation of Other Bottlenecks into the Basic Model

One type of model incorporating manpower constraints where it was desired to treat certain types of labor as free goods is discussed in Chapter 8. This model is intended for use in the evaluation of labor-absorbing projects in the public sector. Within the private sector, the problem is somewhat different. Labor costs are a cost to the firm, so must be included in the costs of the project, and any financial constraints may still apply (they need not—there are no financial constraints in the problem in Chapter 8). What is needed is an additional constraint or constraints to handle the limitations of scarce labor of a given type.

For this purpose we can use the same basic model developed in Sec. 9.4, for which Equations (1)-(3) still apply, adding to it an additional set of constraints of the form

$$\sum_j X_j d_{jt} \leq L_t \tag{9}$$

where d_{jt} is the number of man hours of input required for project j in period t and where L_t is the number of such hours available in the period.

The dual of this problem becomes

$$\text{minimize} \quad \sum_t P_t C_t + \sum_t w_t L_t + \sum_j U_j \tag{10}$$

$$\text{subject to} \quad \sum_t P_t C_{jt} + \sum_t w_t d_{jt} + U_j \geq b_j \tag{11}$$

$$P_t, \ w_t, \ U_j \geq 0$$

---

[9] For further discussion see Weingartner, *op. cit.*, pp. 39-44.

The new dual variable, w_t, is a shadow price reflecting the marginal productivity of the type of labor subject to constraint in the period in question, expressed as the addition to output resulting from the addition of an hour of the labor input. The w_t may be used to evaluate the desirability of adding to the labor force. Additions may not be possible in the short run, as training or seasoning may be needed before the addition becomes effective, but the multiperiod structure of the model enables future requirements to be evaluated against training costs. Material bottlenecks may be handled in a similar manner.

9.10 Shifting Funds between Periods

The model developed so far has assumed that funds cannot be carried over from one period to the next. This is a rather artificial restriction which we are better off without, and we can eliminate it by altering the budget constraints in a simple fashion. The objective function remains unchanged, but the constraints become

$$\sum_j \sum_{t=1}^{n} X_j c_{jt} \leq \sum_{t=1}^{n} C_t \tag{2b}$$

Because the c_{jt} are on a present value basis, this formulation implicitly assumes that funds carried over can be invested until needed at the cost of capital rate.

To alter our example to permit shifting funds between periods we form the new constraints

$100X_1 + 100X_2 + 100X_3 + 100X_4 + 100X_5 + 100X_6 + 60X_7 \leq 380$

$100X_1 + 100X_2 + 100X_3 + 100X_4 + 100X_5 + 100X_6 + 96X_7 + 91X_8 + 91X_9 + 91X_{10}$
$\quad + 91X_{11} + 91X_{12} + 91X_{13} + 54X_{14} \leq 725 \tag{2c}$

$100X_1 + 100X_2 + 100X_3 + 100X_4 + 100X_5 + 100X_6 + 96X_7 + 91X_8 + 91X_9 + 91X_{10}$
$\quad + 91X_{11} + 91X_{12} + 91X_{13} + 87X_{14} + 183X_{15} + 183X_{16} + 183X_{17} + 83X_{18}$
$\quad + 83X_{19} + 83X_{20} \leq 1039$

Using these revised constraints gives us the new optimum solution:

$X_1 = 1.0$	$X_6 = 1.0$	$X_{11} = 0$	$X_{16} = 1.0$
$X_2 = 1.0$	$X_7 = 0$	$X_{12} = 0$	$X_{17} = 1.0$
$X_3 = 0$	$X_8 = 1.0$	$X_{13} = 1.0$	$X_{18} = 0$
$X_4 = 0.17$	$X_9 = 1.0$	$X_{14} = 0$	$X_{19} = 0$
$X_5 = 0$	$X_{10} = 0$	$X_{15} = 1.0$	$X_{20} = 0$

Added present value in this case totals $634,100.

Using this version of the model, funds will not be shifted from period 1 to period 2 to ease the period 2 constraint unless there is a project in period 2 which would have been rejected using the simple constraint which represents a more productive use of funds than one of the projects adopted in the earlier period. Here, funds are shifted into period 3 to complete projects 16 and 17.

9.11 Shifting Projects between Periods

Another artificial feature of the model is that the timing of expenditures appears to be fixed. However, this is really not the case since all conceivable schedules for the construction of a project can be shown as separate but mutually exclusive projects. Thus provision for shifting project 1 between periods 1 and 2 can be made by considering the following projects:

TABLE 9–7
SHIFTING PROJECTS BETWEEN PERIODS

j	b_j	C_{j1}	C_{j2}	C_{j3}	Y_{j2}	Y_{j3}
1 70		100	0	0	20	20
21 . . . . . 69.4		90	9	0	18	20
22 . . . . . 68.8		80	18	0	16	20
23 . . . . . 68.2		70	27	0	14	20
24 . . . . . 67.6		60	36	0	12	20
25 . . . . . 67.0		50	45	0	10	20
26 . . . . . 66.4		40	54	0	8	20
27 . . . . . 65.8		30	63	0	6	20
28 . . . . . 65.2		20	72	0	4	20
29 . . . . . 64.6		10	81	0	2	20
30 . . . . . 64.0		—	91	0	0	20

If these projects are included, as mutually exclusive alternatives, i.e., subject to

$$X_1 + \sum_{j=21}^{30} X_j \leq 1$$

the solution will tell within 10 percent how much of the project should be shifted from one period to the next. Similar sets of alternatives can be constructed for each project that can be rescheduled. While this process seems relatively cumbersome, a linear programming formulation requires the use of an electronic computer in any event, and the desired degree of budget flexibility can be considered at relatively little added cost.

Here again, the project will not be shifted unless doing so frees funds for more profitable employment. Allowing for such shifts, to the extent that construction schedules can be rearranged, is a way to minimize the difficulties resulting from solutions which direct the construction of fractional projects in the simpler model.

9.12 Considering Cash Generation within the Budget Period

As mentioned in Sec. 9.5, the model is the multiperiod equivalent of the benefit-cost ratio ranking discussed in Sec. 9.3, and ignores the possibility of reinvesting proceeds from earlier periods at rates of return in excess of the cost of capital. This being the case, it is not surprising that multiple rate of return projects were ignored. Cash throwoff can easily be incorporated into the analysis, however. The present values of the cash throwoff in periods 2 and 3 are shown in Table 9-6 as Y_{j2} and Y_{j3} respectively. Our objective function remains unchanged but we incorporate net cash outlays instead of capital expenditures into the budget constraints which take the form:

$$\sum_j X_j (C_{jt} - Y_{jt}) \leq C_t \qquad (2d)$$

Treating the constraints in this fashion, and continuing to permit funds to be carried forward, we replace (2c) with

$$100X_1 + 100X_2 + 100X_3 + 100X_4 + 100X_5 + 100X_6 + 60X_7 \leq 380$$
$$80X_1 + 70X_2 + 40X_3 + 90X_4 + 94X_5 + 92X_6 + 93X_7 + 91X_8 + 91X_9 + 91X_{10} + 91X_{11}$$
$$+ 91X_{12} + 91X_{13} + 54X_{14} \leq 725 \qquad (2e)$$
$$60X_1 + 45X_2 - 20X_3 + 82X_4 + 90X_5 + 83X_6 + 88X_7 + 73X_8 + 64X_9 + 37X_{10} + 82X_{11}$$
$$+ 86X_{12} + 84X_{13} + 85X_{14} + 183X_{15} + 183X_{16} + 83X_{17} + 83X_{18} + 83X_{19}$$
$$+ 83X_{20} \leq 1039$$

Our new optimum values are:

$X_1 = 1.0$	$X_6 = 1.0$	$X_{11} = 1.0$	$X_{16} = 1.0$
$X_2 = 1.0$	$X_7 = 0$	$X_{12} = 0$	$X_{17} = 1.0$
$X_3 = 0$	$X_8 = 1.0$	$X_{13} = 1.0$	$X_{18} = 0.4$
$X_4 = 0.8$	$X_9 = 1.0$	$X_{14} = 0$	$X_{19} = 0$
$X_5 = 0$	$X_{10} = 0$	$X_{15} = 1.0$	$X_{20} = 0$

Comparing this solution with the previous one, which permitted funds to be carried forward, it will be seen to have directed an increase in the investment in project 4 and to have added project 11 out of the funds flow from earlier projects.

9.13   Some Practical Difficulties in the Use of Multiperiod Models

In our discussion of linear programming models, we have only considered some of the simpler formulations possible. More complex models can be built which are not confined to the capital rationing case and which take into account various types of borrowing opportunities. These models permit simultaneous selection of optimal budgets and plans for financing them under conditions of certainty. While this problem is complex enough, it is still exceedingly simple in relation to the difficulties of operating in an uncertain world. Their use in practical situations to date has been limited; there is little doubt, however, that it will grow.

One of the chief obstacles to their use is that they require a complete specification of the available projects which will be available for consideration in future periods. While there are some industries, such as public utilities, where long run planning is sufficiently advanced to permit such specification, there are others for which it is simply not feasible. The projects to be considered next year and the year after may still lie a long way back in the research "pipeline," from which the form of their eventual emergence, let alone its timing, is virtually impossible to predict.

This need not be a fatal flaw, for rational behavior in the face of uncertainty merely requires that we make the best estimates possible and recalculate our strategies as more information comes to light.[10] If our expectations of the future are sufficiently well-formed and of such a nature that interperiod relationships are of sufficient importance that systematic incorporation into a comprehensive model seems necessary, then they should be used.

Casual interperiod relationships can be handled without resort to such models. If a firm is giving serious consideration to building a new plant in five years time, this should be taken into account in any decisions to spend money on improving facilities in the present

---

[10]R. Bellman, *Dynamic Programming* (Princeton: Princeton University Press, 1957), p. 83.

plant. "Urgency" criteria, such as those discussed in Sec. 9.3, can be used to select projects for postponement and otherwise adapt the single period model to cover many situations.

PROBLEMS

1. A company is considering the construction of a new plant which can be built in one year at a cost of $1,000,000. It can be completed in 6 months on a "crash program" basis at a cost of $1,100,000, or stretched out over two years at a total cost of $1,000,000. Benefits from the new plant are worth $1,800,000 if it is constructed in a year's time, at the company's 14 percent cost of capital. What items should appear
   (a) in the objective function
   (b) in the constraint set
of a linear programming model to reflect these alternatives?

2. Project 1 costs $100,000 and has a present value of $155,000 if completed this year, $165,000 if completed next year. Project 2 costs $20,000 and has a present value of $28,000 if completed this year, $31,000 if completed next year. Which project should be postponed if the firm is operating under capital rationing conditions?

3. Using the data in Table 9-6, construct a linear programming model which could be used to construct a capital budget on the assumption that
   (a) Projects 1 and 2 are mutually exclusive
   (b) Project 8 is dependent on the construction of project 4.
   (c) Budgets available are $300,000, $300,000, and $250,000 in the three periods, but funds can be carried forward from one period to another.
   (d) Projects 3, 4, 9, 10, 13 and 14 require scarce engineering services, to the extent of 3 man-years each. Only two men are available, but they can start work on a project prior to its construction.

CHAPTER 10

Risk and Uncertainty
in the Decision Process

10.1 Nature of the Problem

Risk exists because we are unable to make perfect forecasts. If we could, we would never make unprofitable decisions, could plan to meet all commitments with precision, and life would be very dull indeed. While handling risk in the decision process poses problems, conceptual and practical, it is here that the decision maker plays his vital role in society. In a static society there is no risk; bearing the risks associated with economic change is the basic social function undertaken by the entrepreneur, and in the views of a number of economists[1] profit is the reward for providing this service.

Economic theorists have attempted to distinguish between risk and uncertainty. The usual basis for such a distinction is whether the probability distribution of outcomes is known or unknown.[2] In our view, with one exception, such a distinction is obsolete or rapidly becoming so. It rests on a frequency concept of probability which has been subject to serious challenge.[3] Even when the frequency concept of probability is inadmissible, because of the uniqueness of the event, we usually have, or can develop by simulation techniques,[4] fairly valid ideas about the probability distribution of possible outcomes, and it

---

[1]F. H. Knight, *Risk, Uncertainty and Profit* (Boston: Houghton Mifflin, 1923); J. A. Schumpeter, *The Theory of Economic Development* (Cambridge: Harvard, 1934).

[2]Knight, *op. cit.* Alternatively, uncertainty can be regarded as the case where compounding of probabilities, i.e., the consideration of probability distributions of probability distributions is necessary. See A. G. Hart, "Risk, Uncertainty, and the Unprofitability of Compounding Probabilities" in *Studies in Mathematical Economics and Econometrics* (Chicago, 1942), pp. 110-18.

[3]F. P. Ramsay, *The Foundations of Mathematics* (London: Macmillan, 1931); L. J. Savage, *The Foundation of Statistics,* (New York: Wiley, 1954).

[4]H. A. Meyers, ed., *Symposium on Monte Carlo Methods* (New York: Wiley, 1956).

makes sense to utilize such information to the fullest extent possible in making decisions.

The exception arises where outcomes depend on the consciously chosen strategies of competitors, customers, or suppliers, where the number of participants in the market is small, and where the opponents' strategies will be chosen to maximize their anticipated utilities. A more elaborate theory of behavior is needed for such situations, and is provided by the theory of games.[5] Its application to capital budgeting will be examined briefly in the next chapter. We prefer to reserve the term uncertainty for this type of conflict situation and to speak of risk in the simpler situations where some kind of probability distribution, objective or subjective, can be generated.

Risk, as we have defined it, can be classified in a number of ways, depending for example on whether it is the result of vagaries in the market place or of intrinsic stochastic properties of the production function. We need not go into such detail here, though we shall retain the distinction between *operating risk* (fluctuations in earnings before interest and taxes) and *financial risk* (additional fluctuations in earnings per share induced by the use of leverage in the capital structure).[6] We shall be concerned with how this sum is affected by the choice of projects and how its level may be controlled.

Risk, to the firm, is the possibility of unforeseen fluctuations in its cash flow—of deviations of cash flow from its most probable or expected value. All risk arises from such deviations; more specialized ideas of risk are derivative from risk defined in this manner. For example, the risk of insolvency arises because of the possibility that a succession of unplanned cash deficits will exhaust liquid assets and leave the firm unable to meet commitments as they fall due.

Can risk be measured? In principle it can; whenever we can derive a probability distribution of outcomes we can measure its dispersion which will serve as a measure of risk. In practice it may be quite difficult and many practical businessmen as well as leading economists have argued against it.[7] The principal arguments against it seem to be that so many variable factors must be considered in attempting to evaluate risk that it is either impossible, too time consuming, or too expensive to do so with enough accuracy to be of any use. A sec-

---

[5]J. Von Neumann and O. Morgenstern, *The Theory of Games and Economic Behavior* (3d ed.; Princeton: Princeton University Press, 1953).

[6]R. W. Johnson, *Financial Management* (2d ed.; Boston: Allyn and Bacon, 1962), p. 48.

[7]Cf. A. G. Hart, *loc. cit.*

ond problem is that even if we had accurate measurements, the state of theoretical development has been such that we would not have been able to use them operationally. It is our view that neither of these arguments remains valid. The computational argument was valid until the advent of the electronic computer; it is no longer so. The development of theory, as we shall see, leaves a great deal to be desired. The model to be presented in the next chapter is an operational, if imperfect, means of handling measurable differences in risk in a capital budgeting situation.

How should risk be measured? Cash flows are not known with certainty, but are random variables; in place of a series of cash flows C_t, we can define a joint probability distribution of cash flows for the corresponding periods. Distributions of cash flows in successive periods may be independent of one another, but it will not ordinarily do to assume that they are. By discounting, we were able to compress the two-dimensional series of cash flows into either of two alternative measures of desirability, internal rate of return or a benefit-cost ratio. Discounting will enable us to reduce the dimensionality in the risk case as well, but will no longer yield us a single number. In place of an internal rate of return, we now have a probability distribution of internal rates of return; in place of a benefit-cost ratio, a probability distribution of benefit-cost ratios.

If we consider each possible series of cash flows, we may calculate an internal rate of return for each one. The spectrum of possible rates of return may be arrayed along the x-axis of a graph as in Fig.

FIGURE 10–1
PROBABILITY DISTRIBUTION OF RATES OF RETURN

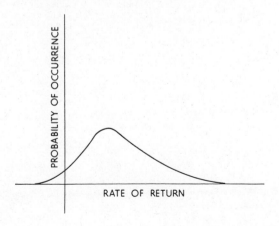

10-1; we may measure the probability of each possible rate of return occurring along the y-axis.[8]

Alternatively, we can calculate the benefit-cost ratio for each possible stream and construct the probability distribution of benefit-cost ratios, as in Fig. 10-2. For these respective probability distributions, we can calculate the usual measures of central tendency, of dispersion, of skewness and kurtosis described in elementary statistics textbooks. We will in this chapter and in Chapter 11 make use of the concept of *net present value*, which may be defined as the present value of benefits minus the present value of costs at a given discount rate. This concept was discussed in Sec. 3.8. We will examine the actual construction of such distributions later in this chapter; at this point we wish to examine why risk should be considered and in what ways it is appropriate to attempt to measure it.

FIGURE 10-2
PROBABILITY DISTRIBUTION OF BENEFIT-COST RATIOS

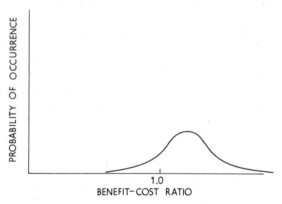

10.2   How Should Risk Be Considered?

Risk is a fact of business life, and some provision must be made for it, if only to ensure the firm's survival. Could we not, however, take sufficient account of it by utilizing the expected values of the probability distributions we have been examining, trusting these to work as actuarial equivalents to the rate of return or benefit-cost ratio in the certainty case?

Our answer must, in general, be no. First of all, an attempt to

-----

[8]Note that there may be a number of possible cash-flow sequences which have identical rates of return.

maximize expected income under conditions of risk has long been recognized as capable of leading to ridiculous decisions, such as paying an infinite sum to play the notorious St. Petersburg game.[9]

Second, it is contrary to observed behavior, in that most firms hedge certain risks and insure against others, at a cost which is in excess of the expected value of receipts from the contract. Finally, although limited liability relieves the shareholder of the threat of losses in excess of the amount invested, lesser losses are transmitted to him, either as reduced dividends or capital losses.

Starting from the observation that insurance is a frequently bought commodity, we are led to the premise that most people have an aversion to risk and are willing to pay something (accept a reduced expectation of income) to avoid it. It has been pointed out that many people also buy Irish Sweepstake tickets if they can get them and that this behavior implies a preference for, rather than an aversion to, risk.[10] This seeming paradox can be resolved either by assuming a certain form of the utility function or by assuming that people distinguish between different risks, and have different aversions or affinities to them. An alternative explanation is also possible. We will return to this point later, and proceed for now on the assumption that business risks are sufficiently homogeneous to be explained by the same utility function.

Given that people have an aversion to business risks and are willing to forego income in order to avoid them, what is the tradeoff function which links the two and tells us how much income they are willing to forego to reduce risk by a given amount?

To answer this requires a brief excursion into utility theory. While measurable utility is an economist's artifact which makes most businessmen (and many economists) uncomfortable, we have to assume its existence in order to resolve our problem. Some of the decision rules which have been prepared make explicit use of the utility concept; as we shall show, the problem can be resolved without using it directly, and we prefer to do so.

Utility, in classical economic theory, is a measure of the satisfaction derived from the ownership or use of some commodity. For our pur-

---

[9]D. Bernoulli, "Exposition of a New Theory on the Measurement of Risk" (1730) reprinted in *Econometrica*, Vol. 22 (1954), pp. 23-36.

[10]M. Friedman and L. J. Savage, "The Utility Analysis of Choices Involving Risk," *Journal of Political Economy*, Vol. 56 (1948), reprinted in A.E.A., *Readings in Price Theory* (Homewood, Ill.: Irwin, 1952), pp. 57-96.

poses we need only be concerned with the utility of money and can measure it by any index which is unique to a linear transformation, i.e., the units of measurement may be multiplied or divided by any arbitrary constant and the zero point is arbitrarily fixed.[11]

We can derive such a measure by taking two arbitrary sums, say $1 and $1,000,000, and assigning to these the respective utilities of 0 and 1. To derive the utility of any sum between these amounts we need, in principle, merely to ascertain the probability U_i at which the individual is indifferent between having the sum S_i with certainty and a lottery ticket offering:

(a)$1,000,000 with probability U_i, or
(b)$1 with probability $(1 - U_i)$

It can be shown that U_i is a measure of the utility of the sum S_i which meets our requirements.[12]

If we assume that more money is preferred to less, and that additional increments of wealth are less highly valued than earlier increments, then it can be shown that the expected utility of a random amount with mean value $\overline{X}$ and standard deviation σ_x is given by an expression of the form

$$U(X) = \overline{X} - a\sigma_x{}^2 \tag{1}$$

where a may be termed the coefficient of risk aversion.[13] If we maximize not income, but utility, as seems intuitively reasonable,[14] we maximize a function similar to (1) which implies that the tradeoffs between expected income and its variance are linear, their slope being given by the coefficient of risk aversion, a.

If this is rational behavior for individuals, what is rational behavior for firms, assuming they seek to maximize the welfare of their share-

---

[11]This is the kind of index of temperature which was in use prior to the discovery of absolute zero and which is still used in the Fahrenheit and Centigrade Scales.

[12]J. Von Neumann and O. Morgenstern, *op. cit.*, pp. 617-33.

[13]Strictly speaking, this requires that we assume the utility of money function to be quadratic or that it can be tolerably well represented in the neighborhood of its mean by a Taylor series expansion from which all terms beyond the quadratic have been dropped. The former assumption is stronger but probably more honest. For the demonstration see D. E. Farrar, *The Investment Decision Under Uncertainty* (Englewood Cliffs, N. J.: Prentice-Hall, 1962), pp. 20-21.

[14]See also H. M. Markowitz, *Portfolio Selection: Efficient Diversification of Investments* (New York: Wiley, 1959), Part IV, and J. Rothenberg, *The Measurement of Social Welfare* (Englewood Cliffs, N. J.: Prentice-Hall, 1961), Chap. 10.

holders? While a rigorous demonstration is too involved to be pursued here, we shall merely note that shareholders' tradeoff functions between expected income and risk in their portfolios affect their demand functions for individual securities, so that we can derive for each security a set of expected income-risk combinations for which market price is unchanged. This set is consistent with individual preferences (remains on his indifference curve) or gives him a higher price than he would have obtained had his own preferences been followed by the firm (thus placing him on a higher indifference curve). The set of combinations at which market price remains unchanged is an indifference curve expressing the market's risk preferences. The firm seeking to maximize shareholders' welfare will seek the highest attainable position on this risk-indifference map. The risk-expected income tradeoffs for the firm need not be linear. There are some interesting corollaries to this.

First of all, risk preferences of individual shareholders do not count, except insofar as departures from them are fully compensated, so that it is the risk-taking attitudes of the entire investing public which must be considered.

Second, since all securities are, from the investor's point of view, substitutes, differing from one another only in their expected yield and in their respective riskiness, the market-determined risk preference map for all publicly held firms would be identical in a perfect market when both operating risks and financial risks are taken into account. This of course has to be modified to take account of market imperfections which have segmented the market into submarkets each with its own risk preference map. This does not mean that individual companies within the submarket (or all companies if the perfect capital market assumption is retained) will seek the same position on the risk preference map or end up with identical levels of risk. Individual companies will have different opportunity sets open to them, depending on their initial position and their success in generating projects. It does mean, however, that they should evaluate risks in similar fashion and behave similarly when confronted with similar risks. Closely held corporations, whose shares are not freely traded, will probably evolve risk preferences related to the personal preferences of controlling shareholders.

The risk preference function for the firm tells us how the market valuation process responds to changes in either the size or the variability of the firm's income stream. Since we are interested in selecting a capital budget which maximizes the market value of the firm, we need to know not only the way in which a given stream will be evaluated by the market, but the way in which individual projects affect the size and variability of the income stream, or adopt some decision criterion which takes these factors into account.

We can measure risk by using any of the available statistical measures of dispersion and applying these to the probability distributions of outcomes. Equation (1) suggests the use of the variance of the earnings stream, but alternative measures such as the interquartile range or the range between other specified probability limits can be used in suitably constructed models. In the model we develop in Chapter 11, the coefficient of variation, or the ratio of the standard deviation of the net present value to its expected value, is used as a more convenient measure.[15]

10.3 Calculating the Probability Distribution of Outcomes

To calculate the probability distribution of outcomes, it is necessary to go back to the forecasts of individual revenue and expenditure items which were used to prepare a forecast of cash flow. Instead of single-valued "point" estimates for each of these variables for each year, it is now necessary to specify their probability distributions and the extent to which there are interrelationships between the variables. These are then used to identify possible outcomes, to calculate the respective rate of return or benefit-cost ratio for each outcome, and to calculate the probability of occurrence in each case.[16]

The following examples will indicate the basic steps in the procedure.

Example 1

A firm is contemplating installation of a widget chopper. The company's engineers estimate the installed cost of the chopper at $100,000, but experience indicates that they are sometimes overly optimistic. Accordingly, the following is the estimated probability distribution for capital cost of the chopper:

---

[15]This discussion assumes that a measure of dispersion is a sufficient indicator of risk for decision-making purposes and implicitly ignores the possibility that other attributes of the probability distribution, e.g., skewness and kurtosis, may be important. The discussion also ignores the effect that covariation between the results of a given firm and those of other firms may have on investors' demand for the firm's shares and thus on its value. It is felt that these effects are of secondary importance in most cases.

[16]Cf. F. A. Lutz and V. Lutz, *Theory of Investment of the Firm* (Princeton: Princeton University Press, 1951), pp. 184-87.

Probability of occurrence	Capital cost
0.90	100,000
0.10	120,000

The chopper will turn out 1,000 tons of chopped widgets per year for 10 years, all of which can be sold. Labor and other operating costs are independent of widget prices and are estimated to vary according to the following probability distribution:

Probability of occurrence	Annual labor & other operating costs
0.25	10,000
0.50	12,000
0.25	15,000

The selling price of chopped widgets is variable and is related to the price of raw widgets, the only raw material used in the process. Prices of the two will vary according to the following joint probability distribution:

Price of raw widgets	Price of chopped widgets, $ per ton				
$ per ton	50	55	60	65	70
20	0.03	0.05	0.02	0	0
25	0.06	0.12	0.10	0.02	0
30	0.01	0.02	0.16	0.10	0.01
35	0	0.01	0.02	0.15	0.02
40	0	0	0	0.03	0.07

This joint distribution can be compressed to give us the following probability distribution of the annual choppers' margin earned:

Annual gross margin	Probability of occurrence	
$20,000	(0.01 + 0.01)	= 0.02
25,000	(0.06 + 0.02 + 0.02 + 0.03)	= 0.13
30,000	(0.03 + 0.12 + 0.16 + 0.15 + 0.07)	= 0.53
35,000	(0.05 + 0.10 + 0.10 + 0.02)	= 0.27
40,000	(0.02 + 0.02 + 0.01)	= 0.05
		1.00

There are no taxes on income.

Each of these annual margins can be associated with any of the three possible labor and operating cost figures and with either one of the possible capital costs. There are thus 15 possible receipt streams and 2 possible capital costs, a total of 30 possible outcomes.

The probability of each of the receipt streams can be found by multiplying the probability of each annual gross margin by the probability of each of the possible associated annual operating costs. Thus we have the following combinations, with annual receipts shown in brackets in the body of the table:

Annual gross margin	Annual labor and operating costs		
	10,000 (p=0.25)	12,000 (p=0.50)	15,000 (p=0.25)
	(10,000)	(8,000)	(5,000)
20,000 (p=0.02)	0.0050	0.0100	0.0050
	(15,000)	(13,000)	(10,000)
25,000 (p=0.13)	0.0325	0.0650	0.0325
	(20,000)	(18,000)	(15,000)
30,000 (p=0.53)	0.1325	0.2650	0.1325
	(25,000)	(23,000)	(20,000)
35,000 (p=0.27)	0.0675	0.1350	0.0675
	(30,000)	(28,000)	(25,000)
40,000 (p=0.05) . . ͜.	0.0125	0.0250	0.0125

Several of these combinations produce an identical annual annuity; we can compress the data slightly by combining those which are identical into the following tabulation of annual annuities:

Size of annual annuity		Probability of occurrence
5,000		0.0050
8,000		0.0010
10,000	(0.0050+0.0325)	0.0375
13,000		0.0650
15,000	(0.0325+0.1325)	0.1650
18,000		0.2650
20,000	(0.1325+0.0675)	0.2000
23,000		0.1350
25,000	(0.0675+0.0125)	0.0800
28,000		0.0250
30,000		0.0125

Each of these annual annuities can be combined with either of the two capital costs to give an internal rate of return. Internal rates and their respective probabilities are given in the following tabulation (enclosed figures in the body of the table are estimated rates of return):

Annual annuity	Capital cost			
	100,000 (p=0.90)		120,000 (p=0.10)	
5,000 (p=0.0050)	(negative)	0.0045	(negative)	0.0005
8,000 (p=0.0100)	(negative)	0.0090	(negative)	0.0010
10,000 (p=0.0375)	0	0.0337	(negative)	0.0038
13,000 (p=0.0650)	(5.0%)	0.0585	(1.5%)	0.0065
15,000 (p=0.1650)	(8.1%)	0.1485	(4.3%)	0.0165
18,000 (p=0.2650)	(12.4%)	0.2385	(8.2%)	0.0265
20,000 (p=0.2000)	(15.0%)	0.1800	(10.5%)	0.0200
23,000 (p=0.1350)	(19.0%)	0.1215	(14.0%)	0.0135
25,000 (p=0.0800)	(21.4%)	0.0720	(16.2%)	0.0080

These probabilities may be summarized in the following tabulation, and are sketched in Fig. 10-3.

Rate of return %	Probability
negative	0.0188
0 – 4.9	0.0567
5 – 9.9	0.2335
10 – 14.9	0.2720
15 – 19.9	0.3095
20 – 24.9	0.0720

FIGURE 10-3

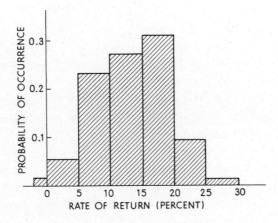

We cannot calculate an expected rate of return in this case because we have not assigned any value to the negative rates of return which occur in several cases.

Example 2

An oil company is considering drilling a wildcat well in search of oil on its prospecting permit in the Canadian Arctic. The well will cost $2,000,000, but its cost can be charged against other corporate income for tax purposes. The corporate tax rate is 50 percent. The company's geologists estimate that, because of the remoteness of the location, the chance that oil will be found in sufficient quantity to warrant further development is approximately 1 in 20. Net present values, at the company's cost of capital, of developing and operating fields of various sizes are shown in Table 10-1, along with the probabilities of their occurrence. These reflect the net present values of oil produced less the cost of developing the field. Benefit-cost ratios, taking account of the tax writeoff as a benefit which is certain are also shown in the table.

TABLE 10-1
POSSIBLE OUTCOMES—ARCTIC OIL VENTURE*

Size of field	Probability of occurrence	Net present value of field $000	Benefit-cost ratios
dry hole	0.949	0	0.50
A	0.004	$ 300	0.65
B	0.010	2,000	1.65
C	0.018	9,000	5.00
D	0.013	42,000	21.50
E	0.005	190,000	95.50
F	0.001	900,000	450.50

This is an example where underlying continuous distributions have been approximated by discrete distributions having a relatively small number of classes. This example, which is drawn from a real business situation, is perhaps an extreme example of a highly skewed distribution of possible outcomes. The expected benefit-cost ratio in this case is 2.98, but this value is entirely due to possible extremely favorable outcomes which have very low probability. Whether it is sufficient to attempt to evaluate projects of this nature by considering merely the expected return and its dispersion is questionable.

_____

*Adapted from data in G. D. Quirin and A. D. Hunt, "A Method of Evaluating Investment Opportunities in Wildcat Acreage," *Proceedings of the Sixth World Petroleum Congress* (Frankfurt, 1964), Sec. VIII, pp. 65-75.

10.4 The Use of Simulation

Instead of attempting to calculate probabilities directly, as was done in the above examples, using discrete probability distributions, it is possible to use simulation to develop synthetic "samples" which give probabilities approximating continuous distributions to any desired degree of accuracy. Basically, the approach requires the specification of the underlying probability distributions and their interrelationships, which are then used to draw, at random, values of the underlying variables, with frequency proportional to their respective probabilities. Rates of return or net present values are then calculated for each set and another set selected. Using computers, it is possible to repeat this process a large number of times, thus synthesizing the probability distribution of outcomes. The process is continued until further calculations no longer affect relative frequencies. Unfortunately, we cannot go into simulation techniques further here. Many excellent treatments are available elsewhere.[17] Simulation techniques have been used to handle the problem of generating probability distributions of outcomes in capital budgeting situations.[18]

Deriving the probability distribution of outcomes does not constitute an adequate "analysis" of the problem of investment decisions under risk. It is only the starting point for such an analysis. Providing a manager with a set of roughly bell-shaped curves and the information that these represent probability distributions of possible outcomes leaves him in square zero as far as picking a budget is concerned, even if he has complete faith in the accuracy of the figures. What he needs is a valid decision criterion for selecting projects, once he has derived the probability distributions. Before attempting to construct such a criterion, let us examine some of the criteria which have been proposed.

10.5 The Use of Payback as a Supplementary Criterion

Many firms which retain payback do so because they feel that forecasting for periods in excess of the payback period is impossible and because it prevents them from exposure to excessive risk. Many

---

[17] A simple but usable introduction can be found in E. H. Bowman and R. B. Fetter, *Analysis for Production Management* (rev. ed.; Homewood, Ill.: Irwin, 1961). See also H. A. Meyers, ed., *Symposium on Monte Carlo Methods* (New York: 1956), Chap. 11.

[18] D. B. Hertz, "Risk Analysis in Capital Investment," *Harvard Business Review*, Vol. 42 (January-February, 1964), pp. 95-106.

firms which have abandoned payback as a measure of desirability retain it as a supplementary hurdle which projects must pass, in the hope of protecting themselves against risk. Among budgeting systems that attempt to make explicit provision for risk, this is perhaps the most common type of provision. It is therefore pertinent to examine what kinds of risks payback protects against, and how.

In the type of single-valued estimate usually considered, payback is simply a comparison of expected aftertax cash flows for the first few years with initial outlays. It does not protect against unforeseen poor outcomes in these initial years, which are admittedly the easiest to forecast but are also the most crucial from the point of view of solvency. It protects instead against bad results subsequent to the payback period by ignoring them entirely. Thus it may accept the highly risky but short-lived project and reject long-lived projects which are virtually risk free since it is not a measure of risk but (an inadequate) one of profitability. It has been claimed that it is a protection against obsolescence, but a leading critic has rightly pointed out that keeping existing equipment around until proposed replacements offer quick payback is a virtual guarantee of obsolescence.[19] In this respect its operation is likely to be perverse. It is difficult to envisage situations in which its use as a supplementary criterion could afford systematic protection against risk. In those situations in which it would be operative it merely imposes certain constraints on the time-shape of the expected stream of cash flows, but none whatever on their variability. As such it is a protection only against the long-term environmental risk resulting from a rate of economic growth and growth in markets below that forecast, and not a particularly useful one.

10.6 An Arbitrary Increase in Earnings Requirements

Another rule of thumb is to insist on a rate of return somewhat above the cost of capital, or a benefit-cost ratio in excess of 1.0. This notion is perhaps derived from the rather loose notion of a "risk premium" found in much of the literature of economics. Presumably the idea is that by requiring all projects to indicate an expected rate of return in excess of the cost of capital, the balancing of projects that fail to do as well as anticipated by those that do better will yield a return which is at least equal to the cost of capital. This contains the germs of at least two fallacies.

---

[19]G. Terborgh, *Business Investment Policy* (Washington: Machinery and Allied Products Institute, 1958), p. 32.

The first is the notion that outcomes of all projects are independent, so that fluctuations may be expected to cancel one another, in the same manner as samples drawn from the same population with replacement. In fact, there is a substantial interdependence between projects, to the extent that their profitability is dependent on environmental conditions, i.e., the business cycle and the rate of economic growth.

The more subtle and dangerous fallacy lies in assuming that expected profit and risk are unrelated. To the extent that profitability is dependent on prices of products and inputs, it is influenced by the price system. As long as there are some competitive influences on the price system, we should expect it to yield a constellation of prices which makes more risky projects offer higher expected rates of return, i.e., a premium for bearing the risk. An arbitrary raising of requirements standards across the board will tend to exclude low risk-low return projects and concentrate on high risk-high return projects, thus having an effect exactly opposite to that intended.

We may of course raise requirements in such a way as to require high risk projects to offer a higher rate of return, while permitting low risk projects to get by with less. This cannot, however, be done arbitrarily with any assurance of achieving the desired results. We shall endeavor to develop a technique for doing this which is not arbitrary.

10.7   The Use of Certainty Equivalents

Lindsay and Sametz offer an approach to the evaluation of risky projects which involves the application of utility discounts to alternative possible outcomes, reflecting an assumed declining marginal utility of money.[20]

To see how the scheme works, let us examine a firm whose utility of money is described by the following schedule:

Additional funds	Average utility
0-2000	1.0
2001-4000	0.9
4001-6000	0.8
6001-8000	0.7

Table 10-2 gives conditional outcomes for two projects, both costing $1,500.

TABLE 10-2
PROBABILITY DISTRIBUTION OF OUTCOMES OF PROJECTS

Project A			Project B		
Conditional present value	Probability	Expected present value	Expected present value	Probability	Expected present value
3,000...... ⅓		1,000	4,500	⅓	1,500
2,000...... ⅓		667	500	⅓	167
0...... ⅓		0	0	⅓	0
	1.0	1,667		1.0	1,667

Following Lindsay and Sametz, we can multiply the expected present values by the utility of the conditional outcome to derive values discounted for the decreasing marginal utility of money. These are shown in Table 10-3. Note that we must use average utility for the respective outcomes, not marginal utilities as Lindsay and Sametz do.[21]

TABLE 10-3
UTILITY-ADJUSTED DISTRIBUTION OF OUTCOMES OF PROJECTS

Project A				Project B			
Outcome	EPV	Average utility	Expected utility	Outcome	EPV	Average utility	Expected utility
3,000...	1,000	0.9	900	4,500	1,500	0.8	1,200
2,000	667	1.0	667	500	167	1.0	167
0	0	1.0	0	0	0	1.0	0
			1,567				1,367

Following the Lindsay-Sametz criterion, we should accept only project A, which is clearly safer. To this extent the criterion does what it is supposed to do.

However, suppose that we have projects A' and B' with the same outcomes, but project B' costs only $1,350, and that the outcomes of each are independent. Following this criterion, we should accept both. Table 10-4 shows the joint probability distribution of outcomes and the resulting utility valuation.

---

[21]*Ibid.*, p. 56-57. The reason for this is that the high income cases include a portion of income of the high marginal utility, e.g., the first $2,000 in our example, and another portion of lower marginal utility.

TABLE 10–4

UTILITY ANALYSIS OF JOINT PROBABILITY DISTRIBUTION OF PROJECT OUTCOMES

Conditional present value	Probability	Expected present value	Average utility	Expected utility
7,500. . . . . . 1/9		833	0.7	583
6,500. . . . . . 1/9		722	0.7	505
4,500. . . . . . 1/9		500	0.8	400
3,500. . . . . . 1/9		377	0.9	339
3,000. . . . . . 1/9		333	0.9	300
2,500. . . . . . 1/9		277	0.9	249
2,000. . . . . . 1/9		222	1.0	222
500	1/9	44	1.0	44
0. . . . . . 1/9		0	1.0	0
	1.0			2,642

Note that in this case, each individual project had an expected utility worth more than its cost. Yet the two of them together have an expected utility less than the cost of doing both. This problem arises out of the assumed diminishing marginal utility of money. In order to make this method usable, we should consider total utility of combined projects outcomes plus existing operations. Note that the difficulty cannot even be resolved by the expedient of considering all possible combinations of the projects under examination. In this instance, A' is acceptable and B' is acceptable, but accepting these two possibilities is equivalent to accepting the combination $A' + B'$, which is unacceptable.

A suitably devised sequential budgeting approach which examines all projects might yield a solution, however. A further objection to the approach (if one is needed) is its reliance on a subjective evaluation of utility by management. How the utility estimates are derived is not indicated,[22] nor is there any indication of their relationship, if any, to the utility functions of the shareholders. As a practical matter, we suspect most managers would prefer not to employ the utility concept if it could be avoided. So do we.

10.8 Adjustments in the Discount Rate

Use of a graduated discount rate to compensate for risk is quite widely practiced, though the required premiums are frequently arbitrary.

One method of estimating the required premium has been suggested by Solomon. He advocates a rather complicated procedure involving the assignment to each project of an imputed borrowing quota, the de-

---

[22] The references cited are not helpful in this regard.

duction from cash flows from the project of imputed debt amortization charges, to yield a rate of return on the equity requirement, which is then compared with the cost of equity in deciding whether to undertake the project.[23] The riskiness of the project determines its imputed borrowing power. This proposal is equivalent to a system in which projects are assessed using a weighted average of the cost of debt and equity. For those projects which do not alter the risk of the firm, the appropriate debt-equity mix to use in making the analysis is simply the weighted average cost of capital for the firm. For projects of above average risk, which increase the operating risk of the firm, a higher rate would be required, calculated by weighting the company's present debt and equity costs in accordance with the following formula

$$k_r = Bk_d + (1-B)k_t \qquad (2)$$

where: B is the imputed borrowing power, as a fraction of the total funds required for the project

k_d = the cost of debt
k_e = the cost of equity
k_r = the required cost of capital for the evaluation of the project

Formula (2) may also be used to calculate the required rate of return for projects of below average risk. These would incorporate an above-average borrowing component and would require lower rates of return for approval (or benefit-cost ratios better than 1.0 at a lower discount rate) than the project of average risk.

This approach requires an estimate of borrowing power for each project. Such an estimate could no doubt be obtained from an examination of lending practices or a study of capital structures. It would be preferable, however, if the borrowing fiction could be bypassed and a direct relationship between variability and required earnings calculated.

10.9 Deriving the Risk Preference Function

We have already discussed the nature of the risk-preference function, which was presented above as Equation (1)

$$U(X) = X - a\sigma_x^2$$

---

[23] E. Solomon, "Measuring A Company's Cost of Capital," *Journal of Business* (October, 1955), reprinted in Solomon (1959), pp. 139-40.

As the risk associated with a given expected income increases, its value drops. In effect, it is capitalized at a higher rate. We have, therefore, a tradeoff between risk and the required rate of return which may be approximated by:

$$k = k^* + b\frac{\sigma_x}{\overline{X}} \tag{3}$$

where k is the required rate of return, k^* is the required rate of return on risk-free income and $\frac{\sigma_x}{\overline{X}}$ is the coefficient of variation in income.[24]

Suppose for a sample of 10 firms we have estimates of price and current dividends, and an estimate of the growth rate derived by fitting a logarithmic trend using least squares and an estimate of risk, computed in this case as the standard error of the estimate of current earnings deflated by the expected value of earnings to remove the scale factor as shown in Table 10-5, then we can derive estimates of k, by applying the following formula:

$$k = \frac{D}{P} + g \tag{4}$$

These can then be correlated with the risk variable to give estimates of the appropriate rates for projects of varying riskiness. Such a graphic correlation is shown in Fig. 10-4.

TABLE 10–5
CALCULATION OF REQUIRED k FOR DIFFERENT DEGREES
OF RISK FROM MARKET DATA

Company	P	D	D/P	g	k	Risk as % of expected earnings
A	60	2.25	0.0375	0.040	0.0775	17
B	45	1.80	0.0400	0.030	0.0700	16
C.	20	1.00	0.0500	0.035	0.0850	22
D	18	1.50	0.0833	0.010	0.0933	25
E	85	3.00	0.0353	0.045	0.0803	20
F	150	4.00	0.0267	0.060	0.0867	22
G	100	1.25	0.0125	0.090	0.1025	30
H	12	1.00	0.0833	0	0.0833	21
I	36	1.45	0.0403	0.020	0.0603	6
J	27	1.00	0.0351	0.040	0.0751	14

[24]W. F. Sharpe, "Risk Aversion in the Stock Market" *Journal of Finance*, Vol. XX (September, 1965), pp. 416-22, is an empirical study analogous to that suggested here.

FIGURE 10–4

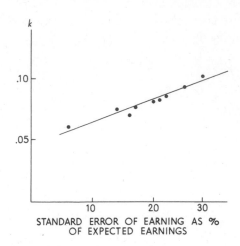

STANDARD ERROR OF EARNING AS %
OF EXPECTED EARNINGS

An alternative procedure is the following. It makes use of the Modigliani-Miller proposition that the value of a firm is independent of its capital structure and is found by capitalizing a pure equity stream at the rate appropriate for its risk class. It assumes further that equities offering equivalent risks will sell at similar capitalization rates, irrespective of the risk class of the companies from which they are derived. Knowing the capitalization rate for the pure equity stream (the company's long run cost of capital) it is possible to calculate the capitalization rates for equity streams preceded by fixed charges of given amounts. Since risk, expressed in terms of the coefficient of variation of earnings, may also be expressed as a function of the level of fixed charges to be deducted from the pure equity stream, we can derive estimates of the capitalization rates for any company from its weighted average cost of capital, its cost of debt schedule, and the standard deviation of its unlevered earnings.

In this example consider the no growth case. Let

c = the no-debt capitalization rate
i = cost of debt (after tax)
n = number of shares
k_e = capitalization rate on equity
P = price per share
L = amount of debt
M = market value of the firm
$\overline{Y}$ = expected earnings, before fixed charges
σ_y = the standard deviation of earnings

From the Modigliani-Miller theorem, we have

$$M = \frac{\overline{Y}}{c} \tag{5}$$

$$= L + nP \tag{6}$$

$$= \frac{iL}{i} + \frac{\overline{Y} - iL}{k_e} \tag{7}$$

$$k_e = \frac{\overline{Y} - iL}{M - L} \tag{8}$$

Relative risk is expressed

$$R = \frac{\sigma_y}{\overline{Y} - iL} \tag{9}$$

In a concrete example, suppose we have

$M = 1,000,000$
$\overline{Y} = 100,000$
$\sigma_y = 30,000$
$c = 0.10$

and the cost of debt schedule expressed in Table 10-6. Table 10-6 shows the calculated level of k_e and R for various levels of debt. Results are shown in Fig. 10-5.

TABLE 10-6

CALCULATION OF REQUIRED k FOR DIFFERENT DEGREES OF RISK FROM INTERNAL DATA

Debt as % of capital	L	i	iL	$\overline{Y} - iL$	k_e	R
0	0	–	0	100,000	0.10	0.300
10	100,000	0.02	2,000	98,000	0.109	0.306
20	200,000	0.02	4,000	96,000	0.120	0.312
30	300,000	0.022	6,600	93,400	0.134	0.322
40	400,000	0.024	9,600	90,400	0.151	0.333
50	500,000	0.027	13,500	86,500	0.173	0.348
60	600,000	0.031	18,600	81,400	0.203	0.369

FIGURE 10–5

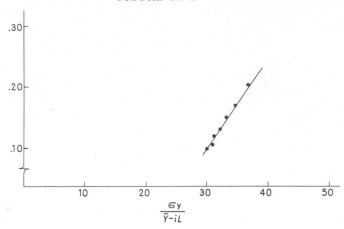

Since the Modigliani-Miller proposition is really a statement of a longrun tendency towards equilibrium, caution should be exercised in using estimates derived in this fashion. It is probably better to use estimates based on observations of the market's valuation of other firms in differing risk categories, particularly when substantial change in relative risk is being considered.

Estimates of k derived from either source, of course, give us an estimate of its average value for the firm as a whole, as risk changes, and are not estimates of the marginal rate of discount to be applied in evaluating projects whose risk differs from that of existing operations. Calculating such a rate is difficult and is not necessary to resolve the problem of selecting those projects which maximize the present value of the firm.

It should be noted, however, that the capital cost estimates derived in this fashion are estimates for the firm, not necessarily for individual projects, and relate to the riskiness of the firm, not to the riskiness of individual projects. The relationship between project risk and corporate risk is neither simple nor direct, as we will discover in the next chapter. As a consequence we cannot use the risk-adjusted capital cost estimates in the simple, direct fashion suggested in Sec. 10.8.

PROBLEMS

1. A farmer is considering the installation of an irrigation pumping system on his 640 acre farm. In "average" years (2 out of 5) he gets a crop of 20 bushels per acre. In years of above-average rainfall (1 in 5) he gets 30, and in drought years (2 in 5) he gets 10. By installing

the system he hopes to get 30 consistently. Cost of the system is $30,000, and its annual operating cost (cash only) is $2,000. He can depreciate the equipment for tax purposes on a 30 percent declining balance basis and is in a 20 percent marginal tax bracket. Estimated price of the product is as follows:

Price	Probability
1.50	0.25
2.00	0.50
2.50	0.25

He expects to use his system only until a gravity irrigation system is installed by the Department of Agriculture. He feels that the chance of this being done in less than 5 years is only 1 in 20, that it is equally likely to occur in 5, 6, 7, or 8 years, and that it is again 1 in 20 that it will be as much as 9 years before the system is installed.

Assuming the farmer's cost of capital is 8 percent, calculate a frequency distribution of benefit-cost ratios.

2. Select a sample of 10 companies. Using their 10 year record of earnings and other data from *Standard and Poor's* or *Moody's*, calculate their cost of capital and relative riskiness. Determine the relationship between these two variables.

3. Take one of the companies which has a cost of capital and relative risk near the middle of your sample. Using the single-company method, by estimating the effect of changes in leverage, calculate the relationship between risk and the cost of capital. How does your answer compare with that obtained in Problem (2)?

CHAPTER 11

Project Selection under Risk and Uncertainty

11.1 Project Risk and Corporate Risk

In Chapter 10 we examined the problem of estimating the riskiness of a single project. In our analysis of why risk ought to be taken into account, we noted that there is a systematic relationship between the riskiness of a firm, defined as the variability of its income, and its market valuation. Because of this relationship, a firm which seeks to maximize the market value of its shares must limit the level of risk it accepts in its overall operations. However, because the relationship between the riskiness of projects and overall corporate risk is complex, we cannot apply standards of risk aversion which might be appropriate to the corporation as a whole to the analysis of individual projects. A basic fault, even of the better selection criteria discussed in Chapter 10, is that they attempt to do just this.

We cannot apply corporate standards to individual project analysis because corporate riskiness does not necessarily vary directly with project risk and may, in fact, vary inversely with it. When we combine any two operations, each of which generates income as a random variable, we get a single probability distribution of income in which the two separate probability distributions of the individual projects are merged. The expected value of the income for the resulting distribution will be the sum of the expected values of the original distributions. The coefficient of variation of the new distribution is unlikely to be any greater than that of the most variable of the original distributions (barring the case where the expected income of one is negative) and may well be substantially less, because fluctuations in the income from one project may be offset by fluctuations in the income of the other. This, of course, is the principle underlying insurance and the diversification of investment portfolios.

For the existing operations of a firm, we can define the present value of cash flows from existing operations at cost of capital k_j as M_{oj}. $[M_{oj} = \sum_t Q_t(1+k_j)^{-t} - \sum_t C_t(1+k_j)^{-t}]$

M_{oj} is a random variable, having mean $\overline{M}_{oj}$, which we will refer to as the expected net present value of existing operations at k_j, and standard deviation σ_{oj}. The coefficient of variation of M_{oj} is $\sigma_{oj}/\overline{M}_{oj}$.

A project i which is being considered as a possible addition to existing operations, has a present value of benefits V_{ij} and of costs C_{ij}, at a cost of capital k_j. Both V_{ij} and C_{ij} are random variables but we will follow the convention of netting any deviations from C_{ij} against the corresponding benefits, treating only the latter as a random variable having mean $\overline{V}_{ij}$ and standard deviation σ_{ij}. The coefficient of variation in net benefits from project i is $\sigma_{ij}/\overline{V}_{ij} - C_{ij}$.

If we combine project i with the existing operations of the firm, we will get an expected net present value for the firm of

$$\overline{M}_{fj} = \overline{M}_{(oj+ij)} = \overline{M}_{oj} + \overline{V}_{ij} - C_{ij} \tag{1}$$

The coefficient of variation in the net present value of the firm is given by:

$$\frac{\sigma_{fj}}{\overline{M}_{fj}} = \left[\left(\frac{\overline{M}_{oj}}{\overline{M}_{fj}}\right)^2 \left(\frac{\sigma_{oj}}{\overline{M}_{oj}}\right)^2 + \left(\frac{\overline{V}_{ij} - C_{ij}}{\overline{M}_{fj}}\right)^2 \left(\frac{\sigma_{ij}}{\overline{V}_{ij} - C_{ij}}\right)^2 + \frac{2\,Cov_{oi,j}}{\overline{M}^2_{fj}} \right]^{\frac{1}{2}} \tag{2}$$

$Cov_{oi,j}$ is the covariance between the net present values, at discount rate k_j, of the firm's existing operations and the proposed addition.[1] This is a new variable, which we have not had before and which our analysis of risk in Chapter 10 did not provide. It can be calculated from

$$Cov_{oi,j} = \sigma_{oj}\sigma_{ij}\,r_{oi,j} \tag{3}$$

where $r_{oi,j}$ is the coefficient of correlation between the respective net present values. Because it plays a key role in determining the effect of the project on corporate risk, and thus in determining whether

---

[1]For the derivation of (2), see G. U. Yule and M. G. Kendall, *An Introduction to the Theory of Statistics* (14th ed.; London: Griffin, 1950), pp. 326-27.

the project should be accepted, we must extend the analysis of Chapter 10 to provide it. This is done in Sec. 11.2, below.

To see how Formulas (1) and (2) work, let's examine a numerical example. Suppose we have

$$
\begin{array}{ll}
\overline{M}_{oj} = 1{,}000 & \overline{V}_{ij} = 300 \\
\sigma_{oj} = 100 & C_{ij} = 200 \\
\sigma^2_{oj} = 10{,}000 & \sigma_{ij} = 10 \\
& \sigma^2_{ij} = 100
\end{array}
$$

Regardless of the value of $Cov_{oi,j}$, the expected net present value of the firm, using Formula (1) is given by:

$$
\begin{aligned}
\overline{M}_{fj} &= 1{,}000 + 300 - 200 \\
&= 1{,}100
\end{aligned}
$$

It will be noted that the relative variability of the proposed project is identical to that of the existing operations:

$$
\frac{\sigma_{oj}}{\overline{M}_{oj}} = \frac{100}{1000} = 0.10
$$

$$
\frac{\sigma_{ij}}{V_{ij} - C_{ij}} = \frac{10}{300 - 200} = 0.10
$$

The first case to consider is the case in which the net present value of the project is perfectly correlated with that of the firm's existing operations, so that

$$
r_{oi,j} = 1.0
$$

We calculate covariance using Formula (3). The relative variability of the combined operation, given by Formula (2) is:

$$
\frac{\sigma_{fj}}{\overline{M}_{fj}} = \left[\left(\frac{1{,}000}{1{,}100} \right)^2 (.10)^2 + \left(\frac{100}{1{,}100} \right)^2 (0.10)^2 + \frac{2(100)(10)(1.0)}{(1{,}100)^2} \right]^{\frac{1}{2}}
$$

$$
= \left(\frac{.01(1{,}000{,}000) + .01(10{,}000) + 2000}{1{,}210{,}000} \right)^{\frac{1}{2}}
$$

$$
= \left(\frac{10{,}000 + 100 + 2000}{1{,}210{,}000} \right)^{\frac{1}{2}}
$$

$$
= 0.10
$$

As we might have suspected all along, adding a project with a net present value just as variable as that of existing operations, and perfectly correlated with it, leaves risk unchanged.

Now consider the case where the project is uncorrelated, so that $r_{oi,j} = 0$. In this case, the last term in Formula (2) vanishes, and we get:

$$\frac{\sigma_{fj}}{\overline{M}_{fj}} = \left(\frac{0.01(1,000,000) + 0.01(10,000)}{1,210,000} \right)^{\frac{1}{2}}$$

$$= \left(\frac{10,000}{1,210,000} \right)^{\frac{1}{2}}$$

$$= 0.0915$$

Here, the independence between the two distributions gives a diversification effect, so riskiness is reduced. As a third example, consider the case where there is a negative correlation between the project and the original operation so that the project may be expected to prosper if the original operation languishes, and *vice versa*. Let $r_{oi,j} = -1.0$, and we get

$$\frac{\sigma_{fj}}{\overline{M}_{fj}} = \left(\frac{0.01(1,000,000) + 0.01(10,000) - 2,000}{1,210,000} \right)^{\frac{1}{2}}$$

$$= \left(\frac{10,000 + 100 - 2,000}{1,210,000} \right)^{\frac{1}{2}}$$

$$= 0.0818$$

As we might expect, a stronger diversification effect is present in this case and risk is further reduced.

Finally, consider project n which has the same net present value as project i but is subject to greater variability, so that we have:

$$\overline{V}_{nj} = 300$$
$$C_{nj} = 200$$
$$\sigma_{nj} = 20$$
$$\sigma^2_{nj} = 400$$
$$\sigma_{nj} / \overline{V}_{nj} - C_{nj} = 0.20$$

The reader can confirm for himself that if $r_{on,j} = 1.0$, project n increases the riskiness of the combined operation from its initial level.

However, if $r_{on,j} = -1.0$, we have

$$\frac{\sigma_{fj}}{\overline{M}_{fj}} = \left(\frac{0.01(1,000,000) + 0.04(10,000) + 2(100)(20)(-1.0)}{1,210,000} \right)^{\frac{1}{2}}$$

$$= \left(\frac{10,000 + 400 - 4000}{1,210,000} \right)^{\frac{1}{2}}$$

$$= 0.0727$$

Here, we have achieved a greater reduction in risk from the initial level represented by existing operations by using a "riskier" project, i.e., one exhibiting a higher relative variability in possible outcomes. This is a general result.

Where there is a negative correlation of project value with the value of existing operations, the *riskier project* is preferable from the point of view of *reducing the risks of the firm*. (It may even be acceptable if the expected return of the project is negative. An example of such a "project" having negative expected value but high negative correlation with possible losses is the purchase of fire or business interruption insurance.) It is also apparent that when a project's outcome is sufficiently uncorrelated with the outcomes of existing operations, it may be undertaken despite very high relative risk, providing the cost is small and the expected return sufficiently positive. This may be the clue to an alternative resolution of the Friedman-Savage paradox noted earlier.

The reasons for these relationships will be more obvious from an examination of Fig. 11-1 to 11-3. Fig. 11-1 shows the effects of combining two operations which have high positive correlation. The income series in Fig. 11-1a is perfectly positively correlated with that in Fig. 11-1b. The combined series in Fig. 11-1c is the result of adding the two series, period-by-period, with weights of 4 and 1 respectively. In Fig. 11-2, two series of equal variance which show perfect negative correlation are combined with 4:1 weights. In Fig. 11-3, the same basic series used in Fig. 11-1 and 11-2 appears with a weight of 4, but is combined with a more widely fluctuating series which is given a weight of 1. Comparison of Fig. 11-2 with Fig. 11-3 shows how greater riskiness in the second series operates to further reduce fluctuations in the combined stream.

Any scheme for selecting a capital budget which seeks to take explicit account of risk in a satisfactory manner must consider the

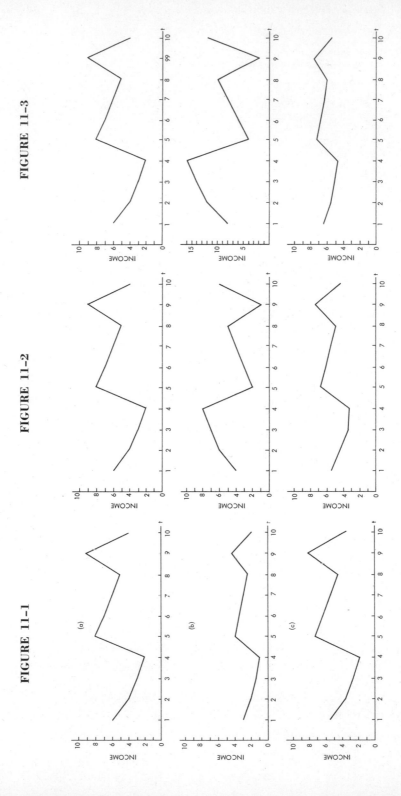

correlation between project value and that of the company's existing operations.

The important pioneering work in this area is that of Markowitz.[2] His decision model was developed to handle security portfolios, and is not directly applicable to the problem of capital budgeting. The model which we develop in this chapter is an heuristic adaptation of Markowitz' portfolio selection model, which attempts to take account (and advantage) of the peculiarities of the capital budgeting problem. These render it quite simple, computationally, and make the use of judgment to modify the selection somewhat simpler than it would be using Markowitz' quadratic programming technique.

11.2   Estimating Interrelationships between Projects

Formula (2) expresses the basic relationship between the riskiness of an individual project, the riskiness of the firm's existing operations and the resulting riskiness of the firm. By regarding "existing operations" at any stage in the budget selection process as consisting of the initial operations of the firm plus all the projects which have so far been adopted, we can estimate the impact of any additional project on the combined risk. However, as we noted, to apply Formula (2) we need the estimated covariances between projects. Where do we get these?

In Chapter 10 we described a simulation procedure used to derive probability distributions for present values of project benefits. In order to derive covariances, it is necessary to modify this procedure by using the basic probability distributions of the economic environment to generate not just the probability distribution of outcomes for a single project, but the joint probability distribution of outcomes for the project and the firm's existing operations. From the resulting pairs of values for M_{oj} and V_{ij}, we can calculate, using the usual techniques of regression analysis, relationships of the following form:

$$V_{ij} = a_{ij} + b_{ij} M_{oj} + u_{ij} \qquad (4)$$

These express the present values of the projects as functions of the present value of the existing operations. The residual term, u_{ij} is added to take account of the variation in V_{ij} which is not accounted for by

---

[2]H. Markowitz; *Portfolio Selection* (New York: Wiley, 1959).

the variation in M_{oj}. It is assumed to have the following properties:

$$Cov\,(u_{ij},\,u_{nj})=0$$
$$Cov\,(u_{ij},\,M_{oj})=0$$
$$\bar{u}_{ij}=0$$

The covariance between the value of project i and that of the initial operation is given by:

$$Cov_{oi,j}=b_{ij}\,\sigma_{oj}{}^{2} \tag{5}$$

The coefficient of correlation, $r_{oi,j}$ is given by

$$r_{oi,j}=\frac{b_{ij}\,\sigma_{oj}}{\sigma_{ij}} \tag{6}$$

While we have used $r_{oi,j}$ in conjunction with Formula (3) in the examples above, it will usually prove more convenient to work directly with covariances.

When we have decided to combine project i with the initial operations and wish to examine the relationship with an additional project n, we can derive the standard deviation of the combined value of o and i using Formulas (1) and (2), while the covariance between them is given by:

$$Cov_{o+i,n,j}=\frac{b_{nj}(\bar{M}_{oj}+\bar{M}_{ij})\sigma_{oj}{}^{2}}{\bar{M}_{oj}+\bar{M}_{ij}} \tag{7}$$

where $\bar{M}_{ij}=\bar{V}_{ij}-C_{ij}$.

The extension of Formula (7) to the case where we have a set P of projects already chosen is:[4]

$$Cov_{o+P,n,j,}=b_{nj}\left(\frac{\bar{M}_{oj}+\sum_{i\epsilon P}b_{ij}\bar{M}_{ij}}{\bar{M}_{oj}+\sum_{i\epsilon P}\bar{M}_{ij}}\right)\sigma_{oj}{}^{2} \tag{8}$$

---

[4]Formulas (4) and (8) can be derived from the treatment by Markowitz, *op. cit.*, p. 100 (n. 1).

11.3 Outline of a Sequential Selection Process

We can compute, using Formulas (1) and (2), the expected net present value and risk level of the firm which result from combining any project with its existing operations. Both Formula (1) and (2) however, give values for these variables at a specified capitalization rate. However, neither net present value nor its standard deviation are invariant under a change in capitalization rates. A basic difference between the no-risk case and the case where risk is taken into account is that, in the latter, changing the level of risk changes the discount rate. In the no-risk (or constant-risk) case, the effect of a project on the value of the firm is to add its net present value to that of the existing operations. When risk is allowed to change, the impact is twofold, as follows:

(a) The change in risk causes a change in the discount rate which changes the valuation of existing operations,

(b) It adds its own expected net present value, at the new discount rate to that of existing operations.

The change under (a) may be either positive or negative, depending on whether risk is decreased or increased, respectively.

In the no-risk case, since the only impact of the project on the value of the firm is through its own net present value, the requirement that the latter be positive or that the benefit-cost ratio exceed 1.0 is sufficient to lead to maximization of the present value of the firm. Because of the second-order effects in the risk case, which operate through changing the discount rate, this rule is no longer sufficient. Instead of being able to pay for the project an amount not exceeding the present value of its benefits, we can afford to pay for it an amount not exceeding the sum of

(a) The change in the expected valuation of existing operations due to the change in discount rate (positive or negative), *plus*

(b) The expected present value of benefits, from the project, at the new discount rate.

If the present value of costs of the project does not exceed this total, then the project increases the market value of the firm, and should be adopted. The effect of this rule is to require projects which increase the riskiness of the firm (irrespective of their own riskiness) to meet a higher standard than the 1.0 benefit-cost ratio, and to allow those which reduce its riskiness to meet a lower standard.

This rule forms the basic criterion for project acceptance. We cannot, however, select projects by considering them as individual additions to firm's existing operations or we will run into the same sort of difficulty we encountered in Sec. 10.7, where two projects were each acceptable individually, but were not acceptable in combination. We must consider combinations of projects and attempt to add the set of projects which makes the maximum addition to the present value of the firm. Rather than attempting to do this by enumeration, i.e., by considering all possible combinations of projects, we will examine projects in a particular sequence which will normally result in having to examine fewer combinations.

Consideration of the projects in sequence is made possible by the fact that, for normal projects, net present value is inversely related to the discount rate. Consequently, any project which is acceptable at a given discount rate will remain acceptable at any lower rate. If we start at the highest discount rate and move to successively lower rates, we can add projects to the budget which will never have to be deleted.

To reach the starting point where the highest discount rate applies, it is necessary to find the project which causes the greatest increase in risk, relative to the existing operation. Using Formula (2), we can calculate the impact of each project on the risk of the firm. By taking the ratio of the risk of the firm so calculated to the riskiness of existing operations, we obtain an index of marginal riskiness. The first step in our selection process is to list all projects in descending order of their index of marginal riskiness.

We then proceed to an examination of the top project on the resulting list. Using the coefficient of variation of the combination of this project with existing operations, and using the market risk-preference function derived from the analysis presented in Chapter 10, we can estimate the applicable cost of capital.

With this discount rate we evaluate the expected net present value of existing operations, add the expected present value of the benefits from the project, then deduct the expected net present value of existing operations at the initial cost of capital to determine how much we can afford to pay for the project. If this amount is in excess of the present value of the project's cost at the new cost of capital, the project is accepted, and we proceed to the evaluation of the next project. If it is not, it is placed at the bottom of a list of provisionally rejected projects, which will be reevaluated after one of the projects on the initial list has been accepted. It is not rejected outright, because acceptance of one of the projects farther down the initial list may so dilute its risk-increasing potential as to make it acceptable.

Evaluation of the next, and subsequent projects, is carried out in the same manner, except that present values and risk levels for the original operation combined with all previously accepted projects are used for comparison purposes. The process continues, with the list of provisional rejects reintroduced after each project acceptance, until the initial list has been exhausted and the list of provisional rejects has been gone through from beginning to end without accepting any project. Projects remaining on the provisionally rejected list at this stage are then rejected.

The following section will illustrate the application of the model.

11.4 Application of the Sequential Selection Model

Company X has a current market value of \$100,000, and a current cost of capital of 10 percent. Its estimate of the way the market will evaluate changes in its risk level is given in Table 11-1. Current risk $(\sigma_{oj}/\overline{M}_{oj})$ is 0.30.

TABLE 11–1
MARKET RISK PREFERENCE SCHEDULE: COMPANY X

Risk $-\dfrac{\sigma_{fj}}{\overline{M}_{fj}}$	k
0	0.04
0.05	0.05
0.10	0.06
0.15	0.07
0.20	0.08
0.25	0.09
0.30	0.10
0.35	0.11
0.40	0.12
0.50	0.14

Company X is considering a number of projects, basic data concerning which are presented in Table 11-2. It is assumed for this example that σ_{ij} and b_{ij} do not change as the discount rate changes. This may not be a safe assumption in an actual case, but has been adopted here for the sake of simplicity.

The first step is to calculate an index of marginal riskiness for the projects. This is done by calculating $\sigma_{fj}/\overline{M}_{fj}$ for the combination of each project with existing operations, dividing the result by $\sigma_{oj}/\overline{M}_{oj}$.

These calculations are shown in Table 11-3. Values of the resulting index above 1.0 as in the case of project A indicate that combining the project in question with the original operation would increase the risk of the firm. Values below 1.0 indicate that the project is risk reducing.

TABLE 11-2
PROJECTS TO BE CONSIDERED: COMPANY X

| Project | Expected present value of benefits ($\overline{V}_{ij}$) | | | Present value of costs (C_{ij}) | | | σ_{ij} | b_{ij} |
	$k=0.08$	$k=0.10$	$k=0.12$	$k=0.08$	$k=0.10$	$k=0.12$		
A	100,000	75,000	60,000	52,000	50,000	49,000	40,000	1.3333
B	250,000	230,000	200,000	215,000	200,000	190,000	20,000	0.3333
C	138,000	135,000	132,000	31,000	30,000	29,000	25,000	$-$ 0.1000

TABLE 11-3
INDEX OF MARGINAL RISKINESS,
AVAILABLE PROJECTS: COMPANY X

Project	$\sigma_{fj}/\overline{M}_{fj}$	$Index=\dfrac{\sigma_{fj}\overline{M}_{oj}}{\sigma_{oj}\overline{M}_{fj}}$
A	0.418	1.39
B	0.336	1.12
C	0.162	0.54

Since the ranking of projects by the index of riskiness leaves the list of projects in its original order, we can start our selection process by looking at project A.

Project A raises the relative risk of the firm to 0.418. Referring to Table 11-1, we conclude that if it were adopted, Company X's cost of capital would rise to $k=0.124$, which we round to 0.12.

Effects, on expected present value of existing operations, of shifting from a discount rate of k_1 to k_2 are given by

$$M_{o2} = \frac{M_{o1}k_1}{k_2} \tag{9}$$

Formula (3) is an approximation which effectively calculates an implicit perpetuity at the original discount rate and recapitalizes it at the new rate. Applying Formula (3) in this case give us

$$\overline{M}_{0,0.12} = \frac{(100,000)(0.10)}{(0.12)}$$

$$= 83,333$$

The expected net present value of the benefits from project A, discounted at $k = 0.12$ is, from Table 11-2, \$60,000. The combined value of the firm incorporating project A is the sum of these amounts, \$143,333. But the firm is worth \$100,000 without project A, so it can afford to pay an amount up to \$43,333 for A if it is to benefit from the addition. Since the present value of A's costs, at $k = 0.12$, is \$49,000, adding A alone would lead to a reduction in the value of the firm and A must be provisionally rejected.

Since we did not adopt project A, move on and consider project B. B would raise the firm's relative risk to 0.336 (Table 11-3) and give us a new cost of capital $k = 0.107$ (Table 11-1, interpolating). At $k = 0.107$, the existing operation would be revalued downward once again, this time to

$$M_{O,0.107} = \frac{(100,000)(0.10)}{(0.107)}$$

$$= \$93,500$$

By interpolating in Table 11-2, the expected present value of benefits from B at $k = 0.107$ is \$219,500. This would raise the combined "worth" of the firm to \$313,000. Since its worth without project B was only \$100,000, it can afford to pay up to \$213,000 for project B. Since the present value of B's cost is only \$196,500 at $k = 0.107$, we would increase the value of the firm by adopting it. B is, therefore, the first project from the group to be selected.

We may now proceed to reevaluate project A, which we provisionally rejected earlier. The *rationale* behind reconsidering it is the possibility that its risk-increasing characteristics might be sufficiently diluted when it is added to a larger basic operation that it becomes acceptable. To examine this possibility, we must examine the effect of its possible adoption on the riskiness of the firm's operations as augmented by the adoption of project B.

First of all, we need the covariance between project A and the planned operations represented by the budget already adopted. Applying Formula (7), we get the following:

$$Cov_{O+B,A} = 1.333 \left(\frac{93,500 + 0.3333(23,000)}{116,500} \right) (30,000)^2$$

$$= 4 \left(\frac{101.2}{116.5} \right) \times 10^8$$

$$= 3.48 \times 10^8$$

We now apply Formula (2) to get the relative risk of the combination. This is carried out using the net present values at the 10.7 percent discount rate applicable to the already-adopted budget.

$$\frac{\sigma_{fj}}{\overline{M}_{fj}} = \left[\left(\frac{116.5}{136.6}\right)^2 (0.336)^2 + \left(\frac{20.1}{136.6}\right)^2 (1.6)^2 + \frac{2(3.48)\times10^8}{136,600^2} \right]^{\frac{1}{2}}$$

$$= (0.1750)^{\frac{1}{2}}$$

$$= 0.418$$

By coincidence, the effect of increasing the size of the operation to which A must be added is just offset by the risk-increasing effect of project B. To be a little more precise this time around, the cost of capital for a level of risk of 0.418 is, by interpolation, 0.124. The value of the adopted budget at 12.4 percent is given by:

$$\overline{M}_{O+B,0.124} = \frac{116,500 \ (0.107)}{(0.124)}$$
$$= \$100,600$$

At 12.4 percent, project A is worth \$57,000 (extrapolating). The firm, at 10.7 percent without project A is worth \$116,000. The amount we can afford to pay for project A is given by:

$$\overline{M}_{O+B,0.124} = \$100,000$$
$$\overline{V}_{A,0.124} = \underline{\quad 57,000}$$
$$\$157,000$$
$$-\overline{M}_{O+B,0.107} = \underline{-116,500}$$
$$\$\ 41,100$$

Since A costs an estimated \$48,800 at 12.4 percent, it must be rejected provisionally once more.

We now proceed to consider project C.

Applying Formula (7), we derive first:

$$Cov_{O+B,C} = -0.10 \left(\frac{93,500 + 0.3333(23,000)}{116,500} \right) (30,000)^2$$

$$= -0.261 \times 10^8$$

and risk:

$$\frac{\sigma_{fj}}{\overline{M}_{fj}} = \left[\left(\frac{116.5}{220.8} \right)^2 (0.336)^2 + \left(\frac{104.3}{220.8} \right)^2 (0.238)^2 - \frac{2(0.261)}{(22.08)^2} \right]^{\frac{1}{2}}$$

$$= (0.0430)^{\frac{1}{2}}$$

$$= 0.207$$

This is indeed a substantial reduction in risk, and reduces our effective cost of capital to 8.1 percent, interpolating in Table 11-1. This leads to an upward revision in the valuation of existing operations:

$$\overline{M}_{O+B,\,0.081} = \frac{116{,}500 \ (0.107)}{(0.081)}$$

$$= \$154{,}000$$

At 8.1 percent, Project C is worth \$137,900. The amount we can afford to pay for Project C is given by:

$$\overline{M}_{O+B,\,0.081} = \$154{,}000$$

$$\overline{V}_{C,\,0.081} = \frac{137{,}900}{291{,}900}$$

$$- \overline{M}_{O\,+B,\,0.107} = \frac{-106{,}500}{\$185{,}400}$$

This amount exceeds the cost of project C, hence C should be adopted. Note that in this case, it exceeds even the benefits of C, which implies that C would be a profitable acquisition even if its benefit-cost ratio, at the applicable cost of capital, were below 1.0. This is due to its remarkable risk-reducing properties.

As the firm is now, at least on paper, much larger and better diversified than it was earlier, can it afford to reconsider the individually-risky project A?

Its covariance is now obtained by applying formula (8), using present values at $k = 0.081$ for the calculation.

$$Cov_{O+B+C,\,A} = 1.3333 \left(\frac{123.6 + 0.3333(30.4) - 0.1(106.9)}{260.9} \right) (30{,}000)^2$$

$$= 1.9 \times 10^8$$

Risk, including A, is now given by:

$$\frac{\sigma_{fj}}{\overline{M}_{fj}} = \left[\left(\frac{260.9}{298.3} \right)^2 (0.207)^2 + \left(\frac{37.4}{298.3} \right)^2 (1.07)^2 + \frac{3.8}{(26.09)^2} \right]^{\frac{1}{2}}$$

$$= (0.0562)^{\frac{1}{2}}$$

$$= 0.237$$

At this level of risk, our cost of capital would rise to 8.7 percent. This would give the following reevaluation of planned operations:

$$\overline{M}_{O+B+C,.087} = \frac{260,900(0.081)}{(0.087)}$$

The amount the firm can pay for Project A is:

$$
\begin{array}{ll}
\overline{M}_{O+B+C\ 0.087} = & \$243,000 \\
\overline{V}_{A,0.087} = & \underline{84,700} \\
& \$327,700 \\
-\overline{M}_{O+B+C,0.081} = & \underline{-260,900} \\
& \$66,800
\end{array}
$$

As A costs only \$51,300, it can be justified. The steps in our analysis indicate that A could only be justified if C were adopted as well, to offset the risk of A.

11.5   Evaluating Investments under Risk: Some Further Comments

The last two sections have been devoted to developing and explaining the use of a decision rule for selecting projects which differ in risk. It is only one of a number of models which can be developed from Markowitz' basic work.[5]

---

[5]Besides Markowitz' study referred to earlier, the following are significant contributions to the theory of the investment decision under risk:

M. J. Gordon, "Security and Investment: Theory and Evidence," *Journal of Finance*, Vol. XIX (December, 1964), pp. 607-18.

J. Lintner, "The Valuation of Risk Assets and the Selection of Risky Investments in Stock Portfolios and Capital Budgets," *Review of Economics and Statistics* (February, 1965), pp. 13-37.

J. Lintner, "Optimal Dividends and Corporate Growth Under Uncertainty," *Quarterly*

While the basic theory upon which such models must be based is still in a state of rapid development and will require further sorting out before anything approaching a consensus is attained, the vital ingredients of any successful model can be distinguished. These include:

(a) A specification of the basic relationships between project risk and corporate risk.

(b) A basic valuation model which embraces an adequate definition of risk and specifies the relationship between risk and market price in an operationally useable fashion.

(c) A selection procedure which utilizes (a) and (b) to select projects which maximize the market value of the firm.

Given a definition of risk, (a) flows readily from a consideration of the joint probability distribution of project outcomes. Thus, it is not a serious problem. Similarly, there are several possible approaches to the selection procedure problem, ranging from outright enumeration and evaluation of all possible project combinations, which is always a feasible, if somewhat cumbersome approach to the problem, through a structured evaluation of selected combinations such as that presented above, to the use of mathematical programming as developed in Markowitz' portfolio selection model. The structured combinatorial approach we have outlined appears to offer a substantial saving over complete enumeration in terms of the number of combinations which have to be considered. We have not made any direct comparisons between it and quadratic integer programming in terms of computational speed and cost. Neither (a) nor (b) appears to raise any serious difficulties, however.

The basic weakness in all decision rules arises from our rather weak understanding of risk and its relationship to valuation. Some authors have postulated the existence of a corporate utility function.[6] This

---

Journal of Economics (February, 1964), pp. 68-71.; J. Lintner, "Security Prices, Risk, and Maximal Gains from Diversification," *Journal of Finance*, Vol. XX (December, 1965), pp. 587-616.; J. Lintner, "The Cost of Capital and Optimal Financing of Corporate Growth," *Journal of Finance*, Vol. XVIII (May, 1963), pp. 292-310. W. F. Sharpe, "A Simplified Model for Portfolio Analysis," *Management Science*, Vol. IX (January, 1963), pp. 277-93.; W. F. Sharpe, "Capital Asset Prices: A Theory of Market Equilibrium Under Conditions of Uncertainty," *Journal of Finance*, Vol. XIX (September, 1964), pp. 425-42. J. Tobin, "Liquidity Preferences as Behavior Toward Risk," *Review of Economic Studies*, (February, 1958), pp.65-86.

[6] R. Lindsay and A. W. Sametz, *Financial Mangement* (Homewood, Ill.: Irwin, 1963); M. J. Gordon, "Security and Investment, Theory and Evidence," *Journal of Finance*, Vol. XIX (December, 1964), pp. 607-18.

may or may not be related to market valuation. Assuming the existence of such a function seems to imply a philosophical position on
the nature of the corporation somewhat akin to that of the medieval
realists on the problem of universals. We reject this approach not
because of our doubts concerning the existence of such a utility function, (though these are considerable) but, like Ockham, because we
feel that all the necessary decisions can be made without referring to
it. Even in this context, however, it is not clear that we do not have
to consider the skewness and kurtosis of the probability distribution
of outcomes as well as the expected value and dispersion.

Among those whose models like ours imply dependence on market
criteria, there is some question as to just what are the dimensions
of risk which the market evaluates.[7]

Are these restricted to the first two moments of the probability
distribution of outcomes, or not? Are they complicated by the interrelationships between different companies in investors' portfolios? It
is easy to have recourse to the type of general equilibrium model in
which everything depends on everything else. The most important
function of theory, augmented by empirical research to the extent
necessary, is to tell us which variables enter into such a model with
zero or near zero coefficients, i.e., which ones don't matter. In our
opinion, it has been rather conclusively demonstrated that dispersion
of outcomes matters, although the precise functional form of the
relationship is not too clear from the empirical evidence. On the other
hand, there is little as yet to indicate that more exotic variables need
to be taken into account.

11.6   Risk in the Public Sector

Most parts of the decision process outlined in the previous sections
can be adapted for use in the public sector as well. While the private
firm must consider the market's evaluation of risk, the government
need not do so, but may substitute its own risk-preference function.
The problem does not lie in the decision mechanism if risk preferences
are given but in deciding just what this risk-preference function should
be. Several mutually exclusive points of view exist, as usual.

The first, often but not exclusively identified with Budget Bureaus
and Treasury Boards, is that it is the taxpayers' money which is being
spent and that we must not gamble with the taxpayers' money. This

---

[7]Cf. especially, W. F. Sharpe, *op. cit.* (1964); J. Lintner, *op. cit.* (December, 1965).

view requires that the public sector exhibit a much stronger risk aversion than the private sector, with infinite aversion manifesting itself at a relatively low level of risk. It also forbids offsetting losses in one activity, the result of risks taken which turned out badly, with gains elsewhere. The decision process described above is not a satisfactory one for a decision unit having such a viewpoint, as it depends on such offsets. We could develop a decision process which would select projects rationally, in accord with such a precept, but have chosen not to do so in the hope that irrationality in the decision process will offset the basic irrationality of a rule of this type.

A second view is that government activities, except for the traditional (18th century?) functions of government, should be limited to those projects which are too risky to be undertaken by private enterprise. This implies a diametrically opposed risk preference function to that implicit in the first view. Government budgets should exhibit risk affinity rather than risk aversion and might include anything, provided it is risky enough, i.e., too risky for the private sector. Despite the logical difficulty, there are some commentators on government activity who appear to hold this view before the fact, and the first view after the fact, at least in cases where the risk comes home to roost. We shall reject this view also, if only because its application would lead to completely irresponsible spending practices, in which all soberly conceived projects were rejected in favor of reckless adventures.

Among the authorities in this field, Eckstein favors the application of an interest rate differential to reflect "risk,"[8] but apparently favors its application in the evaluation of all projects irrespective of their riskiness. He gives no recommendations as to how it should be calculated, except that all evidence from the private sector is expressly rejected.[9] Hirshleifer, Milliman, and DeHaven correctly point out that the only allowance required is to cover risk aversion, where benefit-cost ratios are calculated on the basis of expected values, but regard the existence of risk aversion as questionable. They would prefer to use some of the evidence of the private capital market in determining the allowance for risk aversion.[10] Neither study devotes

---

[8]O. Eckstein, *Water Resource Development* (Cambridge: Harvard, 1961), p. 88.

[9]*Ibid.*, pp. 89-90.

[10]J. Hirshleifer, J. C. DeHaven, and J. W. Milliman, *Water Supply, Economics, Technology, Policy* (Chicago: University of Chicago Press, 1960), pp. 139-41.

much attention to this problem, or to methods of estimating variability in outcomes, for that matter.

The best guide that we can suggest at the present time is that
government ought to use the risk-aversion of the private sector as a
starting point and not depart from it without good reason. It is, of
course, the risk aversion not of the community as a whole but of investors as a group that is effective in the market place, and there
may be reasons for departing from it.

To the extent that domestic markets are subject to large scale buying and selling from abroad, the risk preferences of the market may
be those of foreigners and not those of nationals. If the country is
dependent on capital imports and the government borrows abroad, it
can ignore the risk preferences of foreign investors at its peril and
might better seek another way of demonstrating its independence.

If, as frequently happens in underdeveloped countries and sometimes
elsewhere, domestic private capital is timid, exhibiting strong risk-
aversion through custom or because large parts of domestic savings
are channeled through financial intermediaries having very conservative portfolio policies, there may well be a need for the government
to assume the role of innovator and undertake risks which the private
sector would reject out of hand. This does not mean throwing caution
to the winds, but rather that the government should show a lower
degree of risk aversion than does the private sector, providing it can
do so without raising doubts in the minds of foreign investors concerning its solvency.

Again, where there is strong evidence of public sentiment in favor
of a more liberal attitude toward risk-taking, there is no reason why
the government ought not to bow to it despite the apparent evidence
of conservatism in this respect among investors.

While there is good reason to be more daring in this regard, it
should be noted that in the case of underdeveloped countries, there
are pressures tending to force politicians beyond this limit. These are
most obvious in the case of multiparty democratic countries, but exist
elsewhere as well. The party in power has to choose between a gamble
which, if it comes off, will produce tangible betterment in living standards in a hurry and a more responsible program which will build a
substantial base for future growth, at little risk, but yield little
obvious improvement in living standards. It will, in many cases, choose
the gamble. If the gamble pays off, it will retain office. If it fails, the
party will be booted out, but if it is not taken they're likely to be
booted out anyway, because the opposition is certain to promise the

moon. The only sobering influences here are donors of aid, international agencies and international investors whose risk aversion curbs this temptation. It is well that it is curbed, for risk aversion is needed to preserve capital where it is scarce. That such pressures exist even in totalitarian countries is evidenced by China's abortive "Great Leap Forward" in the 1950's.

The paradox is that while there are pressures on countries whose situation dictates strong risk aversion to throw caution to the winds, it is precisely in those countries which are wealthy, and which can afford to take a few risks, that the "Treasury mind" dominates and risk aversion in excess of that of the market place restricts risk taking in many government activities. This view is, of course, expressly rejected in its application to certain activities (outer space, hydroelectric and nuclear power development, irrigation, etc.) which are politically fashionable, while others (education in some areas, care of the insane, urban renewal in most areas) continue to be hamstrung by it. A reallocation of government spending, which applied private sector risk preferences across the board would, we suspect, produce far more spectacular results than any reasonable subsequent adjustment in government risk aversion designed to offset the obvious deficiencies of private sector risk aversion as a measure of social risk preferences.

11.7 Conflict Situations: The Uncertainty Case

In Chapter 10, we restricted the use of the term uncertainty to those cases in which the firm faces a rational opponent or a small number of them and in which the outcomes of projects are dependent on the actions taken by opponents, thus are *not* random variables, though their value is unknown. In such cases it is *not* possible to express possible outcomes in terms of a probability distribution. The appropriate mathematical tool for the analysis of risk is the calculus of probabilities, here it is the theory of games. The market structure where this situation develops is one characterized by small numbers of participants, i.e., bilateral monopoly, oligopoly, or oligopsony.

There have been no significant attempts to develop a satisfactory theory of capital budgeting based on game-theoretic models of the behavior of the firm. To the extent that economic implications of the theory have been developed, these have been implications for price theory and not for capital theory.[11] The following suggestions do not

---

[11]Cf. M. Shubik, *Strategy and Market Structure* (New York: Wiley, 1961).

constitute a rigorous application of game theory to the problem; such an application is well beyond the scope of this book.

First of all, the basic data of an oligopolistic market, such as the demand for its product, are random variables to which the theory of probability applies. Changing fortunes of firms in such a market are the result of risk factors and strategy choices, but there is no evidence that the capital market makes any distinction between the two. It is apt to regard all variability as due to risk, as we have defined that term, and to capitalize unstable income streams accordingly. Nor is there any evidence that it should do otherwise, except that in doing so it may underestimate risk. Variance due to parameter shifts may be measurable, that due to changes in strategy may be infinite. A sample variance can be computed for any sample of data but is not a reliable estimator of the population variance, which is infinite.[12]

A second fundamental problem is that most capital budgeting problems turn out to be not games of the simple two-person zero-sum variety for which all solutions are known, but n-person games, for which all solutions are not known.

Finally, the concept of a mixed strategy, which plays a fundamental role in finding solutions to the two-person zero-sum games into which all larger games must be resolved, is unappealing, at least intuitively, in the capital budgeting situation. It is quite feasible to quote prices, day by day, in accordance with some predetermined probability distribution. It is not possible to vary the number of one's plants or service stations in the same fashion, since construction takes time, cannot be kept secret, and is irreversible in the short run.

Game theory, at its present stage of development, cannot give us a completely valid model for use in this capital budgeting situation. In the meantime, the practical man who must reach decisions should use the risk model developed above, recognizing that it must be based on subjective probability distributions which may not be strictly correct. Projects where the conflict element is of predominant importance may be omitted from the inital selection process and subjected to a separate analysis which attempts to take account of game theoretic principles, along the lines of the following example.

_____

[12]One theoretical frequency distribution which would fit such data is the Pareto Distribution. See B. Mandelbrot, "The Variation of Certain Speculative Prices," *Journal of Business*, Vol. 36 (October, 1963), pp. 394-419. For evidence that observed yields on the Toronto Stock Exchange appear to fit this distribution, see Janet Smith, *A Simulation Model of Portfolio Investments* (Unpublished B.Comm. thesis, University of British Columbia, 1965).

Example—Interdependence Recognized

In a moderately sized town there are two banks, the First National and the State. Both have, at the moment, single offices in the down-town shopping area. The First National has adopted its capital budget, and has considered all projects except the addition of two new branches. Estimated cost of capital is 5.5 percent, and the following estimates are based on present values calculated at that rate. Value of the shareholder's interest in First National at present, after certain additions, is estimated at $3,000,000. Suppose each new branch costs $1,000,000. If the State Bank doesn't build any new branches, the value of the First National will be increased as follows, after deducting all costs:

	Value $000	Added benefits	Added costs	Net gain
No new branch	3,000			
New branch location A	3,900	1,900	1,000	900
New branch location B	3,400	1,400	1,000	400
Both new branches	4,000	3,000	2,000	1000

On this basis, the First National should build both branches.

However, there are a couple of other locations in town where new bank branches might be located and on which the State Bank is known to be considering building. Should they do so, values of First National will be as shown in its *payoff matrix* (Table 11-4) which gives its net present value for all strategy pairs which might be chosen by the two competitors.

TABLE 11-4
PAYOFF MATRIX: FIRST NATIONAL BANK

		State Bank's strategy			
		No new branch	New branch C	New branch D	Both new branches
First	No new branch	3,000	2,500	2,600	2,400
National's	New branch A	3,900	3,300	3,100	2,700
strategy	New branch B	3,400	2,850	2,900	2,800
	Both new branches	4,000	3,100	3,400	2,600

To take account of the possible effects of retaliation we must ex-amine the minimum entry in each row, to see in effect what would happen if the competition did its worst. The worst that can happen in each case is that the State Bank builds two branches, in which case the values in the fourth column apply. Selecting that row which has the greatest *minimum* entry gives us the optimum pure strategy for the First National Bank. This is to build branch *B*. We must carry out analysis further, however, and consider the State Bank's payoff matrix. Fortunately, First National has also evaluated the sites and can calculate the values for its competitor quite accurately. These appear in Table 11-5.

TABLE 11-5
PAYOFF MATRIX—STATE BANK

		State Bank's strategy			
		No new branch	New branch C	New branch D	Both new branches
First	No new branch	2,000	2,900	3,200	2,600
National's	New branch A	1,600	2,300	3,000	2,200
strategy	New branch B	1,800	2,200	2,800	2,400
	Both new branches	1,400	1,900	1,500	2,000

State Bank's optimum countermove against First National's decision to build branch *B* is to build branch *D*. If it does so, FNB will be worth $2.9 million. If, however, FNB could be sure of this beforehand, it would choose to build both branches, for this is its optimum counterstrategy to *D* and makes its value $3.4 million.

But suppose, for some reason, FNB can lure SB into moving first. Overall, SB's optimum strategy can be found by examining Table 11-5 to find which column has the largest minimum element. This is the fourth column, and SB's optimum strategy is to build both branches. It it does so, FNB would be better off to build branch *B*, and its value would be only $2.8 million. It is potentially worth a great deal to First National to get State to commit itself first, and to *C* only rather than to both branches. It is only slightly inferior from State's point of view, much better from *A*'s. As a minimum, it may choose to wait, hoping that State will not do both at once. As a maximum, there are opportunities for collusion or merger, providing legal hurdles can be cleared. Merger is probably out in this 2-bank situation because of the Clayton Act, even if the Comptroller of the Currency should consent, but there are many strategies short of this that are not illegal. For example, FNB might suddenly become a bit uncooperative in dealing with a large customer whose operations were near site *C*, in the hope that he will tip State's decision in favor of that location.

This is clearly not a zero-sum game of the variety found in elementary expositions of game theory. We cannot go into all of the possible ramifications of nonzero sum games here,[13] but shall explore this particular situation a bit further, by examining the combined payoff matrix for the two banks. This matrix is derived by adding together the respective payoffs in the two individual matrices and appears in Table 11-6.

TABLE 11-6
COMBINED PAYOFF MATRIX—BOTH BANKS

		State Bank's strategy			
		No new branch	New branch C	New branch D	Both new branches
First	No new branch	5,000	5,400	5,800	5,000
National's	New branch A	5,500	5,600	6,100	4,900
strategy	New branch B	5,200	5,000	5,700	5,200
	Both new branches	5,400	5,000	4,900	4,600

This matrix is a condensed version of the payoff matrix for a game played between the coalition of the two banks and a fictitious player "nature," whose only function is to lose what the coalition gains. It does indicate something that was not apparent from our earlier discussion, namely that joint gains are maximized when the combination (A, D) is built. This combination is unlikely to result without collusion, for State's safest strategy is to build both C and D, while First National's is to build B. Game theory does not predict any definite outcome for a situation of this type, but indicates a range of possible outcomes which may be attained by the participants depending on their bargaining ability and the institutional constraints within which they find themselves. Here the possibility of collusion is dependent not only on legal constraints but on the possibility of an exchange of values from one party to another, termed a "side-payment" in the literature of game theory. This need not take the form of a bribe, nor is it likely to in a situation of this kind, but it could take the form of a slightly more generous valuation for the assets of one party to a merger. In this case, if merger could be attained, the combined values would total $6.1 million. Of this amount, FNB would have to

---

[13]But see Von Neumann and Morgenstern, *The Theory of Games and Economic Behavior* (3d ed.; Princeton: Princeton University Press, 1953); R. D. Luce and H. Raiffa, *Games and Decisions* (New York: Wiley, 1957); M. Shubik, *Strategy and Market Structure* (New York: Wiley, 1959) for an introduction and further references.

get at least $2.8 million, the smallest amount it could get by non-participation, while State would have to get at least $2.0 million, the worst it could get on its own, but the way in which the remainder would be divided is indeterminate.

This example is, of course, highly simplified. It is probable that game theory is not yet sufficiently well developed to be a usable tool, particularly in those cases where the number of participants is greater than two or three. However, it is desirable as far as possible to evaluate payoff matrices for one's own firm and for various combinations of firms, in order to see what possibilities are inherent in a given situation and to what extent cooperative behavior might be induced by legally permissible means.

It is here that judgment must be exercised with great care, for these parts of budgets cannot be selected by the mechanical application of a decision rule but are instead dependent on an informed evaluation of possible competitor behavior. To rush into a situation such as the one we have just examined and merely pick the appropriate minimum strategy based only on the firm's own payoff matrix is to forfeit any chance of getting a bigger share of a bigger pie.

This should not be taken as an unqualified endorsement of collusion in aggressively monopolistic strategies on the part of firms in situations of mutual interdependence.

Outright collusion is prima facie illegal and does not therefore constitute a permissible solution under the relevant rules of the game. Failure to recognize interdependence can easily lead, however, to the development of excess capacity, to destructive price wars, and to the other wasteful phenomena of "sick" competition. It remains to be determined whether the misallocation of resources under such conditions may not be, in some cases, greater than that which would result from outright monopolistic practices. This question obviously has ramifications extending beyond the scope of this book.

We suspect that optimum resource allocation is more likely to emerge from a situation where competitors act rationally within the limits set by public policy and where the latter intervenes explicitly in response to obvious malfunctions in the market system, than we are in a situation where we are dependent on the possibility that the actions of competitors, thoroughly irrational in themselves, will somehow lead to and maintain an ideal competitive solution.

APPENDIX A

Present Value of $1.00

Years Hence	1%	2%	4%	6%	8%	10%	12%	14%	15%	16%	18%	20%	22%	24%	25%	26%	28%	30%	35%	40%	45%	50%
1	0.990	0.980	0.962	0.943	0.926	0.909	0.893	0.877	0.870	0.862	0.847	0.833	0.820	0.806	0.800	0.794	0.781	0.769	0.741	0.714	0.690	0.667
2	0.980	0.961	0.925	0.890	0.857	0.826	0.797	0.769	0.756	0.743	0.718	0.694	0.672	0.650	0.640	0.630	0.610	0.592	0.549	0.510	0.476	0.444
3	0.971	0.942	0.889	0.840	0.794	0.751	0.712	0.675	0.658	0.641	0.609	0.579	0.551	0.524	0.512	0.500	0.477	0.455	0.406	0.364	0.328	0.296
4	0.961	0.924	0.855	0.792	0.735	0.683	0.636	0.592	0.572	0.552	0.516	0.482	0.451	0.423	0.410	0.397	0.373	0.350	0.301	0.260	0.226	0.198
5	0.951	0.906	0.822	0.747	0.681	0.621	0.567	0.519	0.497	0.476	0.437	0.402	0.370	0.341	0.328	0.315	0.291	0.269	0.223	0.186	0.156	0.132
6	0.942	0.888	0.790	0.705	0.630	0.564	0.507	0.456	0.432	0.410	0.370	0.335	0.303	0.275	0.262	0.250	0.227	0.207	0.165	0.133	0.108	0.088
7	0.933	0.871	0.760	0.665	0.583	0.513	0.452	0.400	0.376	0.354	0.314	0.279	0.249	0.222	0.210	0.198	0.178	0.159	0.122	0.095	0.074	0.059
8	0.923	0.853	0.731	0.627	0.540	0.467	0.404	0.351	0.327	0.305	0.266	0.233	0.204	0.179	0.168	0.157	0.139	0.123	0.091	0.068	0.051	0.039
9	0.914	0.837	0.703	0.592	0.500	0.424	0.361	0.308	0.284	0.263	0.225	0.194	0.167	0.144	0.134	0.125	0.108	0.094	0.067	0.048	0.035	0.026
10	0.905	0.820	0.676	0.558	0.463	0.386	0.322	0.270	0.247	0.227	0.191	0.162	0.137	0.116	0.107	0.099	0.085	0.073	0.050	0.035	0.024	0.017
11	0.896	0.804	0.650	0.527	0.429	0.350	0.287	0.237	0.215	0.195	0.162	0.135	0.112	0.094	0.086	0.079	0.066	0.056	0.037	0.025	0.017	0.012
12	0.887	0.788	0.625	0.497	0.397	0.319	0.257	0.208	0.187	0.168	0.137	0.112	0.092	0.076	0.069	0.062	0.052	0.043	0.027	0.018	0.012	0.008
13	0.879	0.773	0.601	0.469	0.368	0.290	0.229	0.182	0.163	0.145	0.116	0.093	0.075	0.061	0.055	0.050	0.040	0.033	0.020	0.013	0.008	0.005
14	0.870	0.758	0.577	0.442	0.340	0.263	0.205	0.160	0.141	0.125	0.099	0.078	0.062	0.049	0.044	0.039	0.032	0.025	0.015	0.009	0.006	0.003
15	0.861	0.743	0.555	0.417	0.315	0.239	0.183	0.140	0.123	0.108	0.084	0.065	0.051	0.040	0.035	0.031	0.025	0.020	0.011	0.006	0.004	0.002
16	0.853	0.728	0.534	0.394	0.292	0.218	0.163	0.123	0.107	0.093	0.071	0.054	0.042	0.032	0.028	0.025	0.019	0.015	0.008	0.005	0.003	0.002
17	0.844	0.714	0.513	0.371	0.270	0.198	0.146	0.108	0.093	0.080	0.060	0.045	0.034	0.026	0.023	0.020	0.015	0.012	0.006	0.003	0.002	0.001
18	0.836	0.700	0.494	0.350	0.250	0.180	0.130	0.095	0.081	0.069	0.051	0.038	0.028	0.021	0.018	0.016	0.012	0.009	0.005	0.002	0.001	0.001
19	0.828	0.686	0.475	0.331	0.232	0.164	0.116	0.083	0.070	0.060	0.043	0.031	0.023	0.017	0.014	0.012	0.009	0.007	0.003	0.002	0.001	
20	0.820	0.673	0.456	0.312	0.215	0.149	0.104	0.073	0.061	0.051	0.037	0.026	0.019	0.014	0.012	0.010	0.007	0.005	0.002	0.001		
21	0.811	0.660	0.439	0.294	0.199	0.135	0.093	0.064	0.053	0.044	0.031	0.022	0.015	0.011	0.009	0.008	0.006	0.004	0.002	0.001		
22	0.803	0.647	0.422	0.278	0.184	0.123	0.083	0.056	0.046	0.038	0.026	0.018	0.013	0.009	0.007	0.006	0.004	0.003	0.001	0.001		
23	0.795	0.634	0.406	0.262	0.170	0.112	0.074	0.049	0.040	0.033	0.022	0.015	0.010	0.007	0.006	0.005	0.003	0.002	0.001			
24	0.788	0.622	0.390	0.247	0.158	0.102	0.066	0.043	0.035	0.028	0.019	0.013	0.008	0.006	0.005	0.004	0.003	0.002	0.001			
25	0.780	0.610	0.375	0.233	0.146	0.092	0.059	0.038	0.030	0.024	0.016	0.010	0.007	0.005	0.004	0.003	0.002	0.001	0.001			
26	0.772	0.598	0.361	0.220	0.135	0.084	0.053	0.033	0.026	0.021	0.014	0.009	0.006	0.004	0.003	0.002	0.002	0.001				
27	0.764	0.586	0.347	0.207	0.125	0.076	0.047	0.029	0.023	0.018	0.011	0.007	0.005	0.003	0.002	0.002	0.001	0.001				
28	0.757	0.574	0.333	0.196	0.116	0.069	0.042	0.026	0.020	0.016	0.010	0.006	0.004	0.002	0.002	0.002	0.001	0.001				
29	0.749	0.563	0.321	0.185	0.107	0.063	0.037	0.022	0.017	0.014	0.008	0.005	0.003	0.002	0.002	0.001	0.001					
30	0.742	0.552	0.308	0.174	0.099	0.057	0.033	0.020	0.015	0.012	0.007	0.004	0.003	0.002	0.001	0.001	0.001					
40	0.672	0.453	0.208	0.097	0.046	0.022	0.011	0.005	0.004	0.003	0.001	0.001										
50	0.608	0.372	0.141	0.054	0.021	0.009	0.003	0.001	0.001	0.001												

SOURCE: Robert N. Anthony, *Management Accounting: Text and Cases* (rev. ed.; Homewood, Ill.: Richard D. Irwin, Inc., 1960), p. 656.

APPENDIX B

PRESENT VALUE OF ANNUITIES—$1.00 PER YEAR

Years (N)	1%	2%	4%	6%	8%	10%	12%	14%	15%	16%	18%	20%	22%	24%	25%	26%	28%	30%	35%	40%	45%	50%
1	0.990	0.980	0.962	0.943	0.926	0.909	0.893	0.877	0.870	0.862	0.847	0.833	0.820	0.806	0.800	0.794	0.781	0.769	0.741	0.714	0.690	0.667
2	1.970	1.942	1.886	1.833	1.783	1.736	1.690	1.647	1.626	1.605	1.566	1.528	1.492	1.457	1.440	1.424	1.392	1.361	1.289	1.224	1.165	1.111
3	2.941	2.884	2.775	2.673	2.577	2.487	2.402	2.322	2.283	2.246	2.174	2.106	2.042	1.981	1.952	1.923	1.868	1.816	1.696	1.589	1.493	1.407
4	3.902	3.808	3.630	3.465	3.312	3.170	3.037	2.914	2.855	2.798	2.690	2.589	2.494	2.404	2.362	2.320	2.241	2.166	1.997	1.849	1.720	1.605
5	4.853	4.713	4.452	4.212	3.993	3.791	3.605	3.433	3.352	3.274	3.127	2.991	2.864	2.745	2.689	2.635	2.532	2.436	2.220	2.035	1.876	1.737
6	5.795	5.601	5.242	4.917	4.623	4.355	4.111	3.889	3.784	3.685	3.498	3.326	3.167	3.020	2.951	2.885	2.759	2.643	2.385	2.168	1.983	1.824
7	6.728	6.472	6.002	5.582	5.206	4.868	4.564	4.288	4.160	4.039	3.812	3.605	3.416	3.242	3.161	3.083	2.937	2.802	2.508	2.263	2.057	1.883
8	7.652	7.325	6.733	6.210	5.747	5.335	4.968	4.639	4.487	4.344	4.078	3.837	3.619	3.421	3.329	3.241	3.076	2.925	2.598	2.331	2.108	1.922
9	8.566	8.162	7.435	6.802	6.247	5.759	5.328	4.946	4.772	4.607	4.303	4.031	3.786	3.566	3.463	3.366	3.184	3.019	2.665	2.379	2.144	1.948
10	9.471	8.983	8.111	7.360	6.710	6.145	5.650	5.216	5.019	4.833	4.494	4.192	3.923	3.682	3.571	3.465	3.269	3.092	2.715	2.414	2.168	1.965
11	10.368	9.787	8.760	7.887	7.139	6.495	5.937	5.453	5.234	5.029	4.656	4.327	4.035	3.776	3.656	3.544	3.335	3.147	2.752	2.438	2.185	1.977
12	11.255	10.575	9.385	8.384	7.536	6.814	6.194	5.660	5.421	5.197	4.793	4.439	4.127	3.851	3.725	3.606	3.387	3.190	2.779	2.456	2.196	1.985
13	12.134	11.343	9.986	8.853	7.904	7.103	6.424	5.842	5.583	5.342	4.910	4.533	4.203	3.912	3.780	3.656	3.427	3.223	2.799	2.468	2.204	1.990
14	13.004	12.106	10.563	9.295	8.244	7.367	6.628	6.002	5.724	5.468	5.008	4.611	4.265	3.962	3.824	3.695	3.459	3.249	2.814	2.477	2.210	1.993
15	13.865	12.849	11.118	9.712	8.559	7.506	6.811	6.142	5.847	5.575	5.092	4.675	4.315	4.001	3.859	3.726	3.483	3.268	2.825	2.484	2.214	1.995
16	14.718	13.578	11.652	10.106	8.851	7.824	6.974	6.265	5.954	5.669	5.162	4.730	4.357	4.033	3.887	3.751	3.503	3.283	2.834	2.489	2.216	1.997
17	15.562	14.292	12.166	10.477	9.122	8.022	7.120	6.373	6.047	5.749	5.222	4.775	4.391	4.059	3.910	3.771	3.518	3.295	2.840	2.492	2.218	1.998
18	16.398	14.992	12.659	10.828	9.372	8.201	7.250	6.467	6.128	5.818	5.273	4.812	4.419	4.080	3.928	3.786	3.529	3.304	2.844	2.494	2.219	1.999
19	17.226	15.678	13.134	11.158	9.604	8.365	7.366	6.550	6.198	5.877	5.316	4.844	4.442	4.097	3.942	3.799	3.539	3.311	2.848	2.496	2.220	1.999
20	18.046	16.351	13.590	11.470	9.818	8.514	7.469	6.623	6.259	5.929	5.353	4.870	4.460	4.110	3.954	3.808	3.546	3.316	2.850	2.497	2.221	1.999
21	18.857	17.011	14.029	11.764	10.017	8.649	7.562	6.687	6.312	5.973	5.384	4.891	4.476	4.121	3.963	3.816	3.551	3.320	2.852	2.498	2.221	2.000
22	19.660	17.658	14.451	12.042	10.201	8.772	7.645	6.743	6.359	6.011	5.410	4.909	4.488	4.130	3.970	3.822	3.556	3.323	2.853	2.498	2.222	2.000
23	20.456	18.292	14.857	12.303	10.371	8.883	7.718	6.792	6.399	6.044	5.432	4.925	4.499	4.137	3.976	3.827	3.559	3.325	2.854	2.499	2.222	2.000
24	21.243	18.914	15.247	12.550	10.529	8.985	7.784	6.835	6.434	6.073	5.451	4.937	4.507	4.143	3.981	3.831	3.562	3.327	2.855	2.499	2.222	2.000
25	22.023	19.523	15.622	12.783	10.675	9.077	7.843	6.873	6.464	6.097	5.467	4.948	4.514	4.147	3.985	3.834	3.564	3.329	2.856	2.499	2.222	2.000
26	22.795	20.121	15.983	13.003	10.810	9.161	7.896	6.906	6.491	6.118	5.480	4.956	4.520	4.151	3.988	3.837	3.566	3.330	2.856	2.500	2.222	2.000
27	23.560	20.707	16.330	13.211	10.935	9.237	7.943	6.935	6.514	6.136	5.492	4.964	4.524	4.154	3.990	3.839	3.567	3.331	2.856	2.500	2.222	2.000
28	24.316	21.281	16.663	13.406	11.051	9.307	7.984	6.961	6.534	6.152	5.502	4.970	4.528	4.157	3.992	3.840	3.568	3.331	2.857	2.500	2.222	2.000
29	25.066	21.844	16.984	13.591	11.158	9.370	8.022	6.983	6.551	6.166	5.510	4.975	4.531	4.159	3.994	3.841	3.569	3.332	2.857	2.500	2.222	2.000
30	25.808	22.396	17.292	13.765	11.258	9.427	8.055	7.003	6.566	6.177	5.517	4.979	4.534	4.160	3.995	3.842	3.569	3.332	2.857	2.500	2.222	2.000
40	32.835	27.355	19.793	15.046	11.925	9.779	8.244	7.105	6.642	6.234	5.548	4.997	4.544	4.166	3.999	3.846	3.571	3.333	2.857	2.500	2.222	2.000
50	39.196	31.424	21.482	15.762	12.234	9.915	8.304	7.133	6.661	6.246	5.554	4.999	4.545	4.167	4.000	3.846	3.571	3.333	2.857	2.500	2.222	2.000

SOURCE: Robert N. Anthony, Management Accounting: Text and Cases (rev. ed.; Homewood, Ill.: Richard D. Irwin, Inc., 1960), p. 657.

Glossary of Symbols

The following symbols have been used in various mathematical expressions appearing in this book. Because of a shortage of letters, some have had to be used with more than one meaning. Accordingly, the following listing indicates both meanings, and lists the page numbers at which the symbol is first used with a particular meaning, and where an adequate explanation will usually be found.

a	coefficient of risk aversion	204
b	fraction of earnings retained	104
b_j	net benefits from project j	185
B	net benefits	185
B	imputed borrowing power	216
c	no-debt capitalization rate	218
c_{jt}	cash outlay for project j in period t	193
C	cost of an asset	35
C	present value of costs over the life of an asset	41
C_i	costs of the i_{th} project (excluding direct labor)	172
C_{jt}	present value of the costs of the j_{th} project in period t	185
C_{ij}	present value of costs of project i at discount rate k_j	224
C_t	costs incurred in period t	35
C_t	(as a constraint) cash available in period t	185
$C(t)$	cash outflows at time t (continuous case)	98
$Cov_{oi,j}$	covariance between net present values of existing operations and proposed addition, i, measured at the discount rate k_j	224
d_{ij}	man-hours of labor of type j required for project i	172
d_{jt}	man-hours of labor required for project j in period t	192
D	dividend per share	107
D_t	depreciation charge in period t	35

251

D_t dividend per share in period t 104

E_A expected earnings per share   104

E_t earnings per share in period t 104

g rate of growth   104

i cost of debt   218

k cost of capital, required yield   35

k_d cost of debt   216

k_e cost of equity   216

L amount of debt   218

L_j amount of labor of type j available   172

L_t amount of labor available in period t 192

M market value of the firm   218

M_{fj} present value of the firm, incorporating proposed additions to
           operations, at discount rate k_j 224

M_{oj} present value of existing operations at discount rate k_j 224

n number of shares   218

P par value (bonds)   100

P price per share   107

P_t a dual variable associated with a funds constraint, yielding a
           measure of the marginal productivity of capital in period t 188

Q_t cash inflow in period t 6

r rate of interest or discount   5

r internal rate of return   41

r^* rate of return on book value   104

R coupon or nominal rate of return (bonds or notes)   100

$r_{oi,j}$ coefficient of correlation between net present values of existing
           operations and proposed addition i, measured at discount rate k_j 224

S an initial sum of money   5

σ_{fj} standard deviation of the value of the firm, including proposed
           additions, measured at discount rate k_j 224

σ_{ij} standard deviation of the benefits from project i, measured
           at discount rate k_j 224

σ_{oj}	standard deviations of the benefits from existing operations, measured at discount rate k_j	224
σ_Y	standard deviation of earnings	218
T	marginal tax rate	100
Tc	marginal capital gains tax rate	107
Ty	marginal income tax rate	107
U_i	a utility index	204
U_j	a dual variable, related to the marginal productivity of project j	188
V_t	present value at time t	6
V	present value of benefits over the life of an asset	41
V_i	present value of benefits from project i	172
V_{ij}	present value of benefits of project i at discount rate k_j	224
w_t	a dual variable, associated with a labor supply constraint, measuring the marginal productivity of labor in period t	192
W_t	future worth, amount	5
W	net price received for bonds before deducting issue expense	100n
X_i, X_j	fraction of the ith, jth project undertaken	172
$\overline{X}$	expected income	204
$\overline{Y}$	expected earnings, before deducting fixed charges	218

Index

This book has been set in 10 point Century Expanded, leaded 3 points and 9 point Century Expanded, leaded 2 points. Chapter numbers are in 14 point Bodoni Bold; chapter titles are in 18 point Bodoni Bold italic. The size of the type page is 27 by 45 picas.